THE IMPACT OF RESTORATION CRITICAL THEORY ON THE ADAPTATION OF FOUR SHAKESPEAREAN COMEDIES

THE IMPACT OF RESTORATION CRITICAL THEORY ON THE ADAPTATION OF FOUR SHAKESPEAREAN COMEDIES

Jaquelyn W. Walsh

Studies in Comparative Literature
Volume 36

The Edwin Mellen Press
Lewiston•Queenston•Lampeter

Library of Congress Cataloging-in-Publication Data

Walsh, Jaquelyn W.
The impact of Restoration critical theory on the adaptation of four Shakespearean comedies / Jaquelyn W. Walsh.
p.cm. -- (Studies in comparative literature ; v. 36)
Includes bibliographical references and index.
ISBN 0-7734-7722-5
1. Shakespeare, William, 1564-1616--Adaptations--History and criticism. 2. Shakespeare, William, 1564-1616--Criticism and interpretation--History--17th century. 3. English drama--Restoration, 1660-1700--History and criticism--Theory, etc. 4. Lansdowne, George Granville, Baron, 1667-1735--Knowledge--Literature. 5. English drama (Comedy)--History and criticism--Theory, etc. 6. Burnaby, William, 1672 or 3-1706--Knowledge--Literature. 7. Gildon, Charles, 1665-1724--Knowledge--Literature. 8. Dennis, John, 1657-1734--Knowledge--Literature. 9. Criticism--England--History--17th century. 10. Shakespeare, William, 1564-1616--Comedies. I. Title. II. Studies in comparative literature (Lewiston, N.Y.) ; v. 36.

PR2880.A1 W35 2000
822.3'3--dc21

00-032876

This is volume 36 in the continuing series
Studies in Comparative Literature
Volume 36 ISBN 0-7734-7722-5
SCL Series ISBN 0-88946-393-X

A CIP catalog record for this book is available from the British Library.

The Edwin Mellen Press
Box 450
Lewiston, New York
USA 14092-0450

The Edwin Mellen Press
Box 67
Queenston, Ontario
CANADA L0S 1L0

The Edwin Mellen Press, Ltd.
Lampeter, Ceredigion, Wales
UNITED KINGDOM SA48 8LT

Printed in the United States of America

To my husband, Nick

CONTENTS

FOREWORD

This work would never have come into being had not the late Charles Cannon suggested the topic. I will be forever grateful for his good counsel. For their kind advice, inspiration, and words of encouragement, I will also always remember Louis Dollarhide, T. J. Ray, and the late Evans Harrington. Colby Kullman has been, and continues to be, a constant source of support and motivation throughout the years. In my years at McNeese State University, I have also been extremely lucky to have the encouragement, help, and advice of the Dean of the College of Liberal Arts, fellow Renaissance scholar Millard T. Jones.

Last, but not least, my family deserves the credit for this book. My late parents subsidized my studies for many years. I am only sorry that they, like far too many of the people responsible for this work, are not present to see it in print. I am fortunate, however, to have a wonderful husband and sister who continue to be my most vocal critics (which I greatly appreciate), my strongest motivators, and my firm foundation. I am eternally in their debt.

Lake Charles, Louisiana
10 November 2000

PREFACE

Restoration and eighteenth-century adaptations of Shakespearean plays are a topic familiar to most students of English literature, but one about which many of the same scholars have little specific knowledge. Most have read John Dryden's *All for Love*; many know that Nahum Tate provided a happy ending in order to improve upon *King Lear*. Almost universally, students and professors disparage the neoclassic writers for presuming to doctor the Bard's plays. But few students of literature have read more than one or two of the most famous or notorious adaptations. Even fewer have clear knowledge of the principles guiding the adapter's revisions. The following study by Jaquelyn Walsh, Associate Professor of English at McNeese State University, makes a good start at filling the gap in knowledge. Her years of study and teaching qualify her extremely well, especially in drama of the Renaissance and Restoration.

Research into the reasons guiding such adaptations encounters serious difficulties, but Professor Walsh structured the project strategically. She organized her study around four adaptations of Shakespearean plays by literary figures at the turn of the eighteenth century who wrote literary criticism and other original plays, as well as the adaptations to be discussed. In chronological order, the four plays are *Measure for Measure, or Beauty the Best Advocate* (1700), an adaptation of Shakespeare's *Measure for Measure* attributed to Charles Gildon; George Granville's *The Jew of Venice* (1701), a rendering of Shakespeare's *The*

ii

Merchant of Venice; John Dennis's *The Comical Gallant* (1702), based on *The Merry Wives of Windsor*; and William Burnaby's *Love Betray'd, or the Agreable Disappointment* (1703), a handling of *Twelfth Night*. Bully aware of the scope and magnitude of changes in theatre, literary taste, social manners, and morals between the time of Shakespeare and the turn of the eighteenth century, Professor Walsh systematically explores all the main conceivable reasons for change. And she analyzes the evidence logically, paying due attention both to adapters' stated reasons and the dramatic effects of the changes they made.

The thoroughness of the research and the method of organization make the study yield valuable information about the Shakespeare adaptations and, simultaneously, remind the reader of cultural and historical developments peculiar to the period referred to by various titles emphasizing somewhat different characteristics of British society of the time: the Restoration and Eighteenth Century Period, the Neoclassical Period, the Augustan Age, and the Age of Reason. Getting at rationales for Shakespeare adaptations requires recognition of the new realities of the theatre after the Restoration of the monarchy. Indoor theatres with proscenium stages, relatively limited seating, and elaborate sets had replaced the outdoor theatres of Elizabethan times and changed the socioeconomic status of the audience, the technical possibilities open to theatrical companies, and the economics of theatre in general. The relatively affluent audience and playwrights addressing it had been influenced strongly by French neoclassicism during the court's stay on the continent during the Commonwealth Period, inclining to some extent toward the three unities and simplicity and clarity of language. The licentious court relished comedy of manners based upon sexual adventure; the defenders of drama argued that its purposes were to encourage morality through poetic justice and to improve manners through refinement of language and subject matter. Thus the milieu of the Shakespeare adaptations was quite complex, an interesting time that Professor Walsh's work helps the reader to understand.

It is a tribute to the quality of Professor Walsh's research that her study puts the reader in touch with the contradictions and complexities of the period and does not oversimplify.

Millard T. Jones

Lake Charles, Louisiana

10 November 2000

INTRODUCTION

When the spectre of John Gower stepped onto the stage at the Cockpit in the spring of 1660 "To sing a song that old was sung," he heralded the return of Shakespeare to the English stage after a lapse of almost twenty years. How prophetic the original Prologue to *Pericles* was to be concerning the critics, playwrights, and managers of this new era who indeed believed they were "born in these latter times,/When wit's more ripe," for they would not "accept" Shakespeare's "rhymes" as they were, but felt compelled to improve them often to the point of constructing totally new plays on their foundations.[1] By 1700 Shakespeare's ghost, no longer willing or able to bear the cruelty of the Restoration theater, returned to the stage for a brief moment at the end of an adaptation of *Measure for Measure*. Taunted and tormented by such atrocities as the happy ending supplied to *King Lear* by Nahum Tate, the "doubling" of Ferdinand and Miranda by Dorinda and Hippolito in Davenant and Dryden's *Tempest*, and the inclusion of spectacle to the detriment of the play in almost every Shakespearean revival and adaptation, Shakespeare's ghost raged, "My Plays, by Scriblers, Mangl'd I have seen."[2]

---

[1]William Shakespeare, Prologue to *Pericles*, in *The Norton Shakespeare*, ed. Stephen Greenblatt, et. al. (New York: W. W. Norton and Company, 1997), p. 2718-19.

[2]John Verbruggen, Epilogue to *Measure for Measure, or, Beauty the Best Advocate*,

To anyone who has read Davenant's *The Law Against Lovers*, or even what is perhaps the best of all the adaptations, Dryden's *All for Love*, after having feasted on the vigor of Shakespeare's characters and the magical rhythms of his verse, the charges made in this epilogue seem just and even mild. To the playwrights, poets, and men of leisure who felt they were polishing, not mangling, Shakespeare's plays, on the other hand, the justness of the accusation may have been less apparent. For these men felt they were the enlightened generation; their refinement and learning represented the natural progression of man in the eternal struggle for perfection. In literary endeavor this progression meant the attainment of the "science" Shakespeare lacked, a knowledge succinctly expressed in John Dennis' assertion that "the Rules were absolutely necessary to Perfection."[3] The application of the rules of art to the native genius of Shakespeare could only lead, they believed, to greater beauty, higher moral usefulness, and ultimately perhaps, the "architechtonike"[4] which Sir Philip Sidney saw as the true end of all art. Shakespeare's ghost returned to the stage the following year in a more benevolent mood to vindicate the task the Restoration adapters had set for themselves in the Prologue to George Granville's *The Jew of Venice*. "These scenes in their rough Native Dress were mine;" he proclaimed. "But now improv'd with nobler Lustre shine,"[5] and thus accurately reflected their sentiments concerning his plays. This "nobler Lustre" such men as Bevill Higgons, George Granville, and John Dennis

attributed to Charles Gildon (London: D. Brown and R. Walker, 1700; reprinted by Cornmarket Press, 1969), precedes p. 1. Future references to the play are from this edition and will be included in the text according to page number.

[3]John Dennis, "The Characters and Conduct of Sir John Edgar,"in *The Critical Works of John Dennis*, ed. Edward Niles Hooker, v. 2 (Baltimore: The Johns Hopkins University Press, 1943), p. 196.

[4]Sir Philip Sidney, *An Apology for Poetry* (Indianapolis: Bobbs-Merrill Company, Inc., 1970), p. 23.

[5]Bevill Higgons, Prologue to *The Jew of Venice*, George Granville (London: Ker Lintott, 1701; reprinted by Cornmarket Press, 1969), precedes p. 1. Future references to the play are from this edition and will be included in the text according to page number.

saw in the adaptations shone primarily because of the application of the rules of art.

Founded largely on the observations of Aristotle, Horace, Longinus, Scaliger, Boileau, Corneille, and Jonson, the critical canons of the Restoration, a period roughly encompassing the years 1660-1700 in regards to drama, were tempered by the memory of Shakespeare's genius and fashioned to fit the "genius" of the age. If these rules do not prove the moving force behind every adaptation of a Shakespearean play–and many critics, Kenneth McMillan and George Odell, for instance, discount the consequence–they do exhibit noticeable influence in several of the adapted versions. Oddly enough, since Aristotle's *Poetics* deals with tragedy and promises a treatise on comedy, which is either now lost or never transcribed, and though most critics feel the "rules" apply primarily to tragedy and only secondarily to comedy, several of the adaptations which most closely adhere to these rules are the adaptations of comedies produced in the early eighteenth century–particularly *Measure for Measure* (generally ascribed to Charles Gildon, 1700), George Granville's *The Jew of Venice* (1701), John Dennis' *The Comical Gallant* (1702), and William Burnaby's *Love Betray'd* (1703). This apparent contradiction is compounded considering the moderate esteem the Restoration had for Shakespeare's comedies but made more logical when one remembers that comedy was not only the dominant genre on the stage during the Restoration, but that it also spawned the most significant criticism of the era.[6]

While many modern commentators mention in passing the critical doctrines that influenced the alterations, no one has yet scrutinized the plays in depth with regards to the adapters' own critical beliefs as shown in their criticism

---

[6]Hooker interprets Dennis' conception that "unities should be more strictly observed in comedy . . . because the action of comedy was little and therefore easily kept in bounds. " Edward Niles Hooker, Introduction to *The Critical Works of John Dennis*, v. 2 (Baltimore: The Johns Hopkins University Press, 1943), p. lxxxvi.

and as manifested in their other plays. Each of these particular playwrights as
well as many of the other adapters of Shakespeare produced copious amounts of
criticism in the form of prefaces, prologues and epilogues, and critical tracts.
Despite the petty quibbling he engaged in with Pope and others, John Dennis is
one of the most respected critics of the age and produced many memorable works
of criticism including the "Large Account of the Taste in Poetry" (1702) and "On
the Genius and Writings of Shakespeare" (1712). E. N. Hooker, the editor of
Dennis' critical works, notes his "extraordinarily good taste" in drama and even
goes so far as to say that "it is highly doubtful if another Augustan could be found
who approaches Dennis as a dramatic critic in soundness and sensitivity."[7]
Although of lesser importance as critics, Granville and Burnaby also contributed
critical prefaces to their plays, and Gildon's *Laws of Poetry* put forth his views in
commentary to the Earl of Roscommon's poem of the same title.

For the question "why" still looms over the adaptations.[9]   Almost

Not only did these men write about plays and adapt plays, they also
wrote plays. At least one playwright in this group, William Burnaby, created
plays that are still of some interest, notably *The Reform'd Wife* (1700) and *The
Ladies' Visiting Day* (1701). Other plays by these adapters include Granville's
The She-Gallants (1696), Gildon's *The Roman Bride's Revenge* (1696), and
Dennis' *A Plot and No Plot* (1697).[8]   By juxtaposing these original plays with
the critical views of these men perhaps the reasons behind their alterations of
Shakespeare will be more clear.

[7]Ibid., pp. cxxviii, cxlii.

[8]Granville's *The She-Gallants*, though based on Campistron's *L'Amante Amant*, is his only other comedy and will be used for comparative purposes. Gildon, if he did indeed write *Measure for Measure*, apparently wrote no other comedies.

[9]Although contemporary critics continue to find the aesthetic reasons behind the adaptations problematic, they note various theatrical and political realities as possible catalysts. Stanley Wells, "Elusive Master Shakespeare," *Forum* 11 (1973-74): 2-3; 6-10, sees "sheer

without exception, modern critics, Robert Hume, Hazleton Spencer, and George Odell included, disdain the tampering as being gratuitous and often contemptible. Odell's comments are representative: "Every time I come on one of these alterations . . . I try by every process of historical readjustment to understand what the adapter thought he was doing for Shakespeare; invariably I am forced to

theatrical necessity" as opening the "door to textual adaptations" and sees proof in extant variants "that Shakespeare countenanced alterations to his plays, including omissions, as the result of practical considerations" (8). In *Living Monument: Shakespeare and the Theatre of His Time*, Muriel Bradbrook (Cambridge: Cambridge University Press, 1976) takes a similarly sensible stance with regards to adaptation, noting that "any performance involves some adaptation and selection–as does any other act of interpretation." Bradbrook, in fact, shows why adaptations are necessary and even desirable: "Shakespeare's works now supply the new universal mythology. . . and like all mythologies they are open to adaptation, improvisation, reformation for each individual. . . . The function of myth is to provide a common vehicle whilst allowing an individual application, the adaptable and flexible strength of the plays is improved by the removal of conventional habits and assumptions imposed on the plays by accumulated traditions so that once again they are free to impose their own form, freshly and directly experienced in an alien world" (121-22). Likewise, in "The Spitted Infant: Scenic Emblem and Exclusionist Politics in Restoration Adaptations of Shakespeare" *Shakespeare Quarterly* 37 (Autumn 1986): 340-58, Matthew H. Wikander likens the task of the adapters to that of any producer who attempts to stage a Shakespeare play: "Producing Shakespeare inevitably requires some sort of simplification or exaggeration, if only for intelligibility. In their readings of Shakespeare, the Restoration adapters anticipated ... the kinds of clarifications that modern directors make in reshaping Shakespeare's plays for performance" (358). Although not discussing adaptation per se in her *Shakespeare Verbatim: The Reproduction of Authenticity and the 1790 Apparatus* (New York: Clarendon Press, 1991), p. 24, Margreta de Grazia echoes many of the sentiments expressed by Bradbrook in terms of the "living" nature of the plays: "Yet the very instability of the printed page when viewed as a function of the original itself discourages such a quest for a single and fixed document. Its intractability implies an original resistant to the regimes of both script and print: an original involved in the vagaries of production. The inconsistencies of the printed copy itself attest to a fundamental incompatibility between a play's protean composition and print's or even a script's systematic fixity: it reproduces the provisionality essential to written plays that remain malleable at every stage to the exigencies of performance...." And, even though he abhors the adaptations he reviews, Hazleton Spencer, *Shakespeare Improv'd: The Restoration Versions in Quarto and on the Stage* (New York: Frederick Ungar Publishing Co., 1963), admits that "Reverence for the text of a stage play is a relatively modern refinement–the mere thought of it would have made Shakespeare laugh. No more ruthless tamperer ever lived than he, and he might be the first to reprehend the scholar's anxiety" (p. 373). On a slightly different note, Paulina Kewes' study "Gerard Langbaine's 'View of *Plagiaries*'": The Rhetoric of Dramatic Appropriation in the Restoration" *The Review of English Studies* ns 48:189 (February 1997): 2-18, though it primarily views the changing attitude towards plagiarism (with the focus here on dramatic appropriation) by Langbaine himself and the Restoration in general makes clear Langbaine's belief that "the redaction of texts from the English past, most notably from the pre-Civil War era" is "part of a larger patriotic and cultural project which involves the transmission, preservation, and adjustment of the best in the native dramatic tradition" (16). A political motivation behind the adaptations had been previously pointed to by Sengupta, "Shakespeare Adaptations and Political Consciousness," *Mid-Hudson Language Studies* 4 (1981): 58-67, as well as Matthew H. Wikander (see citation above).

give up the problem." [10] Others, Montague Summers, for instance, believe the "Restoration dramatists had good warrant for their adaptations" because the innovations of the proscenium arch stage, the paucity of trained actors, and the demands of the audience necessitated corresponding changes in the types of plays presented.[11] Likewise, W. Moelwyn Merchant concedes that the adapters were sometimes compelled "in varying degrees" to "modify" Shakespeare's works in deference to "many different criteria of dramatic propriety."[12] In the vein of Summers and Merchant, more recent critics are a bit more forgiving of the adapters. In his discussion of Sir William Davenant's alterations of Shakespeare, Gary Taylor justifies Davenant's actions, and, by extension, those of the other adapters as well, when he notes, "With younger actors and few old plays, he could attract audiences only by creating the theatrical future. In this process he would make even his old plays seem new."[13] Whether or not Davenant's "fiddling" with Shakespeare's plays came from his own desire for innovation or was forced upon him has been debated. Odell says that "Davenant proposed 'to reform and make fitt for the Company of Actors appointed under his direction and command'" nine Shakespearean plays as well as several other Jacobean and Caroline pieces.[14] Utilizing the same records from the Lord Chamberlain's office, John Freehafer concludes that Davenant did not propose the alterations but rather

[10]George Odell, *Shakespeare from Betterton to Irving*, vol. 1 (New York: Benjamin Blom, Inc., 1963), p. 72.

[11]Montague Summers, *Shakespeare Adaptations* (New York: Benjamin Blom, Inc., 1922; reprint edition, 1966), p. cvii.

[12] W. Moelwyn Merchant, "Shakespeare 'Made Fit,'" in *Restoration Theatre*, pp. 195-220. Ed. by John Russell Brown and Bernard Harris. (New York: St. Martin's Press, 1965), p. 200.

[13] Gary Taylor, *Reinventing Shakespeare* (London: Oxford University Press, 1989), p. 14.

[14]Odell, p. 24.

was forced by the terms of the charter to alter all the plays assigned him except his own.[15] Whether Davenant had to adapt the plays of his predecessor, the adaptations he and the playwrights who wrote for the Duke's Company produced became immensely popular. Their popularity was so great, in fact, that the King's Company under the direction of Thomas Killigrew soon began performing their own altered versions even though their charter stipulated no such changes. This truth must reflect some change in the tastes of the audience.

Although Hazleton Spencer claims in the opening lines of *Shakespeare Improv'd* that "it seems unlikely the subsequent course of the drama would have cut a channel materially different"[16] if the Puritans had not closed the theaters, the superficial changes effected by the Interregnum were substantial and included the introduction of the picture-frame stage, which according to Norman Rabkin, no longer "forced" the audience to be "participants" in the action,[17] increased use of scenery and machines, performances by women, and greater emphasis on musical episodes influenced by the new Italian opera.[18] Arthur Gewirtz's study

[15]John Freehafer, "The Formation of the London Patent Companies in 1660," *Theatre Notebook* 20 (October 1965-July 1966):27. Other critics engaged in this debate include: Robert D. Hume, *The Development of English Drama in the Late Seventeenth Century* (Oxford: Clarendon Press, 1976), p. 27, who agrees with Freehafer, and, on the other side, Gunnar Sorelius, "The Early History of the Restoration Theatre: Some Problems Reconsidered," *Theatre Notebook* 33.2 (1979) along with Mongi Raddadi, *Davenant's Adaptations of Shakespeare.* (Uppsala: Almqvist and Wiksell International, 1979), p.21. Katherine West Scheil, "Sir William Davenant's Use of Shakespeare in 'The Law Against Lovers' (1662)," *Philological Quarterly* 76 (1997): 369-87, claims the only mandate in Davenant's charter was the removal of profanity and obscenity and that he chose to make other alterations to the play for the sake of "novelty" (372). Also essential to this study is Christopher Spencer's *Five Restoration Adaptations of Shakespeare* (Urbana: University of Illinois Press, 1965).

[16]Spencer, p. 1.

[17]Norman Rabkin, *Shakespeare and the Problem of Meaning* (Chicago: University of Chicago Press, 1981), p. 81.

[18]Anthony Hammond, "'Rather a Heap of Rubbish Then a Structure': The Principles of Restoration Dramatic Adaptation Revisited" in *The Stage in the 18th Century*, ed. J. D. Browning (New York: Garland Publishing, Inc., 1981), p. 133.

of Restoration adaptations places the primary emphasis on the changing world view of the new era. Although Restoration comedies "often blankly acknowledged the unified world of the earlier comedy," according to Gewirtz, the world they portrayed was "composed largely of antithetical elements which never find a convincing resolution."[19] This *Weltanschauung* is vastly different from Shakespeare's. Robert Weimann characterizes Shakespeare's comedy by noting that "In its theatrical functions and some of its dramatic structure Shakespeare's comedy is older than the Elizabethan age; and it points to a state of society, or more likely, to a vision of Utopia that precludes any *Entzweiung* or alienation between the self and the social."[20] This world view certainly is at odds with that of the Restoration with its preeminence of the social and the "dissociation of sensibility" that T. S. Eliot claimed it brought in its wake.

Other than this philosophical realignment, the major change that came about with the closing is that while public performances were suppressed for the most part, many private theatricals took place in the homes and country manors of the gentry.[21] The exiled nobles with their king were also entertained, not only by French actors in French plays, but also by various English acting companies. George Jolly's troupe, for instance, received support from Prince Charles while in Paris and probably travelled in Europe to entertain other groups of exiles.[21] The banishment of Charles unexpectedly benefited the English poets of his reign, for in Dryden's estimation the exposure to foreign influences produced a much-needed refinement in the wit, language, and manners of the English courtiers and men of letters. Discussing the improvement of English conversation in his "Defence of

[19] Arthur Gewirtz, *Restoration Adaptations of Early Seventeenth Century Comedies* (Washington, D. C.: University Press of America, 1982), p. 111.

[20] Robert Weimann, *Shakespeare and the Popular Tradition in the Theatre: Studies in the Social Dimension of Dramatic Form and Function* (Baltimore: The Johns Hopkins University Press, 1978), p. 260.

[21] Ibid., p. 36.

the Epilogue" (1673), he attributes this refinement to the Court and "particularly the King" whose:

> own misfortunes, and the nation's, afforded him an opportunity which is rarely allowed to sovereign princes, I mean of travelling, and being conversant in the most polished courts of Europe; and thereby of cultivating a spirit which was formed by nature to receive the impressions of a gallant and generous education.

The impact of this education became evident when "at his return, he found a nation lost as much in barbarism as in rebellion."[22] The poets and poetasters of the age, needless to say, wasted no time in reforming the barbaric tastes of their countrymen.

While Charles and his courtiers were in France enjoying the classically "correct" plays of Corneille and Racine and engaging in stimulating repartee with the wits of Europe, English drama on English soil, though not flourishing, was at least surviving. Milton's closet drama, *Samson Agonistes*, reflects even the Puritan interest in the art form, but drama as a literary form by no means replaced the living art form of the theater even in the most repressive days of the Commonwealth. By 1647 the players were flouting the ordinance of 1642 and performing at "The Salisbury Court, the Cockpit, and the Fortune" in what Leslie Hotson refers to as "quite an open and public manner."[23] Unfortunately, the theater became so popular that the playhouses were drawing larger audiences than the churches and Parliament began to enforce the ordinances more strictly. By March 1649, the interiors of the theaters were "dismantled" and to ply their trade the players had to retreat to private houses and the indoor tennis courts of the

---

[22] John Dryden, "A Defence of the Epilogue" in *"Of Dramatic Poesy" and Other Critical Essays*, vol. 1, ed. George Watson (New York: E. P. Dutton and Co., Inc., 1962), p. 181. Future references to this essay will be from this edition and will be noted in the text according to page number.

[23] Leslie Hotson, *The Commonwealth and Restoration Stage.* New York: Russell and

nobility.[24]   Undaunted, the "irrepressible" Roscians of the Red Bull were, Hotson notes, "playing so regularly and with such supreme disregard for the ordinances of Parliament that a raid on 30 December 1654, when they were acting *Wit Without Money*, came as a surprise."[25]   These surreptitious entertainments paved the way for the more open theatricals by Sir William Davenant. As early as April 1656, Davenant was producing private amusements under the guise of "moral representations" with little or no official intervention. He received what almost amounted to legal sanction to perform his *Siege of Rhodes* and later *The Cruelty of the Spaniards*, entertainments useful to the state, he informed Secretary Thurloe in January 1657, since they would "divert" the attention of the public from "'that melancholy that breeds sedition'" and also keep the wealthy in London where they would spend their money and thus improve the economy.[26] Davenant did not have to cajole the Puritans for long, though. In 1660 Charles II triumphantly returned to England.[27]

    With the renewal of the monarchy came a revival of English theater. Davenant notes the close relationship between the two in the Prologue he delivered at the first play presented at court after the Restoration: "The *Laurel* and the *Crown* together went,/Had the same *Foes*, and same *Banishment*."[28]   If the two had been exiled together, they would return together to even greater glory.

Russell, Inc., 1962, p. 24.

[24]Ibid., p. 43.

[25]Ibid., p. 55.

[26]Ibid., p. 55. Even Davenant was not immune to Parliament's disfavor. In 1659 he spent a brief time in prison, not ostensibly for producing theatricals, but for suspected royalist activities.

[27]Ibid., p. 208.

[28]William Davenant, Prologue to Ben Jonson's *The Silent Woman*. Quoted in Hotson, pp. 208-09.

The effect Charles II and his Court wielded on the drama of his reign was not at all superficial. James Sutherland notes the close relationship of Charles and many writers including Rochester, Wycherley, Dryden, and D'Urfey. Charles' patronage extended to literary criticism and even the "genius" of the age, John Dryden, appears to have followed his suggestions in literary matters. Although the court and theater enjoyed an intimate association, or perhaps partly because of this closeness, many Londoners continued to feel that plays were sinful.[29] As a result, the audience represented a much narrower portion of the population than had attended plays in either the Elizabethan or Jacobean eras. Hume speculates that only courtiers and the very wealthy could afford to attend plays due to the high admission prices, between one and two shillings. Ironically, though the audience had become limited more or less to a specific segment of the population and the plays tended to resemble each other in plot, theme, and tone, the playwrights responsible for those plays constituted a more diverse group than ever before in history. J. Paul Hunter refers to this anomaly when he says, "The single most impressive fact about Restoration theater—even more significant than the brilliance of individual plays and performances—is that it attracted almost without exception the most talented writers of the generation, a large and heterogeneous group of them that cut broadly across class lines, something that no other theatrical era had ever done." The narrowing of the audience resulted in what Hunter calls "the narrowed scope of drama," for if courtiers and would-be courtiers made up the bulk of the audience, plays would have to conform to their tastes.[30]

[29]Robert Hume, *The Development of English Drama in the Late Seventeenth Century* (Oxford: Clarendon Press, 1976), pp. 27, 23.

[30]J. Paul Hunter, "The World as Stage and Closet," in *British Theatre and the Other Arts, 1660-1800*, ed. Shirley Strum Kenney (Washington: Folger Books, 1984), pp. 273-74. John Loftis, on the other hand, rejects the notion of the narrowed audience in *Comedy and Society*. Particularly after 1688 he sees audiences that contain a wide range of the populace. Harold Love's "Who Were the Restoration Audience?" *Yearbook of English Studies* 10 (October 1980): 21-44 and "The Myth of the Restoration Audience" *Komos* 1 (1967):49-56 also address this question.

Above all and totally irrelevant of their social status, the Restoration audience, courtier or craftsman, lawyer or apothecary, went to the theater to be entertained. After the victorious return of king and court, they wished to celebrate, to be stimulated, to be titillated, and perhaps even to shock their less sophisticated countrymen who still held puritanical ideals and had not benefited from exposure to foreign influences. The "rules" of art likely played very little, if any, part in their appreciation of a play. Probably the only real bearing–but of no mean importance to the English ego–the rules had on the audience's approval or disapproval of a play was in proving to their French neighbors they were as urbane and knowing as their eternal rivals.[31]

To the playwrights and critics of the age, on the other hand, the rules of art presented a continual source of debate, inquiry, and consternation. The oddest aspect of this dilemma is that it existed not only between different men–Sir Robert Howard and Dryden, for instance–but each critic or playwright faced the dichotomy of genius and "science" in literature within his own psyche and writings. This vacillation was not, of course, unique or original to the English Restoration. Shakespeare, who broke all the rules quite wonderfully, even alludes to the concept of unity of place in *Henry V*: "The King is set from London, and the scene/Is now transported, gentles, to Southampton./There is the playhouse now, there must you sit,/And thence to   France shall we convey you safe" (2.0.34-37). [32] Castelvetro, whose translation and commentary of Aristotle more strictly codified the concepts of the *Poetics* for his generation and those following, comments in his discussion of the epic that "the plot of an epic should contain

[31]Arthur H. Nethercot, *Sir William Davenant: Poet Laureate and Playwright Manager* (New York: Russell and Russell, 1966), p. 383, claims that if "'Evelyn and Pepys are characteristic," the Restoration 'seemed to *prefer* the *adaptations.*"

[32] Citing this passage in *The Theory of Drama in the Restoration Period*, Sarup Singh maintains that Shakespeare subscribed to the view that "the audience is bodily present at the place of the supposed action." Sarup Singh, *The Theory of Drama in the Restoration Period* (Bombay: Orient Longmans, 1963), p. 124.

one action by one person, *not of necessity* but to show the excellence of the poet."[33]   The dilemma does not diminish over the ages but actually becomes the focal point of the opening paragraphs of Lope de Vega's "The New Art of Making Comedies" (1609) as in Pierre Corneille's Dedicatory Epistle to *La Suivante* (1634) when he says, "To know the rules and to understand the secret of skillfully adjusting them to our stage are two very different sciences; and perhaps to make a play succeed nowadays it is not enough to have studied the books of Aristotle and Horace."[34]

If respect for and constraint by the rules co-existed in neoclassical France, this critical ferment was pervasive in Restoration England.[35]   Dryden's criticism contains dialogue after dialogue debating the necessity or even the advisability of rigid adherence to the rules. Far from willing to prescribe strict adherence to the laws of poetry, Dryden, who asserted that he had brought the "exactest rules" of both the English and French stages to his *Secret Love* (1668), affirms in his Letter to John, Lord Haughton, that one should be able "to break a rule for the pleasure of variety."[36]   In his Prologue to the *Double Dealer* he even more explicitly minimizes the importance of the rules when he says:

Time, place, and action may with pains be wrought,

But genius must be born; and never can be taught.

This is your portion; this your native store;

[33]Lodovico Castlevetro, *A Commentary on the "Poetics"of Aristotle,* in *Literary Criticism: Plato to Dryden,* ed. Allan H. Gilbert (New York: American Book Company, 1940), p. 319.

[34]Pierre Corneille, Dedicatory Epistle to *La Suivante,* in *Literary Criticism: Plato to Dryden,* ed. Allan H. Gilbert (New York: American Book Company, 1940), p. 575.

[35]Francis Gallaway, *Reason, Rule, and Revolt in English Classicism* (New York: Octagon Books, 1965), p. 293.

[36]John Dryden, Letter to John, Lord Haughton, in *"Of Dramatic Poesy" and Other Critical Essays,* ed. George Watson, vol. 1 (New York: E. P. Dutton and Company, Inc., 1962), p. 279.

Heav'n, that but once was prodigal before,

To Shakespeare gave as much; she could not give him more.[37]

This prologue supports Singh's contention that Dryden paradoxically found the best example of Corneille's "'one complete action which leaves the mind of the audience in a full repose'" in Shakespeare, who, in Singh's words, "consistently breaks the traditional unity of action yet in his mixed plays achieves a superb emotional unity not so much by leaving 'the mind of the audience in a full repose' as by actively *creating* such a 'repose'."[38] Weimann similarly notes the "unity of taste" which Shakespeare attains, a "multiple unity based on contradictions, and as such allowed the dramatist a flexible frame of reference that was more complex and more vital to the experience of living and feeling within the social organism than the achievement of any other theater before or since."[39] Finally, with Dryden the supreme unity is emotional, the ultimate focus is characterization, and the quintessential achievement of the poet is writing "to the genius of the age and nation" in which he lives.[40] The laws of poetry, in Dryden's estimation, apply only when Nature ordains.

Dryden's tolerant interpretation of the laws of poetry was not to dominate throughout the remainder of the age. The most rigid neo-Aristotelians cannot cease admiring the glories of Shakespeare even while condemning his "errors." Sir Robert Howard, Dryden's brother-in-law and literary arch-rival, propounds the necessity of strict obedience to the rules, yet he was one of

[37]John Dryden, To Mr. Congreve, on His *Double Dealer*, prefixed to Congreve, *The Double Dealer* (1694), in *"Of Dramatic Poesy" and Other Critical Essays,* ed. George Watson, vol. 2 (New York: E. P. Dutton and Company, Inc., 1962), p. 171.

[38]Singh, p. 162.

[39]Weimann, p. 174.

[40]John Dryden, "Heads of an Answer to Rymer," in *"Of Dramatic Poesy" and Other Critical Essays,* ed. George Watson, vol. 2 (New York: E. P. Dutton and Company, Ltd., 1962), p. 214.

Shakespeare's most ardent admirers.   Later critics who tend as a whole to represent a more stringent application of the rules and more intolerance towards breaches of these dictates similarly stand in awe of the "native" genius epitomized by Shakespeare. This viewpoint is perhaps best expressed in the writings of John Dennis, who repeatedly asserts the necessity of the rules, yet notes in a letter about Granville that the one who truly appreciates Shakespeare, in this instance Granville himself, is he "who sees him and reads him over and over and still remains unsatiated, and who mentions his Faults for no other Reason but to make his Excellency the more conspicuous."[41]   Even with Dennis the rules must bow before the greater achievements of genius.   The question nonetheless remains whether or not genius can profit from the refining influence of the laws of poetry. Or, in Dennis' words, "It had then been time to consider whether the genius of Shakespear himself would not have appear'd brighter and more glorious, if he had writ more regularly."   Hooker points out that Dennis' "defence of low and realistic comedy," in "A Large Account of Taste in Poetry" shows "his realization that the playwright must depart from theory to meet the demands of audience, actors, and generally, of theatrical effectiveness."[42]   The adapters of Shakespeare's comedies believed they could, to a certain extent, achieve this goal by unifying Shakespeare's plots, making his characters more consistent, providing balance where they felt it was needed, and simplifying the language, tone, and meaning. Aristotle's divine rules provided the impetus for these changes.

---

[41]John Dennis, "Essay on the Genius and Writings of Shakespear," in *The Critical Works of John Dennis,* ed. E. N. Hooker, vol. 2 (Baltimore: The Johns Hopkins University Press, 1943), p. 17.

[42]Hooker, vol. 1, p. 492.

"There's a Rule for Making a Pudding, but None for Making a Play."
                                        Colley Cibber

CHAPTER I
THE RULES OF ART

Confronted with the alternatives of genius and the rules, Restoration critics and playwrights affirmed the supremacy of the wild strains of genius over the cooler tones produced by the application of the laws of poetry. Reason nonetheless continued to be the watchword of the late seventeenth and early eighteenth centuries. Any praise the later days of the Restoration afforded to the "flash of fancy" best embodied by Shakespeare's plays was thus quickly qualified. Charles Gildon's *Laws of Poetry* succinctly expresses the view of the age when he remarks, "in a good poem there must always shine a great genius, who, tho' it must be born with the poet, and is not to be obtain'd by study and art, yet study and art are absolutely necessary to give this true genius of poetry its full and admirable lustre."[1] That this particular group of men in this particular historical period could adamantly believe in the efficacy of rules in the creation of art remains one of the paradoxes of the Restoration. Anything but reasonable themselves, the great and small of the Restoration marred their personal and professional reputations by their petty bickerings–from the heated arguments between John Dryden and Sir Robert Howard to the vicious name calling engaged

---

[1]Charles Gildon, *The Laws of Poetry* (New York: Garland Publishing, Inc., 1970), p. 22. Future references to this essay will be from this edition and will be noted in the text in the following manner, *LP*, and page number.

in by John Dennis and almost everyone remotely involved in the literary world. These men continued to believe that man's most passionate moments, whether tragic or comic, could be displayed best in plays which adhered to a system of rules based on reason.

The attitude of the Restoration toward regulations of any kind is contradictory. They had lived through a period of great turmoil. The uncertainties, the horrors of the Interregnum, the exile, and the political unrest would naturally have led them to desire the safety of regulations. The discipline they desired, though, was definitely not a moral restriction. Having only recently defeated the Puritans, they were in open revolt against anything that savored of enforced morality. Taking the lead of the French, they discovered the discipline they needed in the rules of art, rules which in no way limited their actual freedom.

By the heyday of the neoclassical period, political and economic security had been reestablished, and moral license was accepted behavior on and off the stage. No longer did artists need to follow the letter of the law of poetry to satisfy any possible psychological needs. Their adherence to these laws, nonetheless, became even more complete. The final decade of the seventeenth century and the first of the eighteenth brought with them a period of commerce, safety and conformity.[2] Conformity and safety ultimately breed revolt, and revolt against the rules became more and more prevalent as the new century progressed. Promptly, but only momentarily dealt with in the early days, the final blow to the reign of the rules significantly came, according to Robert D. Hume, with "the rise in Shakespeare's reputation as a playwright." Despite the continued adaptation of Shakespeare's plays in order to make them conform to

---

[2]See Dennis' "Large Account of Taste in Poetry," in *The Critical Works of John Dennis* ed. E. N. Hooker, vol. 1 (Baltimore: The Johns Hopkins University Press, 1939), pp. 279-95, for a discussion of how this state of affairs produced the "happiest condition in the World, to attain that knowledge of Mankind, which is requisite for the judging of Comedy" (292). Future references to this essay will be from this edition and will be noted in the text in the following manner, LATP and page number.

Aristotelian formulae, Shakespeare's expertise as a craftsman as well as genius began to receive the recognition it deserved. Hume feels that Shakespeare's growing "influence on theory" liberated "forces" that "undermined neoclassical dramatic criticism."[3] The turning point in Shakespeare criticism came in 1709 with Rowe's paean to the genius *and* master playwright in his edition of the collected works.[4]

Exactly what did the force of Shakespeare's imagination undermine? Neoclassical dramatic criticism has its foundation in the dictates of Aristotle, Horace, Quintilian, and Longinus. Even more fundamentally, neoclassical critics claim nature as the basis of the rules of art. In his "Grounds of Criticism in Tragedy," Dryden attempts to show that rules are not "a kind of magisterial prescription upon poets" by quoting Rapin:

> If the rules be well considered, we shall find them to be made only to reduce Nature into method, to trace her step by step, and not suffer the least mark of her to escape us: 'tis only by these that probability in fiction is maintained, which is the soul of poetry. They are founded upon good sense, and sound reason, rather than on authority; for though Aristotle and Horace are produced, yet no man must argue that what they write is true because they write it, but 'tis evident, by the ridiculous mistakes and gross absurdities which have been made by those poets who have taken their fancy only for their guide, that if this fancy be not regulated, 'tis a mere caprice, and utterly incapable to produce a reasonable and judicious poem.[5]

[3]Hume, p. 191.

[4]Gallaway, p. 101. Rowe's edition, interestingly, contains several scenes from the altered versions. Whether Rowe was conscious of this fact is unclear.

[5]John Dryden, "The Grounds of Criticism in Tragedy," in *"Of Dramatic Poesy" and Other Critical Essays,* ed. George Watson, vol. 1 (New York: E. P. Dutton and Company, Inc.,

John Dennis echoes this idea in a letter he wrote to Walter Moyle on 26 October 1695. A true neoclassicist, Dennis finds the idea of rules and nature so inextricably bound that he insists "nothing" which exists in nature can be "great and beautiful without rule and order." His argument does not end with this statement. He elaborates by linking rules with the beautiful and great in Nature as well as by asserting that, in fact, "Nature is Rule and Order itself."[6]   In the remainder of Dennis' letter, he relates the rules to the idea of probability, the essential justification for the use of rules in the drama.[7]

"The sequence of events in *all* comedy," (emphasis mine) in fact, according to Lane Cooper's application of Aristotle's *Poetics* to comedy, "must often run counter to the laws of necessity and probability."[8]   Probability was a necessary adjunct of the world-view of the Restoration critic. Thomas Rymer, for instance, believed that probability in drama would intensify man's faith, particularly through the depiction of poetic justice, "that necessary relation and chain, whereby the causes and the effects, the virtues and rewards, the vices and the punishments are proportion'd and link'd together," which evinces "how deep and dark soever are laid the springs and however intricate and involv'd are the operations" of Providence.[9]   Only rarely did the Restoration critic overtly philosophize about why probability should be observed in the drama. Most, in

1962), pp. 260-61. Future references to this essay will be from this edition and will be noted in the text in the following manner, GCT and page number.

[6]John Dennis, Letter to Walter Moyle, in *"Of Dramatic Poesy" and Other Critical Essays,* ed. George Watson, vol. 2 (New York: E. P. Dutton and Company, Inc., 1962), p. 386.

[7]Probability was also, according to Gallaway, one of the main points of *attack* directed toward the "Mechanick Unities" (124).

[8]Lane Cooper, *Aristotelian Theory of Comedy* (New York: Harcourt, Brace, and Company, 1922), p. 187.

[9]Thomas Rymer, "The Tragedies of the Last Age Consider'd and Examin'd by the Practice of the Ancients and by the Common Sense of All Ages," in *Critical Essays of the Seventeenth Century,* ed. J. E. Spingarn, vol. 2 (Bloomington: Indiana University Press, 1957), pp. 206-207.

fact, related the idea of probability, as the modern audience does, to the rules of drama, or, more specifically, to notions about the unities, decorum, and less frequently the idea of poetic justice. For the audience, probability signified primarily that a play should seem as realistic as possible.

The "Mechanick Rules of the Unities," as both Dennis and Dryden call them more than once, probably were and are the rules most closely associated with the concept of probability in the drama. Drama presents an illusion of reality, and the most simplistic reasoning would assume that in order for a drama to portray reality effectively, it would need to conform as closely as it can to the superficialities of time, place, and action. This rationalization necessarily eliminates the complexities of human action and existence; by the same token, the simplicity and clarity of the approach suit the Restoration concept of the world much more neatly.[10]

The Restoration critic did not have to formulate the idea of the unities to accord with his philosophy of life but was provided with the concept by the classical writers. One of the basic tenets Aristotle suggests in the *Poetics* is that in a play one action should dominate and the time utilized to depict an action should correspond roughly to the actual time necessary to perform it. In Aristotle's words,

> Just as, therefore, in the other mimetic arts a unitary mimesis has a unitary object, so too the plot, since it is mimesis of an action, should be of a unitary and indeed whole action; and the component events should be so structured that if any is displaced or removed, the sense of the whole is disturbed and dislocated: since that wholse presence or absence has no clear significance is not an

---

[10]Gallaway, p. 206. Also see Norman Rabkin's *Shakespeare and the Problem of Meaning* for a discussion of Shakespearean adaptation as a process which "reduces" character and meaning to their lowest terms.

integral part of the whole.[11]

Aristotle's motives for writing the *Poetics* were regrettably misconstrued throughout the Renaissance and Restoration; for, in setting forth the unities, he was not prescribing the only method which could be used to produce an effective play. He was, on the other hand, looking at the plays which had been presented in the Athenian theater and attempting to deduce from them the characteristics which were common to the best plays.

In his study of the various atrocities the Shakespeare canon has been subjected to over the years, *Whatever Happened to Shakespeare?*, Kenneth McClellan partially vindicates Aristotle's role in the Restoration adaptations of Shakespeare in very much the same way the Restoration apologized for Shakespeare's "lawlessness"–by blaming the naïvetè of the age in which he lived. McClellan discovers fault in Aristotle's "small child's preoccupation with plot rather than character" and his equally childlike desire "to divide mankind very definitely into 'the good' and 'the bad.'" The classical starkness of Aristotle's thought led, in McClellan's opinion, to a simplistic classification of the Athenian plays which enabled him to disregard the fact that the Greek plays "continually flout the Unities."[12] Aeschylus, Sophocles, Euripides, and Aristophanes all prove Leo Salingar's observation that "Comedy has usually meant one thing in theory and another in practice."[13] For, even though Greek plays, especially tragedy, depend heavily upon *peripety* rather than a gradual growth and development of character, few of them blindly adhere to the unities of time, place, or action. The *Agamemnon* of Aeschylus, for instance, probably takes place over

[11]Aristotle, *Poetic*, edited and translated by Stephen Halliwell, The Loeb Classical Library, edited by G. P. Goold (Cambridge, Mass.: Harvard University Press, 1995), p. 59.

[12]Kenneth McClellan, *Whatever Happened to Shakespeare?* (New York: Barnes and Noble, 1978), p. 21.

[13]Leo Salingar, *Shakespeare and the Traditions of Comedy* (Cambridge: Cambridge University Press, 1974), p. 1.

a period of several days (some editions mark such a time lapse during the speeches of the Chorus, particularly before the herald comes to announce the entry of Agamemnon). Euripides' *Medea* and Aristophanes' *The Frogs* both contain scenes that some critics consider disruptive of unity of action. The scene in which Aegeus comes to offer sanctuary to Medea and the long debate between Aeschylus and Euripides in *The Frogs* represent two of the more difficult scenes to account for in Aristotelian dramaturgy.

A note concerning Aristotle's actual pronouncements on the unities is in order at this point. Aristotle does not mention unity of place in the *Poetics* at all. Leo Salingar contends that "it was the scene designer not Aristotle or Terence who came to dictate the critical "'law' of unity of place."[14] And, in terms of unity of time, some classical scholars feel that the Renaissance interpreters and commentators place far more emphasis on it than was intended. Dryden himself notes that the Roman dramatist Terence, "who was the best and most regular of them," did not adhere to unity of time in his *Self-Punisher.*"[15] H. B. Charlton in *Castelvetro's Theory of Poetry* claims that Aristotle does not even mention unity of time. He attributes the doctrine to Castelvetro who "was first to formulate the unities of time and place definitely" though Minturno "spoke" of unity of time and Scaliger makes "oblique references" to it. Even the Aristotelian commentators

---

[14]Ibid.," p. 184. Likewise, Gary Taylor attributes the need for unity of place in Restoration plays to the increasing use of realistic scenery: "In Shakespeare's case, changeable scenery also kept reminding audiences and critics of how often Shakespeare changed the scene. His violation of the prescribed unity of place became a recurring theme of literary criticism for the next century; it lay behind innumerable allusions, apologetic or accusing, to his lack of 'Art.' Performance on an unillustrated stage tends to minimize an audience's awareness of shifts in locale; Davenant's 'scenes,' by contrast, served as an inescapable repeated irritant, waving in front of spectators' noses an aspect of Shakespeare they disliked" (*Reinventing Shakespeare* 16). The adaptations support Salingar's and Taylor's assertions, for, while they may not always adhere to the doctrine of unity of place, they almost without exception greatly reduce the number of scene shifts.

[15]John Dryden, "Of Dramatic Poesy," in "*Of Dramatic Poesy""and Other Critical Essays*, ed. George Watson (New York: E. P. Dutton and Co., Inc., 1962), p. 36. Future references to this essay will be from this edition and will be noted in the text in the following manner, ODP and page number.

of the Italian Renaissance were not as adamant about the application of the unities as modern critics sometimes suggest. Charlton comments on Castelvetro's conception of unity of action–of the three unities, the most significant–"Thus, the unity of action is not an inherent necessity, but merely a demonstration of the skill of the poet."[16]   Considering the intellectual superiority the Restoration perceived itself to have over its predecessors, one can assume that this demonstration of excellence would be adequate motivation to keep the unities in their own plays.

Although that "three-headed monster,"[17] the Unities, was rather insignificant as far as the Athenian plays are concerned–the transcript of Aristotle's *Poetics*, after all, consists of only one medium length paragraph in a long treatise to them–later critics as well as translators of Aristotle began to place more emphasis on them. By the time of the English Renaissance, the unities had become almost synonymous with the idea of the laws of poetical drama. Emphasis on the unities was so strong that critics and playwrights of the Renaissance and Restoration failed to recognize them as the true embodiment of classical principles as opposed to a purely theoretical adherence. Leo Salingar points out the inability of the critics to recognize that Shakespeare, though downgraded throughout these periods for his failure to observe the classic laws, actually "applied the principles of classical comedy much more thoroughly than any English writer before him." According to Salingar, Shakespeare's early *Comedy of Errors* "showed that the 'upstart Crow' had not only picked up some of the lessons of classical art, but was prepared to apply them more thoroughly than anyone else."[18] Both *The Tempest* and *The Merry Wives of Windsor* follow

---

[16]H. B. Charlton, *Castelvetro's Theory of Poetry* (Manchester: University Press, 1913), pp. 89, 92.

[17]McClellan, p. 21.

[18]Salingar, pp. 27; 75.

the rules closely enough to show Shakespeare's ability to write plays closely conforming to classical dictates.

The playwrights of the Restoration needed only the influence of the French critics to convince them that, as Corneille says, "It is necessary to observe unity of action, place, and time; that no one doubts." So many of them failed to consider Corneille's thought-provoking addendum that the difficulty arises "in knowing what unity of action is, or how far one can extend this unity of time and place."[19] The best critics of the Restoration could not be certain about what constituted unity of action, time, or place, and their uncertainty, rather than their dogmatism, accounts for much of the critical output centering on the unities. The dialectic of Dryden's "Essay: Of Dramatic Poesy" (1668) set the tone for the coming era since it embodies most, if not all, of the dichotomies characterizing the Restoration's conception of the unities.

On the side of the rules particularly strict observance of the unities, Lisideius praises the French playwrights who are "so scrupulous" in the matter of unity of time "that it yet remains a dispute among their poets whether the artificial day of twelve hours more or less, be not meant by Aristotle, rather than the natural one of twenty-four." Lisideius also praises their similar close adherence to the unity of place, "none of them exceed the compass of the same town or city," and their even "more conspicuous" attention to unity of action, "for they do not burden themselves with underplots, as the English do" (ODP 44-45). Not content to hand down his pronouncements without providing a logical basis for them, Lisideius in the end affirms the justification for the unities in the need for "verisimility" (ODP 47). He uses the example of Shakespeare's history plays to illustrate. Since they span decades in the two or three hours of the presentation, these plays, according to Lisideius, do not "imitate or paint nature." Instead, they "draw her in miniature," even worse, "look upon her through the

[19]Corneille, pp. 575-76.

wrong end of a perspective, and receive her images not only much less, but infinitely more imperfect than life: this instead of making a play delightful, renders it ridiculous" (ODP 47). In response to Lisideius' preference to mechanical verisimilitude, Neander echoes the words of Corneille's "Discours des Trois Unities" noting how restricted a playwright is when he conforms to the rules and how many "'beauties of the stage'" have thus been "'banished from it'" (ODP 63). Dryden repeatedly voices this idea. The first three stanzas of his Prologue to *Secret Love* (1667) adequately summarize Dryden's feelings about the unities:

> He who writ this, not without pains and thought
>
> From *French* and *English* Theatres has brought
>
> Th'exactest Rules by which a Play is wrought.

> The Unities of Action, Place, and Time;
>
> The Scenes unbroken; and a mingled chime
>
> Of *Johnsons* humour, with *Corneilles* rhyme.

> But while dead colours he with care did lay,
>
> He fears his Wit, or Plot he did not weigh,
>
> Which are the living Beauties of a Play.[20]

In a letter "To John, Lord Haughton" (1681), Dryden reiterates the notion that a playwright should be able "to break a rule for the pleasure of variety," (LH 279) as variety is the hallmark of the English genius.

Dryden's "Of Dramatic Poesy" quickly stirred critical debate. One of the first respondents was his brother-in-law and sometime collaborator, Sir Robert Howard, took the unflattering portrait of Crites to represent himself. Steeped in the tradition of the Renaissance playwright, Howard disagreed with the emphasis

---

[20]John Dryden, Prologue to *Secret Love*, in *The Prologues and Epilogues of John Dryden: A Critical Edition* (New York: Columbia University Press, 1951), p. 10. Future references to this essay will be from this edition and will be noted in the text in the following manner, *SL*, and page number.

Lisideius placed on the rules and felt that Crites inadequately countered his arguments. In his Preface to *The Great Favourite*, Howard condemns the "unnecessary understanding of some that have labour'd to give strict rules to things that are not Mathematical," and then proceeds "to make it evident that there's no such thing as What [laws for poetry] they all pretend" by using logic to refute the idea of the unities. He elaborates:

> . . . if strictly and duly weigh'd, 'tis as impossible for one stage to represent two Houses or two Roomes truly as two Countreys or Kingdomes, and as impossible that five houres, or four and twenty houres should be two houres and a halfe as that a thousand houres or yeares should be less than what they are, or the greatest part of time to be comprehended in the less; for all being impossible, they are none of them nearest the truth or nature of what they present, for Impossibilities are all equal and admit no degrees.[21]

Howard did not have to wait long for a response.

Incensed by the narrow interpretation of his "Essay," Dryden came to his own defense. Rather than reassuring his kinsman and now literary rival that they both sided with nature over the rules when the ultimate confrontation came, Dryden took the more human move of producing "A Defence of the 'Epilogue'" (1668). In the "Defence," Dryden decided to play devil's advocate and much more rigidly affirmed the efficacy of the rules than he had done in the "Essay." In his treatment of the unities, for instance, he now asserts that the time of all plays should "be contrived into as narrow a compass as the nature of the plot, the quality of the persons, and the variety of accidents will allow." For comedy, he prescribes a limit of thirty hours; he allows a greater time for tragedy whose "design is weighty" (DE 128). Perhaps more than anything else, Howard's

---

[21]Sir Robert Howard, Preface to *The Great Favourite*, in *Critical Essays of the Seventeenth Century*, ed. J. E. Spingarn, vol. 1 (Bloomington: Indiana University Press, 1957), p. 106.

rational refutation of the unities had stung Dryden into debate. Dryden struck back with bitter satire centering on Howard's discussion of unity of place and then continued by informing Howard that although the stage indeed "cannot *be* two places, yet it may properly *represent* them successively, or at several times" (italics mine), for, after all, the "real place is that of the theatre, or piece of ground, on which the play is acted." At this point in his defense, Dryden adds weight to Howard's feeling that unity of place is not necessary or even desirable in a play, but he approaches the problem from the opposite direction.

In this instance, as in most of his dramatic criticism, Dryden does not blindly advocate the opinion of the classical critics, but rather, appeals to them as authority to back up his own well-considered views.[22]   Although in this debate with Howard Dryden asserts that "Neither the Ancients nor Moderns, as much fools as he is pleased to think them, ever asserted that they could make one place two," his essential justification is not based on what Aristotle or Horace or Scaliger has to say.   The authority he appeals to is "every man's imagination" which "aided by the words of the poet and painted scenes, may suppose the stage to be sometimes one place, sometimes another, now a garden, or a wood, and immediately a camp" (DE 125). If such diversity in the "imaginary place of action" is possible, then unity of action is even easier to contemplate.

In further answering the attack on the "impossibility" of unity of time and place, Dryden ridicules the "absurdity" to which Howard had hoped to "reduce" him and then proceeds to affirm that this absurdity is, in fact, logical—"there are degrees in impossibilities" (DE 129). For, as he has mentioned earlier in the "Defence," the narrower the compass of time and place in a play, "the greater

---

[22]Dryden, "A Defence of the Epilogue," p.125. Future references to this essay will be from this edition and will be noted in the text in the following manner, DE and page number. Dryden explains at the outset of the "Defence" that his "whole discourse was sceptical" framed as it is in the form of a "dialogue sustained by persons of several opinions, all of them left doubtful, to be determined by readers in general" (DE 123).

resemblance they will have to truth" (DE 127).[23]   Well-thought out and logical though it is, Dryden's "Defence" apparently did not convince even him that the unities are of supreme importance in making a good play. By 1690 in the Preface to *Don Sebastian*, he remarks unabashedly that he has "not exactly kept to the three mechanic rules of unity." His deviations from the rules have not been gratuitous, however, but represent a necessary infraction for an English playwright writing for an English audience "given to variety." After explaining the exact way in which the play departs from the unities, Dryden acquits himself by assuring the reader that "to gain a greater beauty, 'tis lawful for a poet to supersede a less." Dryden has thus come full circle in his discussion of the unities to an avowal once more that the play, and not the rules, is the "thing."[24]

The heated debate over the unities embarked upon by Dryden and Howard did not deter the critics of the following generation from attempting once again to decipher the mysteries of the unities. That the dilemma did not diminish over the years is evident in the time span during which Dryden himself addressed the question. Those playwrights who wrote comedy, as Dryden did occasionally, if rather unsuccessfully, appear to have been more lenient as far as the rules, and particularly the unities, were concerned. The Rymers and Granvilles, as a result, lean more strongly to the close adherence to the unities whereas Dennis and Farquahar advocate a pragmatic approach to their application.[25]   The adapters

---

[23] According to Sarup Singh, Dryden "showed that the question of the unities was to be considered, if at all, from a dramatic or an artistic point of view rather than from that of any rigid naturalism" (167). He goes on to note Neander's comment in "Of Dramatic Poesy" that in strictly observing the unities, the author risks "'misrepresenting nature'" particularly in the portrayal of love, the "chief, if not the only, theme of contemporary comedy and tragedy" which made utter "nonsense of the unities" (170).

[24] John Dryden, Preface to *Don Sebastian*, in *"Of Dramatic Poesy" and Other Critical Essays*, ed. George Watson, vol.1(New York: E. P. Dutton and Company, Inc., 1962), p. 49. For a more complete discussion of the major ideas of Restoration playwrights and critics see also Sarup Singh, *The Theory of Drama in the Restoration Period*; Robert D. Hume's chapter on the rules in his *The Development of English Drama in the Late Seventeenth Century* ; and Francis Gallaway's *Reason, Rule and Revolt in English Classicism*.

under consideration here–Dennis, Burnaby, Granville, and Gildon–though they all adapted Shakespearean comedy, constitute members of both critical "camps." Dennis, Gildon, and Burnaby range themselves with those more sceptical of the rules, or at least, those who admit the rules may need to be forsaken every now and then; while Granville is, in Robert Hume's estimation, "wholly on the side of the rules."[26] John Dennis' comments on the unities are characteristic of the later seventeenth and early eighteenth century:

> . . . The Unities of Time and Place are Mechanick Rules which, if they are observ'd with judgement, strengthen the reasonableness of the Incidents, heighten the probability of the Action, promote the agreeable Deceit of the Representation, and add Cleanliness, Grace, and Comeliness to it. But if they are practic'd without Discretion, they render the Action more improbable and the Representation more absurd.[27]

Like many of his predecessors, Dennis did not require the unities as essential to a good play and, indeed, believed a too close observance often harms plays.

The opinions expressed in the dialogue *A Comparison Between the Two Stages*, sometimes attributed to Gildon, similarly waver between an appreciation of the enhancement of plays produced through the application of the unities (Crites) and a desire for the beauties of the kind of play created with only the merest attention to unity (Rambler). Rambler, for instance, feels that "if one Scene brings in another, that a third, and so on, and every scene be wrought

---

[25]Like Dryden, Farquahar had difficulty in clearly aligning himself. In his "Discourse upon Comedy in a Letter to a Friend" (1702), he notes the absurdity of much of the defense of unity of place as Howard had in his Preface to *The Great favourite*. Farquahar later admits a distaste of "rambling Plays," and E. N. Hooker notes that Farquahar's own "practice was opposed to needless change of scene." (455–explanatory note to "Of the Simplicity in Poetical Compositions.")

[26]Hume, p. 183.

[27]John Dennis, "Remarks Upon *Cato*, a Tragedy," in *The Critical Works of John Dennis*, ed. E. N. Hooker, vol. 2 (Baltimore: The Johns Hopkins University Press, 1939), p. 68.

conclusive of one great action at last, the unity may be said to be well enough preserv'd." The example he uses to explain his point does not obtain the approval of Crites, who deems that the two strands of the plot are not tied closely enough together: "the two Actions are carried on without any adherence to each other, and as they are divided all along in the Play, so the Catastrophe of each is different and remote."[28] Crites' statement here significantly does not disavow the "double plot" in itself even though he is referring at this point to a tragedy. Because the discussion is centering on a specific play and not on the general notion of the unities, Crites' true position with respect to the double plot is difficult to ascertain. He appears in other places, however, to be lenient regarding the rules, especially where genius is concerned. After Sullen's paean to Shakespeare, for example, Crites remarks that "no Author ever writ with that Felicity, or had such a prodigious compass of Thought; and tho' some of those Plays that Batterton [*sic*] acted were Historical, and consequently highly irregular, yet they never failed to please" (*CTS* 42-43). Oddly, Crites is much more dogmatic in the application of unity of place when he asserts that the "whole Representation of a Play shou'd be confin'd to one Room, and no more." Realizing that this restriction is too severe for most playwrights, he agrees to limit the place to an "Apartment, a Gallery, a House" but draws the line at street scenes, "for after such a latitude the unity is intirely lost; and the Play may as well take in the compass of half the Globe" (*CTS* 143). As Crites discusses the specifics of the play at hand, a task he perseveres in not from any inherent desire to be contentious but because the prologue of the said play "brags so much of these unities," Rambler comments on the triviality of the scene changes Crites is enumerating. With the *Comparison*, as with Dryden's "Of Dramatic Poesy," the reader must ultimately decide whose opinion is most reasonable.

---

[28] Charles Gildon, *A Comparison Between the Two Stages* (New York: Garland Publishing, Inc., 1973), pp. 130-31. Future references to this essay will be from this edition and will be noted in the text in the following manner, *CTS* and page number.

William Burnaby does not state his ideas on the unities as explicitly as Dennis or Dryden. He touches on unity of action in his Preface to *The Ladies' Visiting Day* when he comments that "In a good play there shou'd be nothing but what rises from the Business of it; the Flowers that appear shou'd grow there, as one in a Garden is worth fifty in a Pot"[29] Burnaby expresses a corresponding view in a letter included in *Letters of 'Wit', 'Politicks' and 'Morality.' Original Letters on Divers Subjects, by Several Hands,* 1701. In his letter, "Letter V. *Wherein are Laid down general Rules to judge of Tragedy and Comedy,*" Burnaby addresses the question of subplots[30] in tragedies finding that they "weaken" the effect of the terror and pity, and he ends his letter with this advice: "Read *Aristotle* and *Dacier* and consider Nature thoroughly" in order to make "a true Judgement of the Drama."[31]

Burnaby's closing encomium adequately sums up the rationale of the age towards the unities; they are necessary, but even more essential is the proper knowledge and application of "Nature." Gallaway asserts that "from a

---

[29]William Burnaby, Preface to *The Ladies' Visiting Day,* in *The Complete Works of William Burnaby* ed. F. E. Budd (London: E. Partridge, The Scholartis Press, 1931), p. 276. This statement is reminiscent of Richard Flecknoe's reference to Suckling's and some others' comparison of Jonson and Shakespeare–"one wittily of his Aglaura that 'twas full of fine flowers, but they seem'd rather stuck then [sic] growing there; as another of Shakespear's writings, that 'twas a fine Garden, but it wanted weeding" [Richard Flecknoe, "A Short Discourse of the English Stage," in *Critical Essays of the Seventeenth Century,* ed. J. E. Spingarn (Bloomington: Indiana University Press, 1957), p. 92].

[30]The double plot is not forbidden in comedy. Aristotle, in fact, finds it suitable to comedy (*Poetics,* p. 87). Giraldi Cinthio believes it to be "much praised in comedy" (254). Giraldi Cinthio, "On The Composition of Comedies and Tragedies" in *Literary Criticism: Plato to Dryden,* ed. Allan H. Gilbert (New York: American Book Company, 1940). The Restoration's love of balance and symmetry made this structure even more desirable for them. Gildon, for instance, remarks in his *Complete Art of Poetry,* vol. 1 (New York: Garland Publishing, Inc., 1970), that the double plot "may do well in Comedy" (244). Future references to Gildon's *Complete Art of Poetry* will be from this edition and will be noted in the text in the following manner, *CAP,* and page number.

[31]Burnaby, p. 460. Burnaby interestingly devotes the majority of his essay to tragedy, his "Taste, Genius, and Inclination leading" him "to Tragedy" (459). Burnaby's craft evidently led him to comedy, though, for his extant plays include five comedies and one adaptation of a comedy.

perspective of two centuries" the modern critic can recognize "direct debts to the Ancients" exerted relatively "little effect on the independent spirit of the major classicists, for the 'neoclassical' Rules were often questioned, frequently modified, and, in general, respected only when it could be shown that Reason and the Rules were the same."[32] Reason and nature, not the Rules, were therefore of supreme importance to the Restoration critic and playwright.

Although the modern reader may think of the neoclassical rules of drama as pertaining primarily to the unities of time, place, and action, the unities constitute only a very small part of the characteristics evaluated by Aristotle and his many disciples. In his study *Reason, Rule, and Revolt,* Gallaway notes that "most critics" regard as "obligatory" not only unity of action, probability, and "imitation of nature," but also decorum, poetic justice, "perspicuity, singleness of artistic purpose, and the moral aim in art."[33] The Restoration critic by no means rests with these strictures. Also significant in his study of the drama are symmetry, clarity, consistency, the advantages of rhyme, blank verse or prose, and an in-depth examination of characterization.

Many of the aspects of drama the Restoration critics considered important were bound to what they considered to be the purpose of the drama. The Restoration had little conception of "art for art's sake." The same was true in the early days of the Restoration when Davenant made clear that the plays presented in his theater were "moral representations, full of lessons concerning the heroic

---

[32]Gallaway, p. 185.

[33]Ibid., p. 197. An interesting article by Derek Hughes, "Providential Justice and English Comedy 1660-1700: A Review of the External Evidence" *The Modern Language Review* 81:2 (April 1986): 273-292, refutes the "moral aim" such critics as J. Douglas Canfield, Aubrey L. Williams, and W. Gerald Marshall attribute to Restoration drama and Restoration comedy in particular. The upshot of Hughes' argument–that the idea of providential justice represents a complex set of beliefs among the religious, as well as in the secular, community during the Restoration–though it is a subtle and accurate examination of the concept of poetic justice–will not be dealt with in the confines of this study. Here what is significant is not whether the playwrights or the audience truly believed in providential justice, but rather, whether the changes made in the adaptations led to an increased perception of poetic justice.

virtues to be pursued and the bad vices to be shunned."[34]   In this instance, the more graphic the depiction of "the bad vices," the more effective the play was considered morally.   Jeremy Collier's attack precipitated the development of a new kind of comedy, the *comédie larmoyante* which stressed the use of role models rather than the portrayal of "bad vices to be shunned."

This response was partially a defensive reaction, especially in the final days of the seventeenth century, to the growing distaste for stage plays provoked by Collier's "Short View of the Profaneness and Immorality of the English Stage."[35]   That the critics and playwrights of the Restoration saw the didactic ends of poetry does not mean that they felt the moral purpose to be the only, or indeed, the chief purpose of art.   In the early days of the Restoration, Dryden's discussion of the advantages of rhyme over prose in plays led him to comment that he is "satisfied if it [rhyme] cause delight."   He adds, "for delight is the chief, if not the only end of poesy; instruction can be admitted but in the second place" (DE 113).   With this problem, as with the other aspects of his criticism, Dryden exhibits the "Janus face" he so frequently assigns to Shakespeare.   He prefaces *Troilus and Cressida* (1679) with the statement that the "general end of all poetry" is "to instruct delightfully,"[36] and his "Parallel of Poetry and Painting" in

---

[34]Philip Bordinat and Sophia Blaydes, *Sir William Davenant* (Boston: Twayne Publishers, 1981), p. 304.

[35]Gewirtz, pp. 20-21, interestingly comments that of the major adapters of Shakespeare's comedies, only Davenant and John Lacy "entirely" eliminate "the ethical framework of the source." Derek Hughes finds that Restoration playwrights may have paid lipservice to the idea of a moral purpose of drama in order to continue to fill the stage with titillation, intrigue, and the escapades of cads and fops, far more interesting to the audiences of the Restoration than the uneventful lives of the virtuous. Even when the playwright *may* have had every good intention in depicting vice "with condemnation" the "unregeneracy of audiences" often "thwarted" that attempt by viewing the vice "with approval" as the Prologue to Colley Cibber's *Xerxes* (1699) points out when it claims, as Hughes notes, that "even Collier's book can serve the interests of vice: 'Girls may read him, not for the truth he says,/But to be pointed to the bawdy plays'" (291).

[36]John Dryden, Preface to *Troilus and Cressida*, in *"Of Dramatic Poesy,"* ed. George Watson, vol. 1 (New York: E.P. Dutton and Co., Inc., 1962), p. 209.

1695 informs the reader that the "chief design of poetry is to instruct;"[37] in this instance, he entirely omits the idea of delight. Dryden's Preface to *An Evening's Love* once again shows his ambivalence. Here he asserts that "the chief end" of comedy is "divertisement and delight; and that so much that it is disputed, I think by Heinsius before Horace his *Art of Poetry*, whether instruction be any part of its employment."[38] Ker notes Dryden's faulty memory here; Heinsius mentions the didactic as essential to comedy. Earlier in the Preface, he says that he knows "no such law [the "law" he refers to here being that comedy is "to reward virtue and punish vice"] to have been constantly observed in comedy, either by the ancient or modern poets."[39]

The moral use of tragedy and the heroic drama are readily apparent, but even comedy has a didactic element according to the critics writing during the Restoration. The ancient law of comedy as related by Dryden in the Preface to the *Mock-Astrologer* demands that it "reward Virtue" and "punish Vice." Restoration comedy all too often did just the opposite as far as Jeremy Collier was concerned, and this infringement prompted his condemnation of the English stage. Had Collier's attack dealt only with the licentiousness of contemporary comedy, it might not have provoked the critical outpouring that resulted. Not content to denounce specific instances of immorality in specific plays, Collier instead damned the stage as a whole, railing that it "seldom gives Quarter to any Thing that's serviceable or significant, but persecutes Worth and Goodness under

[37] John Dryden, "Parallel of Poetry and Painting," in "*Of Dramatic Poesy,*" ed. George Watson, vol. 2 (New York: E.P. Dutton and Co., Inc., 1962), p. 186. Future references to this essay will be from this edition and will be noted in the text in the following manner, PPP and page number.

[38] John Dryden, Preface to *An Evening's Love*, in "*Of Dramatic Poesy,*" ed. George Watson, vol. 1 (New York: E.P. Dutton and Co., Inc., 1962), p. 152. Future references to this essay will be from this edition and will be noted in the text in the following manner, *EL*, and page number.

[39] W. P. Ker, Introduction to *Essays of John Dryden*, vol. 1 (Oxford: Clarendon Press, 1926), p. 150.

every Appearance."[40] Collier's attack produced a great deal of dissension. Not since the Restoration began had the critics exerted such effort to show why the drama was beneficial to the health and welfare of the populace. The response may well have exceeded even the defense of the stage yielded in the early days of the Restoration.[41]

John Dennis stands at the forefront of all the upholders of the Restoration stage. Dennis is unique both in the sheer volume of his defense and the moral fervor with which he proclaims his views. Dennis quickly countered Collier's arguments by appealing to an authority even Collier could not resist. He notes in "The Stage Defended, from Scripture, Reason, Experience, and the Common Sense" that St. Paul himself did not speak out against the drama, "but makes use of it for the conversion and Reformation of Mankind." Dennis contends that when Paul mentions the words of the Greek dramatists in his sermon on Mars Hill (Acts 17:22-31) without warning the listeners against the stage, he is implicitly "establishing the stage by no baser an Authority than that of the Spirit of God himself." Later in the same essay, Dennis refers to Archbishop Tillotson's admonition against those who totally condemn stage plays. He quotes Tillotson's opinion that plays may be "'so framed, and governed by such Rules'" that they are not only entertaining and harmless but might actually be "instructive and useful, to put some Vices and Follies out of Countenance, which cannot perhaps be so decently, nor so effectually exposed and corrected any other Way."[42]

[40]Jeremy Collier, "A Short View of the Immorality of the Stage," in *Critical Essays of the Seventeenth Century* ed. J. E. Spingarn, vol. 3 (Bloomington: Indiana University Press, 1957), p. 256.

[41]Hume thoroughly discusses the reasons behind the insistence of comedy's moral aim in his chapter, "The Comedy of Manners" (*Development of English Drama*). He subscribes to James Sutherland's view that it amounted primarily to "'prestige advertising'" (Hume 213). Perhaps the most complete discussion of this situation can be found in Joseph Wood Krutch's *Comedy and Conscience After the Restoration* (New York: Columbia University Press, 1961).

[42]John Dennis, "The Stage Defended, from Scripture, Reason, Experience, and the Common Sense," in *The Critical Works of John Dennis,* ed. E. N. Hooker, vol. 2 (Baltimore:

Dennis not only argued that the contemporary writers were adequately fulfilling the didactic goals of dramatic literature, but he believed they were accomplishing these objectives better than the ancient poets had. His "Advancement and Reformation of Poetry" compares the effectiveness of the ancient poets, especially the writers of comedy, to that of the modern playwrights and discovers that whether the end of comedy be to delight or to instruct, the moderns "clearly" have the "Advantage." "Modern" comedy instructed better in Dennis' opinion since, unlike ancient comedy whose "*Ridiculum*" was "often out of Nature," contemporary comedy based its *ridiculum* on nature, and was also superior in the "greater Variety of it, both in their Persons and Actions" enabling the "Instruction in the Modern Comedy" to be "more extensive."[43]

The lewdness and licentiousness of the stage which so angered and upset Jeremy Collier are the very elements which induced Dennis to argue the efficacy of the stage in mending manners and morals. Dennis neither approves nor condones the "people" represented in the plays when he commends the inherent morality of the plays themselves. His views come through most clearly in "On the Prophaneness of Comedies," when he writes, "Our Comedies are but Copies of the foolish and vicious Originals of the Age; and 'tis the Business of the Copier to expose, and satyrize, and ridicule those foolish and those vicious Originals." Then he proceeds to examine the state of affairs that was conducive to such works and finds that at the beginning of the Restoration, the court had been "corrupted by foreign Luxury" and returned to "debauch" the "Town" which, in turn, joined forces with the Court to "debauch the stage, because our Comick Poets were

The Johns Hopkins University Press, 1943), p. 306. Future references to this essay will be from this edition and will be noted in the text in the following manner, SD and page number.

[43]John Dennis, "Advancement and Reformation of Poetry," in *The Critical Works of John Dennis,* ed. E. N. Hooker, vol. 1 (Baltimore: The Johns Hopkins University Press, 1939), pp. 224, 226. Future references to this essay will be from this edition and will be noted in the text in the following manner, ARMP and page number.

obliged to copy their Lewd Originals, in order to expose and reform them."[44]   If the comedies of the Restoration contain unseemly characters, the fault lies not with the playwright, but with the age in which he lived. As Dennis states later in a letter to Congreve (25 May 1719) defending Wycherley's *Plain Dealer*, the "Business of a Comick Poet" is "to paint the Age in which he lives, which if he doth not paint, he doth nothing at all."[45] For, in exposing the viciousness and folly of the characters, the dramatist shows the audience "what ought never to be done upon the stage of the world." By enveloping the same folly in ridicule, he attempts to "cure" his spectators of it "by the apprehension of being laugh'd at."[46]

The other adapters under consideration here also deem that comedy has a moral objective. Charles Gildon's commentary on Lord Roscommon's *Laws of*

---

[44]Dennis, SD vol. 2, p. 313.

[45]John Dennis, Letter to William Congreve, in *The Critical Works of John Dennis*, ed. E. N. Hooker, vol. 2 (Baltimore: The Johns Hopkins University Press, 1943), p. 233. The "morality" of Restoration comedy has been the subject of extensive debate over the past few decades. John T. Harwood's *Critics, Values, and Restoration Comedy* (Carbondale: Southern Illinois University Press, 1982), studies the problem in great detail in an attempt to discern whether the theatre reflects or influences society's morals. Important works related to the topic are Norman Holland's *The Dynamics of Literary Response* (New York: Oxford University Press, 1968); Thomas H. Fujimura, *The Restoration Comedy of Wit* (Princeton: Princeton University Press, 1952); C. D. Cecil, "Libertine and *Preciéux* Elements in Restoration Comedy" *Essays in Criticism* 9 (1959):239-53; and G. Wilson Knight, *The Golden Labyrinth: A Study of British Drama* (New York: Norton, 1962). A. N. Kaul, *The Action of English Comedy* (New Haven: Yale University Press, 1970) writes that in Restoration comedy the "idea of innate grace degenerates into the idea of innate gracefulness," while Arthur Gewirtz, *Restoration Adaptations of Early Seventeenth Century Comedies,* asserts that "Restoration comedy is not moral, amoral, non-moral, or even immoral. . . . Rather, it portrays a world which has not yet settled the claims of the individual and society" (xxi).

[46]John Dennis, "Defense of Sir Fopling Flutter," in *The Critical Works of John Dennis,* ed. E. N. Hooker, vol. 2 (Baltimore: The Johns Hopkins University Press, 1943), p. 248. Congreve agrees with this sentiment in the Prologue to his play, *The Way of the World*–"To please this time has been his sole pretense." The following line, however, disavows any didactic purpose in his play when he says, "He'll not instruct, lest it should give offense"; this view probably does not represent Congreve's actual ideas on the moral aim of the drama, for it seems purely a courtesy (possibly satirical) to the audience. If the play happens to "expose some knave or fool," this character was not included to wound the sensibilities of the audience by laughing at their mirror images; for "sure here are none of those" (Congreve, Prologue, 311, ll. 32-35). In his *Amendments to Mr. Collier's . . . Citations* (1698), he espouses views similar to those of Dennis.

Poetry delves into the issue in great detail. He first points out that the "dispute" over the necessity of the *utile* in drama is of relatively recent origin and has been "chiefly promoted by those weak writers who wanted genius and a judgment enough to mingle the *profitable with the pleasant*" and therefore voiced their opinion that instruction was not the poet's purpose. Gildon then looks back at the ancient authors who reinforce his own ideas that poetry without a message is "too weak, and too trifling to be thought of any importance to human happiness. . . . it passes away in a moment, without touching the heart, the only source of great, true, noble, and lasting pleasure."[47]

In his discussion of the pleasant and profitable in drama, Gildon focuses his attention on their application to tragedy, the epic, and satire; and, after a long discussion of the "nature, origin, and progress" (*LP* 138) of each, he examines Horace's *Satires* to illustrate how comic verse may be used to instruct. Although at first such poetry appears to be fit only "to amuse children," on closer observation, it yields valuable lessons. Horace's *Satires* and, Gildon implies, all comedy has as its motivation a desire to

> teach us to conquer vices, to rule our passions, to follow nature, to distinguish true from false, and ideas from things; to forsake prejudice, to know thoroughly the principles and motives of all *our actions, and to Shun that folly which is in all men, who are bigotted to the opinions they have imbibed under their teachers, which they keep obstinately, without examining whether they are well grounded.* In a word, *he endeavors to make us happy for ourselves, agreeable and faithful to our friends, easy, discreet, and honest to all with whom we are obliged to live.* (*LP* 139)[48]

[47]Charles Gildon, *The Laws of Poetry*, (New York: Garland Publishing, Inc., 1962), p. 124. Future references to this essay will be from this edition and will be noted in the text in the following manner, *LP*, and page number.

[48]Though many critics deny the presence of any morality in Wycherley's *Country Wife*, Thomas Fujimura believes that its hero, Horner, adequately summarizes the whole "object of

Gildon expresses his views on the object of comedy more explicitly in a letter affixed to Thomas D'Urfey's *The Marriage Hater Match'd*, affirming that "the Business of Comedy was to expose the general Vices and Follies of the Age." In this instance, he looks more favorably at the *divertisement* of comedy. If perfection in instruction is lacking, he proceeds, then the excellence of the poet's discourse should not be undervalued, "the end of Comedy being Pleasure, as well as Instruction." The poet must pay heed to his vocation as an entertainer as well as teacher, for "let the Moral or Instructive part be never so well writ, the Language never so fine, yet if the Action goes on without any Plot to divert us... it gratifies none of our Passions, without which there can be no Pleasure."[49] According to Gildon, the *dulce et utile* must be interwoven so that one supports and reinforces the other.

George Granville's "Advertisement to the Reader" which precedes his adaptation of Shakespeare's *Merchant of Venice*–Granville entitles it *The Jew of Venice*–begins with what amounts to an apology for his "bestowing so much time and 'Labour'" upon such a comedy. He then excuses himself for his choice of play on the grounds that it contains "so many Manly and Moral Graces in the Characters and Sentiments," and, in the "Epilogue," he remarks the "good Moral and just Thought" of the play. The "Epilogue" also clearly states the role of the drama in exposing and thereby eliminating Vice:

> The present time still gives the Stage its Mode,
>
> The Vices which you practice, we explode:
>
> We hold the Glass, and but reflect your Shame,

satire" in the following: "A pox on 'em, and all that force nature, and would be still what she forbids 'em! Affectation is her greatest monster" (1.1.248-9). Thomas Fujimura, *The Restoration Comedy of Wit* (Princeton: Princeton University Press, 1952), p. 54. (Many of the prologues and epilogues written during this period show at least mention the follies and vices ridiculed in the plays.

[49]Charles Gildon, Preface material to *The Marriage Hater Match'd*, (London: for Richard Parker and Sam Briscoe; Three Centuries of English Drama, 1642-1700, TCD-E-911), prior to p. 1.

Like *Spartans*, by exposing, to reclaim.

The Prologue to Granville's *She-Gallants* expresses the didactic goal of poetry dramatically by having the poet pose as a warrior who "mounts the Stage, to bid Immortal Wars" against "Vice" which has seized the town.

More vocal on the subject than Granville, William Burnaby keeps the morality of the plays in the forefront of the audience's mind by delineating it in his prologues and epilogues. He ends his *Reform'd Wife* with the injunction to the audience to "Let none hereafter Plays Ungodly call,/For this was writ to mortifie you all."[50] As Burnaby explains to the audience, he has presented nothing but the follies which beset each man and woman in an attempt to "reform" them. That Burnaby has not been as licentious or blasphemous in his presentation as was the norm in Restoration comedy does not indicate that he approves of the movement towards sentimental comedy which was beginning in the first decade of the eighteenth century or that he disapproves of the portrayal of more unpleasant characterizations and incidents. The Dedication to Lord Ormond at the beginning of *The Ladies' Visiting Day* more appropriately characterizes his view. Burnaby here apologizes to the ladies who have been offended by his play, but adds that his purpose could only be served by the inclusion of such material. Or, as Burnaby puts it, "He that attempts to put Impudence and Folly out of Countinance [*sic*], may be forc'd to Blush himself" in the process.[51] In his Prologue to Mrs. Centlivre's *The Perjur'd Husband*, Burnaby addresses the problem of morality and pleasure in comedy through the use of satire. He brings the poet before the "bar" of justice to "plead Guilty: And confess the Stage/Has

---

[50]William Burnaby, *The Reform'd Wife* (London: Thomas Bennet, 1700; Ann Arbor, Mich.: University Microfilms, B5745, 1973), p. 192. Future references to this play are from this edition and will be noted in the text according to page number.

[51]William Burnaby, Dedication to Lord Ormond affixed to *The Ladies' Visiting Day*, in *The Complete Works of William Burnaby*, F. E. Budd, ed. (London: E. Partridge; The Scholartis Press, 1931), p. 195.

been immoral and debauch'd the Age."[52] After carefully examining the situation of the times–an era of quibbling lawyers, cheating Magistrates, hypocritical churchmen, cowardly soldiers, and painted Beaux–the poet decides that he will indeed reform the stage, but only when these vices have been obliterated.

Much of the controversy over the purpose of the drama, particularly as related to comedy, focuses on characterization. According to John Dennis, this emphasis is entirely just as "Comedy instructs by its Characters, which not only ought to be drawn truly in Nature, but to be the resembling Picture of our contemporaries, both in Court and Town."[53] Characterization is another dilemma that divides Restoration critics and playwrights. All seem to agree with the importance Dennis assigns to characterization. Hooker comments that in stressing the supremacy of characterization over plot in comedy, Dennis "breaks away from the neoclassic assumption that plot is the main element in comedy, as in tragedy."[54] Dennis explains the reason for assigning the superiority to characterization in his "Large Account of Taste in Poetry" when he asserts that as comedy teaches through the *ridiculum*, the *ridiculum* must first "be in the Characters, or else it cannot be in the Incidents, and consequently there can be no Comedy."[55]

William Burnaby, on the other hand, feels that plot is the "chief Thing" in a play. He looks down upon those writers who produce admirable characters of remarkable wit but who are not able to devise plots adequate to display that wit.

---

[52]William Burnaby, Prologue to Mrs. Centlivre's *The Perjur'd Husband* (London: for Bennet Banbury, 1700; Three Centuries of English Drama, TCD-E-1469), p. 453.

[53]"Sir Fopling," p. 245.

[54]Hooker, p. 470.

[55]"Large Account," p. 294. In discussing Dennis's *The Comical* Gallant, David Wheeler ("Eighteenth-Century Adaptations of Shakespeare and the Example of John Dennis," *Shakespeare Quarterly* 36.4 (Winter 1985): 446), contends, on the other hand, that "For Dennis,

Such writers, according to Burnaby, do not deserve the "Name of a Dramatick Writer, with the best Judges."[56] Although Burnaby's emphasis is different from Dennis', his intentions are the same–the melding of plot and character.

The treatment of characters in the Restoration did not provoke much critical debate. Closely associated with characterization are the concepts of poetic justice, decorum, and consistency–all mentioned by Aristotle in his *Poetics*, critical doctrines which did undergo substantial debate. Perhaps the leniency with which Aristotle spoke of characterization prevented any great dispute over it. Nonetheless, the Restoration presents a fairly united front on the issue, particularly with regards to comedy. Poetic justice is, according to John Dennis, "sufficiently observed if the folly or vice depicted in comedy is exposed to ridicule"[57] and the subject is brought up in relation to the proper function of comedy in society. Decorum was never as strictly applied in England as in France, according to Gallaway. It was, rather, "merged in the more flexible regard for probability." Only those "overly impressed" with the "sanctity of the social order and with the majesty of kings" rigidly upheld the doctrine. Even at its peak in England decorum meant only what Aristotle said it should: that the "actions," "intentions," and "language" of a character should correspond to his station in life, "his sex, his age, and his temperament."[58]

Although the Restoration interpreted Aristotle's decorum and poetic justice rather leniently, it viewed the idea of consistency in character with less

... action is the business of the state, the humours are to be displayed through action rather than through dialogue. Dennis transforms a comedy of language into a comedy of situations...."

[56]William Burnaby, "Critical Essay," in *The Complete Dramatic Works of William Burnaby* (London: E. Partridge; The Scholartis Press, 1931), p. 459.

[57]John Dennis, "The Advancement and Reformation of Poetry," in *The Critical Works of John Dennis*, ed. E. N. Hooker, vol. 1. (Baltimore: The Johns Hopkins University Press, 1939), p. 225. Future references to this essay will be from this edition and will be noted in the text in the following manner, "ARMP" and page number.

[58]Gallaway, p. 163.

tolerance. Aristotle insists on constancy in the portrait, but even more vehemently on realism. "Even if the subject represented is someone inconsistent" Aristotle asserts, "and such character is presupposed, he should still be consistently inconsistent."[59]   In the consistency of characterization, the Restoration leans more strongly to Horace's ideas than to those of Aristotle.[60]

Horace is much more adamant about constancy than Aristotle, proclaiming that if the writer is "bold enough to create a fresh character," he should "let him remain to the end such as he was when he first appeared–consistent throughout."[61]   Charles Gildon echoes Horace's words in his *Complete Art of Poetry* (1719) when he says, "Your Characters must maintain the same Humour, Affectation, & c. thro' the whole Play, which they shew the Audience at the opening of the very first Scene" (265). The Restoration took Horace's dictum to heart and, in Gallaway's words, exhibited characters through the medium of "a ruling passion" which "reduced to order" the intricacies and "subtleties of life."[62] Norman Rabkin views this reduction of the complexities of character as the major change in the Shakespearean plays as they were altered by the Restoration. In Rabkin's opinion, the transition from a world of "animating contradictions" to the "new understanding of life" the Restoration believed itself to possess, led to a "confident definition of character, succinctly expressed by Dryden," a character which is consistent but which does not attempt to reconcile contrarieties.[63]

The desire for consistency in characterization is at one with the

[59]Aristotle, p. 81.

[60]Leo Salingar and A. N. Kaul both stress continuously that although the Restoration claims to follow Aristotle, in actuality, it favors Horace.

[61]Horace, "The Complete Art of Poetry," in *Literary Criticism: Plato to Dryden*, ed. Allan H. Gilbert (New York: American Book Company, 1940), p. 132.

[62]Gallaway, p. 129.

[63]Rabkin, p. 117.

Restoration love for clarity above all else. Clarity and decorum are as important to style as to character; and, as with character, the early Restoration closely follows the strictures of Aristotle and his commentators. Those who succeeded Dryden appear to subscribe to his beliefs so that in the matter of style, the neoclassical ideal reigned. Possibly more than anything else, the disparity of styles epitomizes the difference between Renaissance and Restoration plays. The richness of language necessary to carry the complexity of the Elizabethan-Jacobean world-view is pitted against the stark, clear language of a people who believed the mysteries of life could be resolved through the advancement of knowledge and the application of reason. The Restoration notion of style accords with the classical ideal expressed by Aristotle. According to him, "Excellence of diction means clarity and avoidance of banality,"[64] and if the writers of the Restoration worked at anything, it was to attain such a style.

The poets writing during the early years of the Restoration expressed what almost amounted to a religious fervor as far as language was concerned. Dryden's "Of Dramatic Poesy" and "Defence of the Epilogue" both contain lengthy passages regarding the refinement and improvement of the language since the days of Shakespeare and Jonson. One of the major problems Dryden discovers in Shakespeare, in fact, is his "misuse" of the language. For, he finds in "every page" of every Shakespearean play "some solecism of speech or some notorious flaw in sense" (ODP 171). These "flaws" of Shakespeare offended Dryden's fastidious ear, but he objected even more to the confusion they fostered in the minds of the reader and the audience. In his "Grounds of Criticism in Tragedy," Dryden more

---

[64]Aristotle, p. 109. Note that Leon Golden's translation of *Poetics* uses the words style and diction interchangeably. Aristotle, *Poetics*, translated by Leon Golden with commentary by O. B. Hardison, Jr. (Tallahassee: Florida State University Press, 1981 reprint), p. 39. Compare the Loeb translation, "Excellence of diction means clarity and avoidance of banality. Now, clearest is the diction that uses standard terms, but this is banal...." with Golden's "Diction achieves its virtue in being clear but not mean. The clearest style results from the use of standard words...."

explicitly shows the effect of Shakespeare's "bombast":

> he often obscures his meaning by his words, and sometimes makes
> it unintelligible. I will not say of so great a poet that he
> distinguished not the blown puffy style from true sublimity; but I
> may venture to maintain that the fury of his fancy often
> transported him beyond the bounds of judgment, either in coining
> of new words or phrases, or racking words which were in use into
> the violence of a catachresis. 'Tis not that I would explode the use
> of metaphors from passions, for Longinus thinks 'em necessary to
> raise it; but to use 'em at every word, to say nothing without a
> metaphor, a simile, an image, or a description, is I doubt to smell a
> little too strongly of a buskin. (GCT 257)

Dryden has the word of Aristotle and of Longinus to support him in his desire for
moderation in the use of figures of speech. Aristotle claims that improper use of
ornamental language produces laughter;[65] whereas Longinus warns against the use
of artifice, but adds that "the figure seems to be best when the hearer does not
notice that it is a figure."[66] Sir William Davenant, the first to adapt
Shakespeare's plays, also, according to Gallaway, "was one of the first to attack
the intellectual conceits of the 'metaphysicals'."[67] In his adaptations of
Shakespeare, Davenant attempts to clarify the language and does so to such an
extent, as George Odell claims and most readers will concur, that he robs it of

---

[65]Lane Cooper's application of the *Poetics* to comedy adapts Aristotle's words here to
read: "*An obtrusive employment of the device* of lengthening words will, of course, become
ludicrous . . . . *With metaphors also, and strange words, and the rest, a like effect will ensue if
they are used improperly, and with the aim of causing laughter* " (213). What Aristotle warns
the writer of tragedy to avoid thus becomes a good piece of advice for the writer of comedy to
follow.

[66]Longinus, "On Literary Excellence," in *Literary Criticism: Plato to Dryden*, ed.
Allan H. Gilbert (New York: American Book Company, 1940), p. 170.

[67]Gallaway, p. 160.

every bit of the poetry.[68]

Dryden's call for clarity in dramatic poetry becomes the basis for his defense of the use of rhyme in tragedy. In the "Essay," Neander does not include comedy in his defense of rhyme, but the dispute remains important even in a discussion of comedy as he advocates the use of rhyme to keep the poet from being "too luxuriant," to help his "judgment, by putting bounds to a wild, overflowing fancy" (ODP 90-91). Dryden elaborates on the marks of a good style in his letter "To John, Lord Haughton" when he enumerates the "silent graces": "the purity of phrase, the clearness of conception and expression, the boldness maintained to majesty, the significancy and sound of words, not strained into bombast, but justly elevated; in short, those very words and thoughts which cannot be changed but for the worse."[69] John Dennis favors a similar style in his letter "To Henry Cromwell on the *Vis Comica*" in which he advocates a "simple style" in comedy.[70] The prose writers of the Restoration did well to follow Dryden's advice on style. The adapters of Shakespeare would have done better to ignore it; unfortunately, they too heeded his words.

Considering the Restoration's love for clarity, consistency, and unity, variety would appear to be something they avoided at all costs. In this point, the Restoration once again surprises the reader and audience. Although they frequently admired the French and classical plays for their regular plots, the Restoration applauds English plays more fervently for their greater variety. Keeping in mind the immediate purpose of plays as entertainment, the writers and

[68]Odell, vol. 1, p. 26.

[69]Dryden, "To John, Lord Haughton," vol. 2, p. 278. Future references to this essay will be from this edition and will be noted in the text in the following manner, LH and page number.

[70]John Dennis, "To Henry Cromwell on the *Vis Comica*", in *The Critical Works of John Dennis*, ed. E. N. Hooker, vol. 2 (Baltimore: The Johns Hopkins University Press, 1943), pp. 34-37.

critics realized that the French sort of play could never succeed well with an English audience. The main problem they found with the French plays is that they lacked the diversity that Englishmen had become accustomed to in hundreds of years of stage tradition. When Sir William Davenant, for instance, began to adapt Renaissance plays for the Duke's Men, the major changes he made, aside from the clarification and simplification of language, were to add variety in the form of music, spectacles, and added interest in the plot. Arthur Gewirtz holds that in the addition of "comic diversity for its own sake," Davenant became the "single most propulsive force in the shaping of the great body of Restoration comedy."[71] Davenant's influence is evident most clearly in the other adaptations of Shakespearean comedy. For example, almost all of them contain masques and songs sometimes only remotely connected with the action, as well as additional and unnecessary twists to plot.[72] Though his critical acumen goes beyond Davenant's, John Dryden agrees that the English court cannot bear plays that are too regular. He desires plays that "follow the variety and greatness of characters" which are the literary heritage they have received from Shakespeare, Fletcher, Jonson, and the earlier English comedies (ODP 65). Earlier in his "Essay: Of Dramatic Poesy," Dryden, in Neander's voice, expostulates on the benefits of variety of character and plot. Unlike Davenant, he qualifies his admiration, adding that "the parts" must be "managed so regularly that the beauty of the whole be kept entire, and that the variety become not a perplexed and confused mass of accidents." If the poet follows this admonition, the audience "will find it infinitely pleasing to be led in a labyrinth of design" (ODP 61). Dryden, like Davenant in the matter of variety, does not restrict variety to the inclusion of many characters and complex turns in the plot line, but looks back to the

[71]Gewirtz, p. 34.

[72]Salingar notes that Shakespeare himself almost always made the plots of his plays more involved than the sources had been (20).

"shipwrecks of the Athenian and Roman theatre" to find justification for the inclusion of "scenes, music, dances, and machines."[73] In variety, as in the majority of cases, Dryden remained true to his principles when he wrote his plays. His version of *The Tempest*, for example, makes extensive use of machines–Ariel flew about in the air to the general delight of the Restoration audience. He also greatly expanded the number of songs and the number of characters and introduced new developments in the story line.

John Dennis likewise remarks the need for variety in comedy. In his "Advancement and Reformation of Modern Poetry" (1701), Dennis attempts to show how modern comedy represents an improvement over the comedy of the ancients. Although Dennis is frequently accused by modern critics of being a rigid neoclassicist, his thesis here is that modern comedy is not inferior to the classically "correct" comedy of the Greeks, Romans and French, but, in fact, superior. He attributes this superiority almost solely to the greater variety employed by modern writers. The *ridiculum* of modern comedy is presented in "greater Variety," Dennis asserts, ". . . both in the Incidents and in the characters and that Variety must make it more delightful." He goes on to prove that in the case of comedy, uniformity "takes away from the Surprize," and the surprise is that which provides the lifeblood of the *ridiculum*. Not only does Dennis praise the variety of characters and "fables" of modern comedy, but he commends their "variety of style," thus linking the idea of variety with that of decorum of language. He notes, for example, that Terence's characters speak "with the same Elegance, the same Grace" (ARMP 211) whether they are slave or king and considers the English manner of suiting the language to the character to be much more effective. In his Preface to *The Comical Gallant*, Dennis deplores the inclusion of scenes, machines, and other components of the spectacle "where the

---

[73]John Dryden, Preface to *Albion and Albanus*, in *"Of Dramatic Poesy" and Other Critical Essays* ed. and with introduction by George Watson, vol. 2 (New York: E. P. Dutton and Company, Inc., 1962), p. 42.

business of the Theatre does not require it." He particularly condemns the introduction of "a sort of soft and wanton musick, which has used the People to a delight which is independent of Reason, a delight that has gone a very great way towards the enervating and dissolving their minds." Dennis is not the only critic to feel that the elements of spectacles were all too often thrown in to the detriment of the play. In Gildon's *A Comparison of the Two Stages* Sullen remarks that whereas the addition of "a Song or a Dance" is forgivable in a play, all too often they are "lug'd in by the Head and Shoulders without any relation to the Play' making them appear 'unnatural and monstrous' (*CTS* 48).

Although either Aristotle or his followers spoke out on almost everything related to the drama, the Restoration had only remnants from Aristotle himself on which to base a theory of comedy. Critics have long suspected that Aristotle wrote a book which dealt with comedy comparable to the treatment of tragedy and epic in the *Poetics*.[74] All that remains that can be proven absolutely to be Aristotle's is the brief definition of comedy in chapter five of the *Poetics* which proclaims that "comedy, as we have said, is mimesis of baser but not wholly vicious characters: rather, the laughable is one category of the shameful. For the laughable comprises any fault or mark of shame which involves no pain or destruction...." Aristotle's "missing" treatise on comedy did not prevent his translators and commentators from suggesting theories of their own. Trissino elaborates on the type of actions suitable for comedies: "Disturbances" which do not "involve wounds and deaths, and happy endings" such as "weddings, peaceful agreements, and tranquillity, through which characters issue in peace from the scene." Trissino also devotes a section of his work to the differences and

---

[74]Aristotle, p. 45. Golden's translation says, "As we have said, comedy is an imitation of baser men. These are characterized not by every kind of vice but specifically by 'the ridiculous,' which is a subdivision of the category of 'deformity.'What we mean by 'the ridiculous' is some error or ugliness that is painless and has no harmful effects" (9). Some critics claim that the *Tractatus Coislinianus* is Aristotle's work.

similarities between comedy and tragedy.[75]   Castelvetro interpolates a long section on comedy into his translation of the *Poetics*. In it, he deals primarily with the "proper ends" of comedy, by which he means the "glad" or "sad" outcome of the plot, but he never really formulates a system of judging or writing comedy.[76]

Even though the Greeks and Romans did not bequeath a theory of comedy to the Renaissance and Restoration, they did leave a rather substantial body of Latin comedies as well as a few Greek plays. Leo Salingar comments on the significance of Latin comedy to Shakespeare and the English Renaissance, an influence so strong that it caused comedy to be the dominant theatrical genre in all Europe for over a century. He also remarks the Renaissance transformation of comedy to a form with a "sense of intellectually coherent structure in a new tradition, communicating with the classical past as well as open to the present."[77] The Renaissance, of course, eventually found its supreme voice in the tragedy. The Restoration, however, returned to the dominance of comic drama.

As in every other aspect of the theater, the Restoration was not content to write and perform, but also dissected and theorized in an attempt to define comedy for itself. By this time the French and English writers, most notably Ben Jonson, had developed various theories of comedy. The Restoration, having evolved its own special comedy, had to analyze this "new" comedy and relate it to that of its predecessors.

---

[75]Trissino, "Poetica," in *Literary Criticism: Plato to Dryden*, ed. Allan H. Gilbert (New York: American Book Company, 1940), p. 225.

[76]H. V. E. Perry, *The Comic Spirit in Restoration Drama* (New Haven: Yale University Press, 1925), contends that comedy "cannot be constrained to fit into the narrow limits of a rigidly organized art form" since "by its very essence" it does not have "a well-defined beginning, middle, or end" but rather, "it pervades all life, it is coextensive with it" (63). Perry chides Congreve for attempting to write a "well-made play"–in his opinion an impossibility as comedy is concerned.

[77]Salingar, p. 324.

Dryden once again was one of the first and perhaps the best and most coherent in stating his views. As much as possible, he defers to Aristotle and the classical authors. Like Aristotle, Dryden deems that the persons of comedy must be "of common rank, and their business private, not elevated by passions or high concernments as in serious plays."[78] In his definition of comedy he also reemphasizes the architechtonic end which exposes the "faults" of the characters and attempts to cure the audience of like dispositions. His Preface to *An Evening's Love* more thoroughly examines the proper nature and scope of comedy in relation to that of tragedy:

> The persons in comedy are of a lower quality, the action is little, and the faults and vices are but the sallies of youth, and the frailties of human nature, and not premeditated crimes: such to which all men are obnoxious, not such as are attempted only by few, and those abandoned to all sense of virtue: such as move pity and commiseration, not detestation and horror, such, in short, as may be forgiven, not such as must of necessity be punished.[79]

A cursory glance at Restoration comedy shows that it did not people its plays with "lower quality" characters even though Dryden and Dennis both ostensibly favor them. Dennis in "A Large Account of Taste in Poetry" (1702) repeatedly asserts that low characters are more appropriate in comedy. He qualifies this statement by adding that the "Follies of the Great" are more likely to be emulated and are more visible; therefore, their folly should be exposed to ridicule more frequently.[80]

---

[78]Dryden, "Of Dramatic Poesy," vol. 1, p. 74.

[79]Dryden, *An Evening's Love*, vol. 1, p. 152.

[80]Dennis still prefers "low characters" (LATP vol. 1, 283). He also notes that Wycherley has deviated from the normal mode of writing by showing "a good deal of Humour" in high characters, a rare achievement. Hume points out the disparity between Restoration theory and practice here and shows how the writers, particularly Congreve, attempted to reconcile their

The Restoration discussion on the nature of comedy hinges to a great extent on the dispute over "humours" and "wit" in comedy. Dryden's "Defence of the 'Epilogue'" brings the two ideas together into what amounts to a renunciation of his earlier preference for low characters in comedy. In an examination of Jonson's faults and achievements, Dryden advises the poet to use his plays as a "perfect pattern of imitation" in the matter of "humour," but warns the Restoration playwright to "be more wary than to imitate the meanness of his persons." "If gentlemen "would avoid" the conversation of "Cob and Tib" on "the street," they surely do not go to the theater to be entertained by their foibles (DE 182). In "Of Dramatic Poesy," Dryden defines the English conception of humour to which he subscribes. Humour is

> some extravagant habit, passion, or affectation, particular (as I said before) to some one person, by the address of which he is immediately distinguished from the rest of men; which being lively and naturally represented most frequently begets that malicious pleasure in the audience which is testified by laughter as all things which are deviations from common customs are ever the aptest to produce it. (ODP 73)

In the Preface to *An Evening's Love*, as in the "Defence," Dryden moves away from an orthodox theory to avow that he prefers a "mixed way of comedy, that which is neither all wit, nor all humour, but the result of both" (*EL* 149). He takes Quintilian as his guide and recommends that the writer exhibit "more of the *urbana, venusta, salsa, faceta*" and the other "ornaments of wit" including repartee (149), rather than simply present characters with humours. Later in the Preface, Dryden defends the use of wit against those detractors who claim that it is simpler to write than humour. He counters with the observation that wit actually takes more "imagination" to write and adds that "to entertain an audience

---

"genteel" characters with Aristotelian theory by asserting that Aristotle meant people of "baser" *manners*, not class.

perpetually with humour is to carry them from the conversation of gentlemen, and treat them with the follies and extravagances of Bedlam" (*EL* 150). The raucous exhibition of humour by the Elizabethans did not accord, in Dryden's way of thinking, with the new standards, the new conceptions of life which comedy must now present.

On this point John Dennis disagrees with Dryden. More rigidly neoclassical in his idea of comedy, Dennis reiterates the necessity of the *ridiculum* and goes on to say that the "truly ridiculous in any man is chiefly Humour." He also extols the use of humour, because it is "harder to write than Wit" since wit is dependent only on the operations of "Fancy" whereas humour is produced through the actions of "Judgment," a commodity even more rare. Dennis also prefers humour over wit since it provides "a necessary Occasion for Actions, which Wit does not"; it delineates character better, and thus is more "agreeable to men of Sense, whereas Wit must be often shocking and nauseous to them, because it destroys and confounds the Characters" thereby eliminating a great deal of pleasure from the play. Finally, Dennis asserts that humour is preferable to wit in comedy because humour is a "subordinate passion" and passion is that which "characteristically distinguishes Poetry from Prose."[81]

Burnaby's injunction against the overuse of wit to the detriment of plot, characterization, and the presentation of humour which is the natural outgrowth of the two takes for granted the reader's acquaintance with the terms and does not attempt to redefine them. In *The Complete Art of Poetry* (1719), Charles Gildon, on the other hand, defines humour similarly to Dennis when he calls it "a subordinate or weaker Passion . . . in Persons of a lower degree than those that are admitted in Tragedy." He makes no distinction between affectation and humour, though, only adding that affectation is also "fit for Comedy" since it is ridiculous, too, and should be corrected (*CAP* 265). Gildon's letter to D'Urfey mentions

---

[81]Dennis, "Large Account," vol. 1, p. 282. In "The Advancement and Reformation of Poetry," Dennis defines humour as "a little ridiculous Passion" (vol. 1, p. 225).

humour in the discussion of *The Marriage Hater Match'd*. Gildon praises D'Urfey's play for the "variety of Humours and Characters . . . so truly drawn" but does not discuss humour here except in relation to the specific characterizations.

One of the premier playwrights of the age, William Congreve, pointedly meets the question of humour in his "Concerning Humour in Comedy" (1695). In this letter addressed to John Dennis, Congreve defines humour as that which "naturally arise[s] from the different Constitutions, Complexions, and Dispositions of Men,"[82] a definition in keeping with the medieval and Renaissance traditions. Congreve then proceeds to show what humour is not, by contrasting it with wit. Humour is not wit, in Congreve's opinion, nor is it folly or the presentation of personal defects, strange habits or customs nor affectation. All these characteristics may be included in the portrayal of humour, if the "manner" is "adapted to the Humour" (CHC 244). What differentiates the superficial, learned traits from true humour is that humour is either "born with us, and so of a natural Growth, or else . . . grafted into us by some accidental change in the Constitution, or revolution of the Internal Habit of Body, by which it becomes, if I may so call it, Naturaliz'd" (CHC 246). Humour, which pervades and informs the character and, therefore, "cannot be shewn without a Dissection of Nature," is more difficult to write and produces a superior piece of art as it more truly represents nature (CHC 257).

The Restoration objected to the inclusion of farce in comedy because it exaggerated the humours of the characters and thus went against nature. Dryden examines the difference in farce and comedy in the Preface to *An Evening's Love* and finds that farce "consists" of "forced humours and unnatural events." William

---

[82]William Congreve, "Concerning Humour in Comedy," in *Critical Essays of the Seventeenth Century*, ed. J. E. Spingarn, vol. 3 (Bloomington: Indiana University Press, 1957), p. 243. Future references to this essay will be from this edition and will be noted in the text in the following manner, CHC and page number. In this essay, Congreve does not define wit except for in contrasting it to humour.

Burnaby similarly stresses the "unnatural" quality of farce in his critical letter when he adjures the reader to "not be satisfied with the unnatural Farce of some Poets, which looks like sick Men's Dreams, composed of Parts that no Man can reduce to one Body, and run out of Nature to make you laugh; as if Comedy was only to make us laugh at the Folly of the Poet" (CL 458-9). The critical temper of the era was opposed to farce. John Dennis, who first conceived his play *A Plot and No Plot* as farce, goes against the mainstream in this issue. On second thought, as Dennis perceived the plot to be more "important" and "entirely new," he recast it into the more neoclassically significant form of "low comedy" (Preface).

To exemplify the refinement of their age, the playwrights of the Restoration excluded farce from any comedy. Robert Hume perceives this removal of farcical elements from comedy to be the "weakest spot" in the Restoration's comic drama. He notes that "only a genuine 'mixed' comedy such as Shakespeare's" could encompass the inclusion of wit, romance, humours, farce, music and spectacle "because it reflected the whole of life–the serious, the romantic, the farcical."[83] Removal of farce from comedy eliminates, in his opinion, much of the pleasure, and, as the Restoration failed to note, it also moves comedy further from a true depiction of "Nature."[84]

Unlike farce, which was never really in critical favor during the Restoration, tragicomedy had a fluctuating popularity. Early in the era, in Dryden's "Of Dramatic Poesy," Neander calls it "a more pleasant way of writing for the stage than was ever known to the ancients or moderns of any nation." He upholds this mixture of the comic and tragic because of the concept of *concordia discours*, noting that "contraries, when placed near, set off each other" (ODP 38).

---

[83]Hume, p. 278.

[84]Some of the criticism addressed at farce is more lenient (a strange truth considering the disrepute with which it was held during this period) and, in fact, was raised mainly because entire comedies had "dwindled into vile Farce" (*CTS* 48).

Hume feels that Dryden's interpretation of tragicomedy, reminiscent of Guarini's and Fletcher's, has a great deal to do with his praise of the genre. Guarini, unlike most Aristotelian commentators, had expressed the opinion that the union of comedy and tragedy is not "in opposition to the practice of Nature, and much less to that of Art," but can indeed be "the highest form of poetry." Guarini defines tragicomedy as a drama which

> takes from tragedy its great persons but not its great action, its verisimilar plot but not its true one, its movement of the feelings but not its disturbance of them, its pleasure but not its sadness, its danger but not its death; from comedy it takes laughter that is not excessive, modest amusement, feigned difficulty, happy reversal, and above all the comic order.[85]

Not all the critics and playwrights of the Restoration subscribed to Guarini's notion of tragicomedy. Robert Howard was totally against the mixture of tragic and comic elements in his Preface to *Four New Plays* (1665) on the grounds that it disrupts the tone of the plays and thus does not produce the proper effect on the audience.[86]   The truth is that most tragicomedy written during the Restoration, as Hume asserts, did not accord with Guarini's and Fletcher's ideal, but is, rather, the "mungrell" form that Sidney had warned against and the specific kind of tragicomedy that Lisideius condemns in "Of Dramatic Poesy."[87] As Sarup Singh says, "the witty cynical gallantry of . . . sophisticated court lovers" cannot be successfully interwoven with "the naive fairy-tale romance of the Wicked Usurper, the Fisherman, and the Royal Fondlings."[88]

[85]Guarini, pp. 509, 512.

[86]Sir Robert Howard, Preface to *Four New Plays*, in *Critical Essays of the Seventeenth Century*, ed. J. E. Spingarn, vol. 2 (Bloomington: Indiana University Press, 1957), p. 100.

[87]Hume, p. 57.

[88]Singh, p. 144.

After the heroic play (which saw its heyday from 1664 to 1680, though it regularly appeared on the London stage until roughly 1730) declined and the debate over the morality of early Restoration comedy began to escalate, tragicomedy became the fashion. Beginning with Colley Cibber's *Love's Last Shift* in 1696, the new genre of sentimental comedy was arising which would be developed by Richard Steele in such plays as *The Funeral* (1601) and fully realized in *The Conscious Lovers* (1622). Sentimental comedy provided patterns of imitation rather than objects of ridicule and thereby found favor with the Whigs who had been dissatisfied with the lewdness of the contemporary stage. Charles Gildon disliked this trend and remarked several times the barbarity of tragicomedy, a "mixture wholly monstrous and unnatural." In his "Reflections on Mr. Rymer's *Short View of Tragedy*" Gildon looks at Shakespearean tragedy and places the blame for his inclusion of comical elements on the "Vices of the Age" which dictated that the "Dalilah of the Age must be brought in; the Clown, and the Valet jesting with their Betters."[89] In his *Laws of Poetry* Gildon similarly rejects the combining of comedy and tragedy "things so opposite in themselves," which he accuses the "English writers" of mingling "in spight of nature and reason" (LP 25). How odd then that of all Shakespeare's plays Gildon chose to adapt the one most closely aligned with tragicomedy, *Measure for Measure*.

These excerpts exhibit the schizophrenic nature of Restoration dramatic criticism. Torn between pragmatism and dogmatism, the Restoration critics wanted to follow the lead of French playwrights and establish a dramatic canon which bowed to the dictates of Aristotle, Horace and Scaliger, while, at the same time, emphasizing the social responsibility of drama to the audience even as strongly. A great admiration and awe for the "unteachable" beauties wrought by genius, most vividly exemplifed by Shakespeare's plays, further confused their stand. No wonder that in this age of transition, an age attempting to explore and

[89]Charles Gildon, "Some Reflections on Mr. Rymer's *Short View of Tragedy*," in *The Impartial Critick and Miscellaneous Letters and Essays*, ed. Thomas Arthur Freeman (New

discover its own persona, Shakespeare's plays would also undergo a transformation.

York: Garland Publishing, Inc., 1973), p. 88.

"Time, place, and action may with pains be wrought,
But genius must be born; and never can be taught."
                    Dryden's Prologue to *The Double Dealer*

CHAPTER II

THE ADAPTERS AND THE UNITIES

Modern critics have yet to establish the direct relationship between the application of the unities and the adaptations of Shakespearean and Renaissance-Jacobean plays. Arthur Gewirtz embarked on his examination of *Restoration Adaptations of Seventeenth Century Comedy* fully expecting to find that the neoclassical rules, particularly the unities, accounted for the major changes in the plays only to discover that these edicts exerted little, if any, influence on the adaptations he studied. Gewirtz, as a result, turned his attention to the changing world view embodied in the plays.[1] Gewirtz's expectations and his actual findings reflect those of most of the scholars who preceded him in this study of Restoration alterations. Hazleton Spencer, George Odell, Robert Hume, and Kenneth McClellan all perceive the notion that these adaptations were produced through the stringent compliance with the dictates of Aristotle, Horace, and Longinus to be a misconception if not an absurdity. The high esteem placed on the rules and particularly the unities, evident in the prefixes and prologues affixed to the various adaptations as well as original plays of the period, merely serves, according to modern critics, to point up the self-deception of a people who

[1] Arthur Gewirtz, *Restoration Adaptations of Early Seventeenth Century Comedies*

wished to see themselves as more erudite and sophisticated than their forebears. Now and again a modern critic will note with something between a yawn and a sigh that "here indeed Burnaby (or Granville or Gildon) does actually redesign Shakespeare's plot so that it more clearly accords with the law of unity of action" or "In this instance Dennis eliminates what he saw as needless scene changes." The indifference of these critics strikes the modern reader as justifiable. These adaptations do "mangle" the beauty of Shakespeare's plays and reduce their complex *Weltanschauung* into a simple moral. An attempt to quantify the success of the adaptations with regards to the actual claims of each individual adapter nevertheless remains possible. Granted, the boast of each that he has "improved" Shakespeare may never hold true, but particularly in reference to the unities, many of the adaptations do represent a closer adherence to the neoclassical laws. The four adaptations (as well as the adapters' original plays) under consideration here– Gildon's *Measure for Measure, or Beauty the Best Advocate*, Burnaby's *Love Betray'd*, Granville's *The Jew of Venice*, and Dennis' *The Comical Gallant*– generally adhere more closely to these dictates as the following comparisons will evidence.

Unity of Time

Gildon's Measure for Measure and The Roman Bride's Revenge

The time frame of every play may not always be simple to ascertain. Modern editors may only guess from the contents of a play the approximate time sequence represented by the actions.   Even though this difficulty exists, the reader can easily recognize that two of the adaptations examined here represent a move to a more narrow compass of time. Charles Gildon's *Measure for Measure, or Beauty the Best Advocate* presents a chain of events that spans only a few hours over the actual acting time with no more than a couple of hours' difference

(Washington, D. C.: University Press of America, 1982), p. 111.

between any of the acts. In the original version by Shakespeare, on the other hand, several days elapse between act one, scene one, when Duke Vincentio turns over the reins of office, and scene two; for, not only has the deputy Angelo had a chance to reinstate the ancient law forbidding fornication, but Claudio has already been arrested. Another day passes between scenes four and five of act four, evident in 4.3.119 when the disguised Duke tells Isabel, "The Duke comes tomorrow"[2] and by scene five, he is at the city gates sending advance notice to the city elders. These lapses of time well exceed Dryden's leniently prescribed thirty hours. The expanse of time even in Shakespeare's version does not grossly defy the principle of unity of time as *Macbeth*, for instance, does. Gildon's version, nevertheless, distinctly compresses the amount of time covered by the play. Whether Gildon always kept as strictly to unity of time remains to be seen. In his first play, *The Roman Bride's Revenge*, he does not attain such mastery over unity of time. Although the total time period covered by the play is unclear, in order to be probable at least one day must pass between acts one and three. Between these acts, Portia and Martian have been prevented from marrying by the Emperor who has exiled Martian. After wandering around aimlessly, Martian returns in disguise to see Portia who has become the object of the Emperor's unwelcome attentions. Another time lapse occurs between acts four and five which portray the events of one day and those of the following morning. All these incidents could possibly occur within the recommended thirty hours. If they do, the audience must bring an even greater "suspension of disbelief" to the play, than if it neglects unity of time.

---

[2]William Shakespeare, Prologue to *Measure for Measure*, in *The Norton Shakespeare*, ed. Stephen Greenblatt, et. al. (New York: W. W. Norton and Company, 1997), p. 2072. Future references to this play are from this edition and will be noted in the text in the following manner, *MM* act.scene.line number. Charles Gildon's version of the play is *Measure for Measure, or, Beauty, the Best Advocate* (London: D. Brown, 1700; reprint ed., London: Cornmarket Press, 1969), hereafter noted in the text as *BBA*, page number.

Disappointment alters the time span of Shakespeare's version to make it conform more closely to the law while his other plays either reject or adhere to the rule depending on the demands of their plots. Act one of *Love Betray'd* preserves the unity as all events occur within the playing time, whereas in *Twelfth Night*, scene four takes place after three days have passed. In both plays, acts two, three, four, and five closely follow each other, and the events depicted in each cover the approximate acting time. The incidents of the entire plays represent the passage of six days from the opening in *Love Betray'd* and three months in *Twelfth Night*. This time frame is established explicitly in the final act when the Duke asks Antonio when "Cesario" entered the town and he replies, "To-day, my lord, and for three months before,/No int'rim, not a minute's vacancy,/Both day and night did we keep company."[3] Dumbfounded and a little angry, he responds, "fellow, why words are madness./Three months this youth hath tended upon me" (*TN* 5.1.93-94). Viola/Cesario is shipwrecked in Illyria in act one scene two and comes into the Duke's service in scene four of act one which would mean that the action of the play covers at least three months' time. Moreno and Rodoreague undergo a similar encounter in *Love Betray'd*. Concerning the youth he believes to be Sebastian, Rodoreague asserts, "Today . . ., and for a Month before/(Kept back from storms from making of the Land)/Both day and night did we keep company."[4] Moreno retorts, "Then thou art Mad, Rodoreague, for this Youth/Has been these Six days in my Family,/The constant servant of my wishes" (*LB* 55). When Viola first appears in the play, however, she relates her story to

1969), hereafter noted in the text as *BBA*, page number.

[3]William Shakespeare, *Twelfth Night*, in *The Norton Shakespeare*, ed. Stephen Greenblatt, et. al. (New York: W. W. Norton and Company, 1997), p. 1814. Future references to this play are from this edition and will be noted in the text in the following manner, *TN* act.scene.line number.

[4]William Burnaby, *Love Betray'd, or, the Agreable Disappointment*. London: D. Brown, 1703 reprint ed., London: Cornmarket Press, 1969, p. 54. Future references to this play are from this edition and will be noted in the text in the following manner, *LB*, page number.

Laura, telling her, "I left my Brother, and my House, and six days since, without a Servant, landed here in Venice" (*LB* 12) where she joined the Duke's service. She does not account for the stormy month at sea which she appears to have encountered before reaching Venice according to Sebastian's and Rodoreague's versions. Sebastian claims, "I followed her flight so close, that in a few Hours we came up with the Vessel in which I was assur'd she went; but before we had hail'd 'em, a Storm arose, that separated us; I saw that Vessel sink, and the Plank on which you found me, was all that was left of ours" (*LB*   22). This month, of course, is not included in the action of the play, but, had it been worked into the play, as the three months are in *Twelfth Night*, the sequence of events would be much more believable. Cæsario (Burnaby's spelling) woos and wins Villaretta in one day's time in *Love Betray'd*, whereas Olivia, though moved by Cesario on the first day, has three months' time to become entranced by the "boy" so that in act four she marries his mirror image, Sebastian, despite her avowal in the first act never to marry. As in Gildon's plays, Burnaby's close adherence to unity of time in *Love Betray'd* substantially diminishes its probability.

The Preface to Burnaby's first play, *The Reform'd Wife*, makes the rather odd boast, odd considering the era in which it was written, that he "did not design a just Play" and "had no regards to the Unities."[5]   Despite this avowal, the play transgresses unity of time only very slightly in that its events likely span two to three days at the most. Burnaby returned to strict unity of time in his *Ladies' Visiting Day*. In this case, the brief time span poses no problems in terms of believability of the plot. All the events which take place have been adequately prepared for in the expository material, and when a sudden change occurs, as in

---

[5]William Burnaby, Preface to *The Reform'd Wife*. (London: Thomas Bennet, 1700; reprint ed., Ann Arbor, Mich.:   University Microfilms, B5745, 1973), precedes p. 1. Future references to the play are from this reproduction and will be noted in the text in the following manner, *RW*,   page number.

Lovetoy's immediate decision to marry Prince Alexander, the eccentricity of the character enables the audience to accept the situation despite the brief time she has known her future husband.

Granville's *Jew of Venice* and *The She-Gallants*

The other two adaptations, Granville's *Jew of Venice* and Dennis' *Comical Gallant* do not appreciably change the time covered by the actions of their stories. Granville's *Jew* differs little from Shakespeare's *Merchant*. Each begins with the making of the bond, then moves by act three to the foreclosure by Shylock which was set to occur after three months.   Act four must also take place several (at least one day) days after the third act, for in the meantime Portia has had to journey to Bellario's home from Belmont and then on to Venice for the trial in both versions of the play. Not bound by Shakespeare's fable in *The She-Gallants*, Granville composes an action which can completed within the requisite time span designated by unity of time. In this instance, Granville may simply be utilizing the unity already established in his French source, Campistron's *L'Amant l'amante*.

Dennis' *The Comical Gallant* and *A Plot and No Plot*

One of the attractions of *The Merry Wives of Windsor* for John Dennis may have been the regularity which had previously been noted by Dryden in his "Grounds of Criticism in Tragedy."[6] Both versions of the play, *The Merry Wives* and *The Comical Gallant*, comprise little more than the actual acting time. Dennis' original play, *A Plot and No Plot*, shows a corresponding concern for

---

[6]John Dryden, "The Grounds of Criticism in Tragedy," in *"Of Dramatic Poesy" and Other Critical Essays*, ed. George Watson, vol. 1 (New York: E. P. Dutton and Company, Inc., 1962), p. 247. Future references to this essay will be from this edition and will be noted in the text in the following manner, GCT and page number.

unity of time as all of the incidents follow one after another. In this instance, the critical beliefs of the playwright receive careful attention and are rigorously applied to his creative endeavors.

Summary of Unity of Time

Of the four adaptations, therefore, Gildon's and Burnaby's are the only ones to alter Shakespeare's versions in order to accord with the law of unity of time. Dennis, in the fortunate position of dealing with a play that already conformed to the unities, did not need to make any adjustments in this area. Granville, who boasts of his changes more than the rest, alone keeps Shakespeare's time scheme pretty well intact. The reader must assume that unity of time held little, if any, importance in Granville's evaluation of dramatic excellence.

Unity of Place

Unity of place, unlike unity of time and action, does not comprise a part of the classical critical canon. While confirming the virtual absence of such a doctrine in classical criticism, Renaissance critics in Italy, France, and England nonetheless avowed its usefulness and desirability for contemporary plays. Pierre Corneille sets forth what is ideal and what is acceptable in terms of unity of place in his "Discourse of the Three Unities":

> I should prefer, so as not to incommode the spectator in any way, that one represented before him in two hours and what one displayed to him on a stage that did not change should be kept within a room or a hall, whichever one might choose. But often that is so difficult, not to say impossible, that one must of necessity find some extension in place as well as in time. . . . I believe, then, that we must seek to make this unity as exact as possible, but as it is not fit with every sort of subject, I should

willingly grant that everything taking place in the same city possesses unity of place.[7]

Taken in its broadest terms, unity of place is evident in all of Shakespeare's comedies under evaluation here with the exception of *The Merchant of Venice,* which is set partly in Venice and partly in Belmont. Likewise, all the adaptations with the exception of *The Jew of Venice* adhere to the loose definition of unity of place. The supreme goal of the more dogmatic as well as the most pragmatic remained to have as few changes of scene as possible. They argued that the greater the unity of place, the more sustained the effect and, even more significantly, the greater facility in dramatic presentation since extensive use of scenery was the norm in the Restoration theatre.

Gildon's Measure for Measure and The Roman Bride's Revenge

Although both *Measure for Measure* and *Measure for Measure, or Beauty the Best Advocate* are set within the confines of a single city, the first in Vienna, the second in Turin, Gildon eliminates numerous changes of scene throughout his adaptation. Act one of the original version moves from the Duke's Palace to a street, a friary and finally a nunnery; whereas, the first act of the altered version takes place solely in a large hall of the palace. In act two Gildon introduces a scene change as he moves the action from a room in the palace to a prison. Still, Shakespeare uses twice as many shifts as he goes from the court to Angelo's chambers and from the prison back to Angelo's apartment. Only in act three does Gildon surpass Shakespeare in scene shift, in which he moves from the prison to a hall in the palace while the entire action of Shakespeare's original remains in the prison. In act four Gildon includes more different scenes than he uses in any other act of the play when he sets the action variously in one of Angelo's rooms, a

---

[7]Pierre Corneille, "Discours des Trois Unities," in *Literary Criticism: Plato to Dryden,* ed. Allan H. Gilbert (New York: American Book Company, 1940), pp.578-79.

garden, and the prison. Shakespeare's corresponding act contains two shifts more than Gildon's, and takes the action to three entirely new places as it moves from the moated grange at Saint Luke's to the prison, Angelo's house, the fields outside town, and a street near the city gate. Both plays conclude in one setting: *Measure for Measure* at the city gate and *Measure for Measure, or Beauty the Best Advocate* in a great hall of the Palace. By the end, Gildon's play has undergone a total of eight shifts to four totally different settings while Shakespeare's version has shifted fifteen times to eleven totally different settings. Levison notes that Gildon has unified the setting of the play greatly, as "all the scenes, except Mariana's first appearance in the garden, occur either in the Duke's palace or the prison."[8]   Gildon's play clearly attempts to conform to the doctrine of unity of place.

In *The Roman Bride's Revenge* Gildon once again tries to avoid extraneous change of scene. The first act is set entirely in the grove; the second makes three changes from the Empress's apartments to Portia's and then the street; the third act returns to the palace and moves from Portia's apartments to a gallery; the fourth takes place under the garden wall, in the garden, and in Portia's apartment while the fifth act shifts from a street near the palace to a hall in it. The play has only two scenes which are not set either in or around the palace. In this play even more so than in the altered *Measure for Measure*, Gildon has centered the action almost exclusively on the palace.

Burnaby's Love Betray'd, The Reform'd Wife, and Ladies' Visiting Day

Shakespeare's *Twelfth Night* does not conform as closely to unity of place as his *Measure for Measure* does. Although the bulk of the action occurs in Illyria, two scenes take place on the seacoast near Illyria. Act one scene two

---

[8]William S. Levison, *Restoration Adaptations of Shakespeare as Baroque Art* (Ph.D. dissertation, University of Illinois at Urbana-Champaign, 1972; Ann Arbor, Mich.: University

introduces the shipwrecked Viola on the coast with her fellow survivors as they discuss the loss of her brother and her future plans. Act two scene one parallels this scene with Sebastian mourning the loss of his sister and, like her, preparing to journey to Count Orsino's court. The two scenes must not be set in the same place considering the time scheme. Viola quickly makes her way to Orsino's court while Sebastian apparently takes several months to reach it since the last act occurs three months after the first. The possibility also exists that this scene takes place after the passage of several months during which time Antonio has nursed Sebastian back to health following his shipwreck. If so, this scene could be set at Antonio's house or on a street outside it. In many ways this explanation more adequately accounts for the three-month discrepancy in Viola's and Sebastian's entrance to Illyria. *Twelfth Night* may, therefore, actually have three different locales rather than two. Burnaby eliminated these seacoast scenes and chose instead to set his own version, *Love Betray'd*, entirely in Venice. He tells why he chose Venice rather than Illyria as his setting in the Preface:

> As to the Place of the Scenes, I confess I might have made a better choice for the present condition of a Country. Venice is what first presents it self to us when it is nam'd, and a Duke of Venice wou'd be apt to appear too full of Years, and Grey Hairs for a Lover, but several revolutions have afflicted that State, and their Princes have sometimes been Absolute (Preface to *LB*).

This obvious attention to the scene serves to heighten the probability that Burnaby intentionally unified the setting of *Twelfth Night* in his adaptation as he has not only removed the seacoast scenes, but utilized only four different places as opposed to the six Shakespeare uses. Even more significant than these numbers, the arrangement of Burnaby's scenes displays his concern with unity. *Love Betray'd*, for instance, contains one scene change from Villaretta's (Olivia)

Microfilms, 1973), p. 79.

house to Moreno's (Orsino) while *Twelfth Night* moves from Orsino's to the seacoast, Olivia's house, back to Orsino's and ends at Olivia's house. Act two of *Love Betray'd* contains the most changes Burnaby made in the adaptation as it shifts from Moreno's to Villaretta's and, finally, the Ryalto. Shakespeare, once again, surpasses this number with five shifts: the seacoast (or Antonio's); a street; Olivia's house; Orsino's; Olivia's garden. Burnaby consolidates the setting of act three even more than act two by placing it totally within the confines of Olivia's property and moves it only from the house into the garden while Shakespeare's original moves from the garden to the house, then around and about the garden and into the street. Act four, in contrast, presents a reversal. For once Burnaby disrupts the unity of place established in *Twelfth Night* in which all the action occurs either before or in Olivia's house and garden by including a move from Villaretta's to the Ryalto. Even with this shift, Burnaby changes scene only twice, whereas Shakespeare moves the action three times. As with the two versions of *Measure for Measure*, both of these plays remain in the street setting during the entire final act. By the end Burnaby has moved to four different settings through ten different scene changes while *Twelfth Night* moves to six places in seventeen shifts. Burnaby's inclusion of the Ryalto scenes, though necessary to the plot, disrupts unity of place in some ways but contributes to it if the audience is to imagine that Moreno's house is situated at one end and Villaretta's at the other: a situation Corneille approves of in his treatise. In either case, Burnaby's version remains more unified with regards to place than the original.

Both of Burnaby's other plays, *The Reform'd Wife* and *The Ladies' Visiting Day*, restrict their movement to the confines of London. In this respect, they conform to unity of place. Neither *The Reform'd Wife* nor *The Ladies' Visiting Day*, shows as rigid observance of the law, as *Love Betray'd*. *The Reform'd Wife* undergoes seven, possibly eight scene shifts, to five different locales; while *The Ladies' Visiting Day* is almost on a level with Shakespearean comedy as it shifts scene fifteen times to five distinct settings. *The Reform'd Wife* moves in act one from Astrea's house to the Mall and in two from Lady Dainty's to the Mall. Act three is situated solely in Friendlove's house; four takes place first in Astrea's parlor and dressing room, then in the Mall, and five returns to Astrea's house. This play does not show much digression from the unity employed in *Love Betray'd*. *The Ladies' Visiting Day*, another matter entirely, shifts in act one from the park to Sir Testy's parlor back to the park. Act two begins in Lady Lovetoy's dressing room, moves to her parlor and then returns to Sir Testy's. Act three is more stable and takes place only at the entrance to Sir Testy's or in his parlor. Burnaby dispenses with the centralization of the setting in act four and introduces the greatest number of scene changes in the play as he moves the action from the entrance to Sir Testy's to a room inside, back to the entrance, then to Lady Lovetoy's house and once again to Sir Testy's. The final act takes place at the park and in Sir Testy's parlor. Why Burnaby saw fit to eliminate needless change of scene in his adaptation of *Twelfth Night* and pay little heed to them in *The Ladies' Visiting Day* is uncertain. The exigencies of the plot of *The Ladies' Visiting Day* do not require such extensive scene shifts. He could easily have rearranged a couple of scenes, gotten rid of others, and thereby attained a greater unity. In this instance, Burnaby chose rather to allow the dramatist take over from the critic, and he places the action in the most logical place at the most dramatically effective time to achieve a play much superior to his more critically "correct" *Love Betray'd.*

Granville's *The Jew of Venice* and *The She-Gallants*

Unlike Gildon in *Measure for Measure*, Granville does not restrict his version of *The Merchant of Venice* to one city. Instead, he places his action both in Belmont and Venice just as Shakespeare had. He would have been unable to eliminate the Belmont scenes had he wished, for the whole plot hinges on the two settings. When he hears of Antonio's arrest in act three scene one, Bassanio relates to Portia the story of the loan of three thousand ducats. His guilt overcomes him as the money was, he says, "Rais'd to transport me hither" (*JV* 27). Perhaps Granville could have rid the play of its Belmont scenes. In doing so, he would have lost much of the dramatic effect brought about by the juxtaposition of Bassanio's good fortune and his friend's disaster. Although Granville could not unify the setting by restricting the movement to one city, he drastically cuts the number of scene changes required in each act. In this manner, Granville provides more semblance of unity of place to the play. He reduces the number of scene shifts in each act by half and, when possible, keeps all the action of each act either in Venice or in Belmont; act two, for instance, is located entirely in Venice, first at Shylock's, then on a street; act four takes place in a court in Venice, then at Bassanio's; act five is in Belmont. When he cannot rearrange the scenes so as to avoid a change from one city to the other, he dispenses with all the action in one city and then moves to the other instead of switching back and forth between the two.

Act one of *The Jew of Venice* is set in a street in Venice and then goes to Portia's house in Belmont, and act three takes place at Portia's home, then moves to a prison in Venice. Shakespeare's corresponding acts are quite different. Act one of *The Merchant of Venice* is also set in a street in Venice and then Portia's home; however, the end of the act returns to a public place in Venice. Act three moves even more than act one as it takes place in a street in Venice, proceeds to Portia's house, returns to a Venice street, then heads back to Portia's house and gardens. Granville set the second act solely in Venice. In Shakespeare, by contrast, the action moves eight times in the following order: Belmont, a street in Venice, Shylock's house, street scene, before Shylock's house, Portia's house, Venice, Portia's house. Not only is the number of scene changes excessive, but the act moves back and forth between Venice and Belmont a total of three times. Act four, on the other hand, takes place in a court and on the street both of which are in Venice, while act five is set at Portia's home in Belmont. Strangely enough, in this adaptation, Granville does not reduce the number of settings. Both plays include six different settings. Granville, in fact, devises two new settings for his play. In act two he sets the action in Bassanio's house and in act three he adds a prison scene. The two settings he eliminates are negligible as they are outside either Portia's or Shylock's houses. In the matter of place Granville obviously did not strive for strict unity. If neither Corneille nor Gildon would have been able to applaud his laxity in this case, the scene designer and prop men would have appreciated his efforts, for, if he does not limit the number of sets, he does attempt to cut the number of scene shifts.

    The She-Gallants, on the other hand, conforms to unity of place almost as rigidly as Gildon's *Measure for Measure*. It is set only in three different places, all of which are in London: the Park, Lady Dorimen's house, and the street before her door. Even within Lady Dorimen's house, the action moves only from the toilette to her public chambers. Granville is also able to keep rigid unity within each act. Only act four moves its location from the park to Lady Dainty's chamber. The locale of both acts one and two is the Park; three takes place in Lady Dorimen's toilette; and five at the entrance to her house. As with unity of time, Granville's adherence to unity of place may not be original to him. His careful attention to the needs of those staging the plays is nonetheless evident.

Dennis' *The Comical Gallant* and *A Plot and No Plot*

    John Dennis had a much more "regular" play to alter than his friend George Granville had. *The Merry Wives of Windsor* takes place in and around Windsor. The farthest afield it goes, in fact, is in the final scene of act two and the first scene in act three, which are set in a field near Windsor and a field near Frogmore. Dennis did not settle for this restriction of place but rather limits the movement of his version to three settings, all within the confines of Windsor: Windsor Park, the Garter Inn, and the Bull Inn, a setting introduced by Dennis. *The Merry Wives of Windsor* has more than twice as many, with seven distinguishable settings: Page's house, the Garter Inn, Dr. Caius' house, the field near Windsor, the field near Frogmore, a street scene in Windsor, and Ford's house in Windsor. As is true of the other adaptations and original versions, the number of distinct scenes does not wholly account for the greater unity of place in the altered form. *The Comical Gallant*, like *Measure for Measure*, *Love Betray'd*, and *The Jew of Venice*, also preserves the unity of place by diminishing the number of scene shifts to five from seventeen in *The Merry Wives of Windsor*. Four of the five acts of *The Comical Gallant* occur in one place. Windsor Park serves as the setting for acts one and five and the Pyed Bull Inn for acts three and four. Only act two moves about from Windsor Park to the Garter Inn and back to the Park. Not a single act of *The Merry Wives of Windsor*, in contrast, is set entirely in one place. The final act alone comes close as it advances from Windsor Park to the Garter Inn and then returns to the Park. Acts one and two each contain three shifts. One moves from Page's doorstep to the Garter and Dr. Caius' house. Two winds its way to Page's house again, moves to the Garter, and then proceeds to a field near town. Acts three and four make two additional shifts for a total of five per act. Act three begins at the field near Frogmore, moves onto a street in Windsor, enters Ford's house, goes outside of Page's house, and ends at the Garter. In the fourth act the action once again moves to the streets of Windsor, invades the Garter Inn, returns to Ford's, and then settles in at the Garter. Even though Dennis includes a new setting, the Bull, in his version, *The Comical Gallant* remains a better example of unity of place than *The Merry Wives of Windsor*.

Dennis' first play *A Plot and No Plot* accords with the doctrine even more fully. This play, like *The Comical Gallant*, contains only three settings: a garden (act one), the Playhouse (act two), and Old Bull's House (acts three, four, and five). None of the acts moves from one place to another, and, even more significantly, not a single scene shift occurs after the third act. The play almost reaches the ultimate objective of unity of place: to be situated entirely in one room.

Summary of Unity of Place

Unity of place though not "commanded" by Aristotle, definitely had a bearing on these four adaptations. Each one represents a move toward unity of place either through the centralization of the action in one city as opposed to the surrounding area as is evident in Burnaby's elimination of the seacoast scenes from *Twelfth Night*; in the reduction of the total number of settings, for example, from eleven to four in *Measure for Measure*; or in the number of scene shifts, as in Dennis' *Comical Gallant* which changes only five times whereas *The Merry Wives* switches some seventeen.

Unity of Action

Although usually mentioned first in any discussion of the three unities, the unities of time and place actually function most significantly by helping to focus the action. Unity of action is, after all, what the neoclassical critics judged most crucial in a play even though vacillate as to what constitutes it. Some condone the use of subplots as long as they are intricately woven into the texture of the main plot, while others feel that only one action should be presented. The adapters, oddly enough, did not appear to believe that the interpolation of "masques" and interludes disrupted the continuity of the action. Two of the adaptations, *Measure for Measure* and *The Jew of Venice*, contain such "entertainments," and a third, *Love Betray'd*, originally included a masque which was dropped before the first production, much to Burnaby's dismay. Gildon who, according to Edward A. Cairns, justified his inclusion of this type of entertainment "by citing the authority of Aristotle's remarks about the chorus,"[9] at least attempts to tie the masque in *Measure for Measure, or Beauty, the Best Advocate* thematically into

---

[9]Edward A. Cairns, *Charles Gildon's MEASURE FOR MEASURE, OR BEAUTY, THE BEST ADVOCATE: A Critical Edition* (New York: Garland Publishing, 1987), p. 58.

the basic plot. Escalus presents "The Loves of Dido and Aeneas" in order to soften Angelo's heart so that he will release Claudio. Its effect is quite the opposite, as it moves Angelo to desire Claudio's sister Isabel more and to use Claudio's life as a pawn to obtain her favors. Granville provides no satisfactory reason for his inclusion of the masque "Peleus and Thetis." It merely makes up a part of Bassanio's "good luck," *bon voyage* feast.

For the most part, these adaptations represent a move toward greater unity of action. Every incident in Gildon's *Measure for Measure* relates to the main action: Angelo's attempt to use Claudio's life to seduce Isabel. In order to make the plot more unified, Gildon makes several changes. First, he begins the play by relating Angelo's edict and Claudio's arrest. The original, on the other hand, begins with the departure of the Duke and ends with Escalus and Angelo deciding what Angelo's authority will be. Gildon proceeds from Lucio's and Balthazar's expository exchange to the entrance of Escalus and Angelo who are discussing Claudio's plight. Escalus pleads for Claudio's life to no avail as Angelo avows that he cannot let Claudio go. "What shall I say to Julietta's Friends?" he asks, "whose Injur'd Honour calls upon my Justice" (*BBA* 3). In response, Escalus blames the avarice of her friends for Claudio's situation since, if the conviction stands, she will have to go to a convent and take a vow of poverty. This conversation now reinforces the reason Claudio gives for not openly announcing his marriage to Julietta in act two. At this point a servant enters and announces Isabella, who comes to beg for Claudio's life. She claims that Claudio is really married to Julietta, but the priest who married them is now in France. Angelo refuses to send for the priest but is moved by her beauty. She becomes passionate and asks him to search his own heart for sin. Angelo recoils from the "pointed truths" she speaks but is moved to consider her pleas only to have the opportunity to see her again. The masque which proves "no cure" for Angelo's "distemper;/For every note . . . Seem'd to Sing only Isabella's Beauty" (*BBA* 9) ends the act.

The main plot is not sustained in the first act of Shakespeare's play. After the first scene, Shakespeare introduces Lucio and some gentlemen who stand about for several minutes commenting on the Duke's mission to obtain a treaty with the King of Hungary when Mistress Overdone enters to illustrate graphically the depravity of the city and announce the arrest of Claudio. Pompey the clown comes in, provides a comic interlude in his discussion of Claudio, and then announces that the "houses" in the suburbs are to be razed. At this point, Julietta and Claudio are led in parade. As the couple walk by, Lucio talks to Claudio, who accepts some blame yet claims that he and Julietta are legally married but could not be married by the church because of the dispensation of her dowry. Unlike Gildon's adaptation Shakespeare's version contains no substantial evidence that Julietta's friends wished to obtain her money for themselves. Claudio then asks Lucio to persuade Isabella to plead his case before Angelo. The next scene moves to the friary where the Duke tells the friar he left his post to enable Angelo to enact some dormant laws because things have gone awry in Vienna and also because he wants to see if the "precise" Angelo will be changed by power. In the final scene, Isabel is in the nunnery awaiting her vows and "wishing a more strict restraint/Upon the sisterhood, the votarists of Saint Clare" (*MM* 1. 4. 4-5). Lucio comes to inform her of Julietta's pregnancy and Claudio's arrest.

While every incident enhances plot, theme, and character in Shakespeare's *Measure for Measure*, the action of act one is not really unified in the neoclassical sense of the term. They set the stage for Claudio's conviction and show why the Duke left Vienna, yet the first scene and the friary scene do not actually support the main action of the plot. Gildon's movement of the friary scene to act two, though less effective and much more contrived, does provide an adequate basis for inclusion of the scene in which the Duke details his reasons for leaving the city in Angelo's power. In Gildon's version, the Duke explains his actions only in response to the Friar's information that Angelo, who has "made his false severity/Bawd to his Fame, and Broaker to his Vice/Of Avarice" (*BBA* 17), has married and left Mariana because he could not get her dowry. Act two, which had begun with Angelo's proposition to Isabel to save her brother by giving herself up to "the same Blemish" (*BBA* 10), her subsequent refusal and intention to expose him, and another unsuccessful segment of the masque, ends as the Duke interviews Claudio, who confesses only to the crime of avarice.

Even in Claudio's confession of guilt Gildon strengthens the unity of the plot as Claudio claims he married Julietta secretly to get her dowry from her guardian Pedro, Angelo's "Privado, his Right-Hand" (*BBA* 19). Gildon has taken several of these incidents from act two of the original. He moves the first scene in which Escalus begs for Claudio's life to act one and eliminates the next scene which has Pompey the pimp brought before the court which is unable to find reason enough to hold him. Shakespeare's act concludes by sandwiching the Duke's conversation with Julietta in between Angelo's and Isabella's encounters. The most obvious change that Gildon made here is the removal of the Pompey scene, which, though it points up the injustices of the system, does not actually advance the action.

Gildon made fewer structural changes in act three than in the preceding acts. Here he has the Duke and Friar preparing Claudio for death when Isabel enters to tell him of Angelo's proposition. In Gildon's version, unlike Shakespeare's, Claudio does not press her to submit but, though he would like to live, asks only that she take care of Julietta. When Claudio leaves, the Duke, who has been eavesdropping, proposes to Isabella the plan of using Mariana to trap Angelo. He then leaves but tells her the Duke will return the following day. At this point, the act moves to the palace where Angelo and Escalus are watching the third entertainment and concludes with Isabella accepting Angelo's proposition. The excision of the incarceration of Pompey and Mistress Overdone and the dialogue between the "Friar"/Duke and Escalus help unify Gildon's play to the detriment of characterization and meaning.

Act four of Gildon's play also closely parallels the original. In this instance, Gildon adds a scene of his own devising to show Isabella's agreement to meet Angelo in return for her brother's life. This scene would naturally follow the action of act three. Gildon places Shakespeare's first scene which shows the meeting between Mariana, the Duke, and Isabel after this addition, and eliminates the scene in which Pompey agrees to help Abhorson "cut off a man's head" in order to shorten his imprisonment. Like Shakespeare, he has the Provost preparing Claudio for death as the Duke waits there to hear from the pardon which should be forthcoming but which instead turns out to be an issue hastening Claudio's execution. At this point, Gildon interpolates another scene that has the Duke bringing Claudio and Julietta together in the prison. While they proclaim their love for each other, the Duke and Provost are closeted out of sight as the Duke/Friar convinces the Provost to execute Bernadine and grant Claudio "four days' respite" (*MM* 4.2.148) and presents to the Provost a letter bearing the seal of the Duke announcing his return in two days. Gildon cuts the opening of the next scene, which shows Pompey and Abhorson attempting to execute the drunken Bernardine, and then gives more insight into the Duke's character as he regrets his decision to execute the criminal. The Provost relieves the Duke's conscience by discovering a yellow fever victim, "One Ragusine, a most notorious pirate,/A man of Claudio's years, his beard and head/Just of his colour" to "satisfy the deputy with the visage/Of Ragusine, more like to Claudio" (*MM* 4.3.63-68). The Duke writes to Angelo to tell him of his approach to the city, and the Provost reenters with the head of the pirate. This extensive scene in Shakespeare serves to resolve many of the difficulties of the plot as well as to intensify the audience's perception of the Duke. Gildon nonetheless moves directly to the entrance of Isabella after which the Duke informs her of Claudio's death and of the Duke's arrival the next morning and tells her to meet him with Friar Thomas (Peter in the original) and Mariana before the Duke and Angelo on the following day to "Accuse him home and home" (*BBA* 38). Gildon also eliminates Lucio's appearance as he first mourns with Isabella over the loss of her brother, discusses the Duke's "lechery" with the "friar," and then admits to having fathered a child himself. He moves the following scene which has Angelo and Escalus discussing the Duke's letter to the beginning of act five and cuts the Duke's preparation for entering town as well as the meeting of Mariana and Isabella who discuss their orders from the Duke.

Except for the movement of act four scene six to the beginning of act five, Gildon made no real changes in the action of act five. In both Shakespeare and Gildon the Duke returns, Isabella confronts Angelo with his sin, and Mariana refutes Isabella's claim only to have Angelo deny hers. In Gildon, the Duke openly confesses his part in the scheme. In Shakespeare the Duke goes away to dress in his friar's habit as Lucio discounts anything Friar Lodowick will say by informing the onlookers that this friar had "spoke most villainous speeches of the Duke" (*MM* 5.1.260-61). As the friar denounces the state of affairs in Vienna, Angelo asks if this is the same one who called the Duke "a fleshmonger, a fool, and a coward" (*MM* 5.1.328-29). Lucio replies "yes," runs up to the friar, and removes his hood to discover the Duke. In his version, Gildon sacrifices the dramatic effect of this discovery for the straightforward movement of the action. After the Duke's part in the incident is in the open, Angelo begs for death in both versions and the Duke grants his request, though, in Shakespeare, the Duke has Angelo and Mariana marry before the execution is to be carried out. (In Gildon, they have long been married.) In both versions the Duke pardons the Provost for beheading Bernardine at an hour not sanctioned for executions. The Provost then leaves the stage only to return with Julietta, Claudio, and the living Bernardine in Shakespeare's version; in Gildon's play, the Provost reenters with Julietta and "Bernardine" who, in reality, is Claudio. In Gildon, the Duke forgives Bernardine only to have Claudio revealed. In Shakespeare, Claudio is presented as another prisoner who should have died. Shakespeare resolves the plot by uniting the Duke and Isabella and punishing Lucio by forcing him to marry any one of the women he has wronged and then hanging him. Gildon, of course, eliminates the punishment of Lucio and fades to the final entertainment of the masque.

A comparison of the two plots shows the greater unity of action evident in Gildon's excision of the scenes with Pompey, Mistress Overdone, and Lucio. Gildon excludes the opening scene of the play which, though it sets the stage for the action, is not really essential. Gildon's version also achieves heightened unity through the rearrangement of scenes–particularly notable in his placement of the Duke's explanation of his choice of Angelo as deputy in the second act after the friar tells him of Angelo's true nature rather than in the first act where it contributes to the subplot of the Duke's problems with Vienna instead of the main conflict between Angelo and Isabella. Even Gildon's interpolated scenes, with the possible exception of the exchange between Claudio and Julietta, contribute to what Levison calls this "superficial"[10] unity of action as they advance the plot step by step in a logical sequence with very little left for the audience's imagination.

Gildon's *Roman Bride's Revenge* shows even more concern with unity of action. The whole plot centers around the trials of Portia, the new bride of Martian, who is the leader of the soldiers. At the outset of the act, Perennius is bemoaning the loss of his love to his friend Lætus who suggests he avenge himself with the help of the Emperor. Lætus tells Perennius to "poison" the Emperor's mind against Martian by showing how he clings to the old Junian traditions. The wedding procession passes by and focuses on Portia who is afraid of sending her soon-to-be husband off to war since the earth is behaving portentously. Martian fears something, too, but remembers his obligation to Rome. They are exchanging their wedding vows when the Emperor storms in announcing that Portia cannot marry this traitor. Outraged, Martian claims to have almost single-handedly saved Rome and condemns the Emperor's own efforts as being bloodthirsty acts. This allegation serves to incense the Emperor even more, but he grants Martian life in

10 Ibid., p. 79.

exile after Portia begs him. Like Angelo in *Measure for Measure*, he favors her suit only if she will "learn Compassion"[11] from him. She curses him, but Martian's friend Aurelian advises her to submit to the Emperor while he silently plots revenge.

Act two begins in much the same way as act one. Perennius is now angry at Lætus, since he has a more powerful rival than before. Lætus redeems himself by recounting Portia's plans for revenge and tells Perennius to help her. At this point, the Empress enters planning her own vengeance on Portia. The scene then shifts to Portia's bedchamber where the Emperor surprises the sleeping lady and is attempting to rape her, but is stopped by the entrance of the Empress. Reminding him of the vows they made each other, she begs him to return to her. He begins to feel some pity for her when she embraces him. Angered, he commands her to release him, and "clapping his hand on his dagger" (*RBR* 10), he threatens her with violence. Since he cannot resolve to kill her, he flees but she closely pursues him. In the next scene, the banished Martian is wandering outside Rome. He considers suicide, but his servant Cleander tells him to go to the army to avenge himself and, most importantly, to save Portia.

The third act opens as Martian, in disguise, approaches Portia. After they greet each other, she tells him of her shame at what has occurred. Afraid to hear the details, Martian is relieved to find that she is referring to Aurelian's treachery. As he prepares to leave, the Empress enters to tell Portia she will help her go to Martian. Portia leaves with the Vestal Virgins who are really Perennius and Lætus. At this point, the repentant Emperor comes in ready to return to his wife when Perennius enters, finds their escape route blocked and decides to kill Lætus to absolve himself of blame in helping Portia escape. Feigning disbelief that he has killed his friend, Perennius reveals the Empress Valeria's part in the plot. This

---

[11]Charles Gildon, *The Roman Bride's Revenge* (London: John Sturton, 1697; reprint ed., London: Cornmarket Press, 1969), p. 9. Future references to this play are from this edition and will be noted in the text in the following manner, *RBR* page number.

news leads the Emperor to turn his affections back to Portia, whom he places in Perennius' care until the following day. As the Emperor leaves, Perennius tells Portia he will help her though he intends to rape her.

The fourth act sees Martian waiting for Portia to no avail. Cleander comes to tell him all that has happened, and Martian goes to Perennius' garden to find her. Deathly afraid of Perennius, Portia is walking in the garden expressing her fears when the Emperor comes up. In order to fool him, she submits a little. When he becomes too passionate, she screams, bringing Martian from the shadows to rescue her. Instead, the guards rush in and are commanded to "drag him hence to the Tarpeian Rock; /Dash him to pieces" (*RBR* 37). Perennius enters, keeping to himself the news that Aurelian is leading the army to overtake Rome and avenge his sister's shame. By this time, the Emperor knows of Perennius' stratagems and orders him taken. Perennius draws on the Emperor, but the guards stab him. As he dies on stage, Perennius tells the truth about his plot and boasts of Aurelian's vengeance. Confused, the Emperor leaves as Valeria enters with the plan of dying in his arms. Back in her apartment, Portia decides to emulate Brutus' Portia. To effect her plan, she dissembles to her maid who has been dazzled by "approaching Grandeur" so she will help to murder the Emperor and herself as they take their vows.

The next morning Cleander tells Martian, who has been set free by Aurelian, of Portia's infidelity. He determines to go see the wedding for himself. Upset by Portia's falsehood as she and the Emperor drink her "love philtre," Martian openly scorns her faithlessness as Valeria enters to die in her husband's arms. He takes out his sword, but she stops him and is attempting to explain as the messenger enters with news of Aurelian's "treachery." The Emperor draws on Aurelian but is captured by the guards and begins to feel the effect of the poison. As Portia dies she tells Martian the truth. Torn by grief, Martian kills himself although Aurelian tells him Rome needs him. Aurelian wants to follow his example, but, before he dies, Martian persuades him that he must save Rome.

As this detailed plot summary shows, every action in *The Roman Bride's Revenge* is tied to the main conflict between the Emperor and Portia and to the concept of vengeance. Each character in the play seeks revenge at some point, and every act of vengeance is connected with Portia's plight. The action is highly unified with no digressions or subplots.

Burnaby's Love Betray'd, The Reform'd Wife, and Ladies' Visiting Day

Burnaby's adaptation of *Twelfth Night, Love Betray'd*, represents a complete turnabout from Gildon's two plays. Rather than eliminating the expository material at the beginning of Shakespeare's play, Burnaby's first act is almost entirely exposition. In his version, the curtain opens to the rather callous Villaretta and Emilia discussing a letter from a suitor of Villaretta, who has written a letter even "finer" than those of the Duke, her most ardent admirer. The audience sees more clearly into Villaretta's character when she informs Emilia that she never "quite put[s] him off" because, as she says, "it pleases me to govern him that governs Venice" (*LB* 3). Instead of furthering the plot, Villaretta's admission merely leads to a discussion consisting of pithy sayings about the double standard. The action recommences with the introduction of Moreno, who has come once again to beg her to favor his suit for her hand, but finishes secretly wishing he "cou'd tear the Tyrant" from his "breast." At this point Drances (Sir Toby) enters to pontificate on women and virtue, liquor, and the practical joke he has played on the Butler and Villaretta. The action then moves to Moreno's house where Laura is weeping over Viola's servitude.[12] After a digression on love and the part money plays in it, Viola informs Laura of her love for Moreno

---

[12]This scene is enigmatic since both Laura and Cæsario/Viola appear to have been living in the same household for at least a few days. See page 11, "O my dear Lady Viola! 'tis you, I know it now. The Duke, Madam, took me with him, to wait upon his Sister, And I have liv'd here ever since. I little thought to see your Ladyship my Fellow servant!" and page 12, "I nam'd my self Cæsario, and form'd a Letter, as from one his Highness knew in Paris, to recommend me for his Page--Upon it, Laura, he receiv'd me; lik'd my Person; calls me pretty Youth; makes me sing to him; and sometimes kisses me."

and the mission he has given Cæsario to serve as his emissary to Villaretta.

   Twelfth Night varies the action much more than *Love Betray'd.* At the outset, a lovesick Orsino receives a message from Olivia that "The element itself till seven years' heat,/Shall not behold her face at ample view,/But like a cloistress she will veilèd walk" (*TN* 1.1.25-27). The action moves to the recently shipwrecked Viola, who is grieving over her brother and deciding to go into Orsino's employ for the time being. Rather than following Viola to Orsino's, the next scene thematically parallels the previous one. Here, Sir Toby and Maria discuss the loss of Olivia's brother with Sir Toby's comic animadversions on her behavior. Sir Andrew enters to Sir Toby's exhortations to "Accost, Sir Andrew, accost" (*TN* 1.3.41), and a comic interlude ensues. The fourth scene returns to Viola, who has been with Orsino for three days and is already in love with the man who is instructing her to woo another for him. Maria and the clown open the next scene as Olivia enters to quibble with him over who is the greatest fool. Cesario enters, and woos Olivia to such effect that she is smitten with him.

   In *Twelfth Night* the action is much more various than that of *Love Betray'd.* The first act of *Love Betray'd* centers on the triangle of Villaretta, Viola, and Moreno with every action relating to the problems of the lovers. Even Drances' plot to make the Butler believe Villaretta loves him is directed in this instance at Villaretta's pride (*LB* 10) and not at his pretensions as in *Twelfth Night.* The episode with Sir Andrew Aguecheek is also cut as is the thematically significant exchange between Olivia and the fool.[13] The effect of the more unified plot of *Love Betray'd* is lost on the audience, though, as seemingly half the time on stage is wasted in the bandying of epigrams rather than in advancing the action.

   The brief second act of *Love Betray'd* begins with the opening lines of act one of *Twelfth Night* as Moreno and Cæsario discuss the despair of unrequited

---

[13]This exchange was eliminated by necessity as Burnaby changes Villaretta to a widow from a woman mourning the loss of her brother.

love. Cæsario hints at her love for Moreno while he sends her once more to Villaretta's to "Urge" his "Passion to her" (*LB* 16). In the opening of the second scene, Burnaby sacrifices unity of action as he introduces Dromia, the harpy preying on Drances. As she exits, Cæsario enters with graceful speeches and some honesty to move the heart of Villaretta. The action shifts again in the third scene, which shows Sebastian and Rodoreague discussing Sebastian's situation and even concludes with some very low comedy in the exchange between Sebastian and the eternally hungry Pedro. As they strut off the scene, Cæsario enters followed by Villaretta's footman, who brings him a ring from his lady.

Much of the action of the second act of *Love Betray'd* comes directly from the corresponding act of *Twelfth Night*: Sebastian's story makes up the first scene: the episode with the ring, the second; and Duke Orsino's melancholy, the fourth. In addition, the second act of *Twelfth Night* includes a piece of low comedy in the third scene as Feste, Sir Toby and Sir Andrew revel only to be interrupted by Malvolio's informing them that his mistress disapproves of their behavior; thereby, Malvolio sets the stage for Sir Toby's trick on him. By the final scene of the act, the trick is underway.

Burnaby begins his third act with the trick on Taquilet (Malvolio). He does, as mentioned previously, link this farcical episode to the main plot more securely by having Drances play the trick to dampen Villaretta's pride. After an unsuccessful encounter with Villaretta, Taquilet leaves. Cæsario and Villaretta enter, and he continues the wooing. Unintentionally misleading her by saying he fears his success at proxy lovemaking, Cæsario must flee from her advances. Emilia enters and jabs at Villaretta for falling victim to love, and they plan to consult a physician. The act ends as Rodoreague interrupts the fight involving Taquilet, Drances, and Cæsario.

As in act two, many of the incidents in act three of *Love Betray'd* come directly from the same act in *Twelfth Night*. The continued wooing of Villaretta, the successful duping of Malvolio/Taquilet, the duel between Cæsario and Sir

Andrew/ Taquilet which is interrupted by Antonio/Rodoreague, and Antonio's/ Rodoreague's request for help from the person he believes to be his friend Sebastian, but who is actually Cæsario, appear in both versions of the play. These incidents make up the whole action of Burnaby's alteration. Shakespeare complicates the action in the Sir Andrew Aguecheek subplot which Burnaby makes unnecessary by having Taquilet duel with Cæsario.   The extensive emphasis on Malvolio in the "possession" scene also provides additional action not essential to the main plot, though it improves the comic effect of the play as well as the complexity of the play's meaning. For the most part, Burnaby has unified the action of this act. Not content to eliminate what he saw as "useless" incidents, and furthermore, not content with the incidents Shakespeare has provided, he created an irrelevant and totally contrived action which does nothing to further the plot and only provides occasion for some more of his endless epigrams (this time on the subject of doctors and apothecaries).

Act four begins with a continuation of this new scene. The physician whom Villaretta had called for in act three comes and turns out to be none other than Cæsario who has come to "discover her secrets" (*LB* 37). About the only thing this scene accomplishes is to coarsen Villaretta's character even further as she offers the "doctor" a purse of gold with ten thousand more to come if he helps her to captivate Cæsario. The next scene returns to Sebastian and Pedro searching for the missing Rodoreague when a servant comes and tries to carry Sebastian to Villaretta's, a scene comparable to the first scene of *Twelfth Night* in which the clown attempts to convince Sebastian to follow him to Olivia's. Since he does not go in either version, he is accosted by Drances and Taquilet in *Love Betray'd* and by Sir Andrew and Sir Toby in *Twelfth Night*. In both versions, the fight is interrupted by the lady who takes the bedazzled Sebastian off with her to be married. At this point Burnaby provides a little low comedy in the "courtship" of Emilia and Pedro, and he does away with the continued cozening of Malvolio by the clown and Maria. The new scene of Burnaby's accomplishes nothing, but rather disrupts the action much more than the Malvolio scene which he has already prepared the audience for since the first act. Perhaps Burnaby felt that spending additional time on this intrigue would diminish the effect of the main plot; in eliminating it, he has linked Taquilet's advances to Villaretta's character more clearly. This linking may in itself have proven a barrier to the furthering of this plot. Possibly, he grew fond (somehow) of his creation, Pedro, and wished to focus more of the comic scenes on him rather than Taquilet. His meshing of the characters of Malvolio and Sir Andrew Aguecheek into Taquilet more obviously eliminates the possibility of further gulling of Taquilet. In the next scene, which Burnaby takes from the fifth act, Viola and Moreno enter as she tries to turn him from Villaretta and persuade him to release Rodoreague who saved her from Drances and Taquilet. Both *Love Betray'd* and *Twelfth Night* then move to the entrance of Sebastian and the preparation for the wedding. The fourth act of *Twelfth Night* ends on this note, but Burnaby ends with the mercenary Pedro revelling in the good future about to befall him through his master's marriage.

The fifth act of *Love Betray'd* begins with a new scene as Rodoreague, newly escaped from the soldiers, rushes on stage closely pursued by them. He throws a bag of jewels at them to distract them, but is captured by the captain "who enters at the same time" (*LB* 52). This scene provides Burnaby with yet another opportunity to comment on the state of society with his focus this time on soldiers. It also places Rodoreague on stage for the recognition scene. Shakespeare, on the other hand, must have the guards lead Antonio on the stage for no apparent reason. In both versions, Rodoreague/Antonio accuses Cesario of treachery when the lady Villaretta/Olivia enters to call him "husband." *Love Betray'd* strays from the original at this point and has Moreno violently attack Cæsario. "How has this smiling slave deceiv'd me; And Rodoregue's wrongs are now too Evident: But thou shalt pay for all," he says, as he "offers to stab her" (*LB* 56). In *Twelfth Night*, Orsino's love for Cesario is at war with his passion for Olivia. He raves, but does not cease to love Cesario as is evident in his speech to

Olivia:

> Live you the marble-breasted tyrant still.
>
> But this your minion, whom I know you love,
>
> And whom, by heaven I swear, I tender dearly,
>
> Him will I tear out of that cruel eye
>
> Where he sits crownèd in his master's spite.
>
> Come, boy, with me. My thoughts are ripe in mischief.
>
> I'll sacrifice the lamb that I do love
>
> To spite a raven's heart within a dove." (*TN* 5.1.120-24)

Cesario willingly follows him. Orsino's continued affection for Cesario provides a stronger basis for the conclusion than Moreno's anger in *Love Betray'd*. Moreno, in fact, is kept from killing Cæsario only by the entrance of Laura who proclaims that Cæsario is a woman, a scene not present in the original. In both versions a priest enters at this time and tells them that he indeed married Cesario and Olivia/Villaretta. Sebastian, in *Love Betray'd*, enters and sees Rodoreague in danger as his friend points out the resemblance between Sebastian and Cæsario. *Twelfth Night* provides comic diversion here when Sir Andrew comes in with a 'broken head" pointing out Cesario whom they "took" for a "coward" but whom he discovered to be the "very devil incardinate" (*TN* 5.1.175-176). Only now does Sebastian enter the stage in *Twelfth Night*. He recognizes Antonio and wonders where he has been. The Duke sees "One face, one voice, one habit, and two persons" (*TN* 5.1.208). Since he has no brother, Sebastian is shocked; nevertheless, all is resolved when Viola reveals her true identity. In *Love Betray'd*, Burnaby once again coarsens the action by having a drunken Pedro enter to identify Sebastian as a lady's man newly wed to a rich widow. As Sebastian looks at Cæsario, he comments, "Something while I look dissolves my breast,/And melts down all that's Man" (*LB* 59), and sees his sister's features in Cæsario's face. She reveals her identity to him, and the play ends with Sebastian and Olivia and Orsino and Viola united and Moreno promising to aid Rodoreague. In *Twelfth*

Night, Malvolio comes on stage to proclaim that Olivia has wronged him. She informs him that Maria sent the letter and that Sir Toby has married her in recompense, a situation Burnaby prepares for in the Dromia incident but never capitalizes on. Malvolio exits in a huff, but Orsino sends for Olivia to "entreate him to a peace" (*TN* 5.1.367), and all ends with the preparation for the wedding.

Burnaby thereby unifies the action of *Twelfth Night* by combining the characters of Sir Andrew Aguecheek and Malvolio into Taquilet. He, for some reason, introduces new action with the characters Pedro and Dromia, who appears only once unlike Maria, who plays a relatively significant role throughout *Twelfth Night.* Perhaps Burnaby's most pervasive chantes to the play are infinite epigrams on everything from money and love to soldiers and physicians. Burnaby seems to have been more interested in devising a new character and a few new situations for the play than in unifying its action to accord with the principles of neoclassical drama. All in all, the main line of the action is only slightly more direct, but considerably less pleasing.

In the Preface to his *Reform'd Wife,* Burnaby claims that he "had no regard to the Unities of Action & c.," and a close appraisal of the play supports his statement. In order to rule her aged husband, Sir Solomon, Astrea tells Clarinda that she has pretended a distaste for all men. She also illuminates Sir Solomon's character by establishing him as a man always ready to advise others since he is certain he is possessed of great wisdom and knowledge of the world. Sir Solomon enters, closely followed by a political hawker with pamphlets for either political party. Sir Solomon gets rid of him and tries to persuade Astrea to go to a play even as he derides the depravity of the theater and gloats over his own wife's fidelity. After an argument, Astrea submits. The coachman comes to help them, and the two ladies are off to the theater without Sir Solomon. Clarinda sums up the situation, "Well, thou art a Machiavel, Astrea, I am all astonished, she longs to go, and by a Counterfeit unwillingness makes him against his inclination press her to go, and how happy he thinks himself in having persuaded her to do what he wou'd not have her do" (*RW* 3).

The scene changes to the street where Sir Solomon is praising his wife's virtue as Freeman enters unscathed from the wars and asks his old friend to help him find a profession. Realizing how badly society treats ex-soldiers, Freeman decides to take Sir Solomon's advice to get another man's wife to support him. As Sir Solomon and Freeman are laughing at the husband soon to be cuckolded, Cleremont comes on stage singing, "Drink and drive care away" (*RW* 6). He is despondent because he is unable to win the love of the "sickly lady," Lady Dainty. Here Burnaby introduces a subplot and in so doing disrupts the unity of action, as the Lady Dainty/Cleremont plot is attached only superficially to the main action. Sir Solomon once again offers his well-considered advice to Cleremont to "Cough, Sigh, and Complain; just as you see her" for "what doest ever think to gain a Woman by opposing her?" (*RW* 6). Cleremont has chosen a "cheaper way" and is going to "besiege her so with Songs and Sonnets, that she shall surrender for her own quiet" (*RW* 6). As they go in to test his poem, Freeman and Astrea (masquerading as Cœlia) return to the stage to discuss their developing affair. They plan their rendezvous, and she throws him a purse of money. Amazed at his good fortune, Freeman is musing when his friend Cleremont comes out, then taunts him with disbelief at his plans to marry. Cleremont retorts with claims of her airs, her ills, and, most importantly, her two thousand pounds.

On the following day Lady Dainty is sending word to all her friends as to the state of her health when her doctor, dressmaker, apothecary, and astrologer arrive. She deals with all in the same high-handed manner, exacting what she wants from them. Cleremont enters unannounced, reveals to the audience that he set the astrologer to work, and hides behind a screen to sing to her. She exits in a huff at his impudence. The scene shifts to Clarinda and Astrea. Clarinda admits to having been attracted to a man she saw at the theater the night before, a man Astrea recognizes as her Freeman. She decides to use Clarinda as a ploy to keep suspicion from herself. As they leave, Sir Solomon comes in gayly ridiculing the husband Freeman is about to cuckold and advises Freeman to become acquainted with the husband to throw smoke in his eyes to see if he will prove the old maxim true that one is always fond of the man who cuckolds him. Careless enters to complicate Freeman's life by announcing that he heard a lady with five hundred pounds a year praising his master at the mall. Meanwhile, Clarinda, thoroughly lovesick by this time, is contemplating her state with her maid, Sylvia, when Freeman and Careless just happen by. Freeman thoughtfully asks Careless which is the young woman he heard, since he does not want to fall in love with the wrong one. They banter for a few moments and then scoff at each other to part with Clarinda's "warning" to Freeman, "Nay, I'll rather glory in my indifference, and as a further Proof of it, I walk here every Evening and you shall see that you are not considerable enough to make me forbear one Day" (*RW* 18).

The next act opens as Astrea recounts to Freeman her stratagems to use Clarinda's love for him to hide her own affair with him. He listens to her plan and agrees without knowing the identity of the lady to whom she refers. Astrea goes to fetch Mrs. Friendlove, the bawd, to entertain him while she prepares Clarinda. He is debating whether to marry Clarinda or be Astrea's lover when Mrs. Friendlove enters to provide comic diversion and another interruption of the unity of action. He is amused for a few moments by this woman who is related to everyone, particularly those of the upper classes: "I am some Kin to most of the great Families in England, and I never was two Minutes with any Body of Pedigree, but I found out that I was their Cousin" (*RW* 20). When Astrea enters with Clarinda in tow, he cannot disguise his dismay. In the following conversation, Freeman woos Clarinda by addressing Friendlove who is taken aback when he ends by asking to call on Clarinda. The action moves back to Cleremont and Lady Dainty's physician at this time as he bribes the doctor to prescribe him as physic for his lady. After this brief dialogue, Clarinda and Astrea are discussing how easily Friendlove was taken in when Lady Dainty is announced. She sweeps in, a caricature of *preciosité*, regales them with tales of her day's visit, and denounces the manners and morals of the common sort and even her own kind with "But it is a Reproach to the Honour of a well-bred Woman, to have anything in her Head but the Fashions, or to know any Fatigue but in Idleness" (*RW* 27).

Later that day Sir Solomon is advising Freeman on how to proceed with his romance when he gets an unexpected jolt. As Freeman describes his beautiful lady, Sir Solomon begins to wonder and worry, and when Freeman shows him the letter he received from Cœlia, he knows the truth. Freeman also realizes that Cœlia must be Sir Solomon's wife, but they keep their discoveries from each other and plan the meeting. Cleremont enters and thanks Sir Solomon for his successful advice on how to win Lady Dainty. As he is congratulating Sir Solomon, Freeman goes off to his tryst soon to be followed by the half-mad cuckold. Careless attempts to distract Sir Solomon by telling him about Sir Humphrey Afterwit who has died. Solomon is unable to remember Sir Humphrey until Careless remarks that he left Sir Solomon a great deal of money. Suddenly, thoughts of Astrea's infidelity vanish from Sir Solomon's mind as he follows Careless to collect his money. Freeman comes in and tells Astrea that all is lost. Never at a loss herself, she looks at the letter once again and sends him away telling him she can save them. Astrea sends for Clarinda and decides to let her have Freeman so she can regain her honor. Since Sir Solomon escaped Careless, Careless reenters and suggests that Freeman marry Mrs. Friendlove as a smokescreen. The scene shifts to Lady Dainty who is feebly rejecting Cleremont before she submits to him, and then on to Mrs. Friendlove preparing for her wedding.

Back at Sir Solomon's, the undeceived cuckold tries to kill himself, then wonders if he could be wrong. Astrea is telling the understanding Clarinda the whole truth when her maid Fidelia rushes in to inform her that Sir Solomon is coming to hide behind the tapestry. Clarinda agrees to accept all the responsibility and fears only that she will be jealous. Truly reformed, Astrea promises she will never again make another venture, not because she has been frightened, but because "there is something so Disturb'd, so Hazardous, so full of Fears and Disappointments; That the faint Pleasures that arise don't half atone for the Anxieties that attend 'em" (*RW* 38). When Fidelia announces Freeman, Sir Solomon slips in to see what is afoot. Astrea and Fidelia discuss how things "might have looked," and he is inclined to believe in her innocence even more when she faints away and Fidelia carries on about her inability to lie. Freeman, unfortunately, chooses this moment to dash in and address Astrea as his love. To save themselves, the ladies call him a cutthroat, but he throws the letter before them to retaliate. Astrea looks at it, claiming that it is from Clarinda, her cousin. Sir Solomon, who had left the room before Freeman entered, returns and draws on Fidelia for attempting to betray his lady's honor. Laughing at the jest, Clarinda tells them this whole situation has been a little joke she played on them as her spirits are high, because she is soon to be married and it is Christmas (both times of playfulness and jesting). Astrea, pleased to see how easily Sir Solomon is duped, almost decides to break her vow. At the wedding party, Sir Solomon congratulates himself on his skill in intrigue that has brought the lovers together. Just as everything seems to be fine, Friendlove, who thinks this wedding is to be hers, storms onto the scene in full bridal regalia with Careless. She curses them adequately, then exits. Sir Solomon sees yet another couple to be made as he matches Careless with Sylvia, and the play ends with Astrea's assertion that "The Guilty still with anxious Cares are prest,/The truly Good alone are Blest" (*RW* 45).

Despite Burnaby's claims, *The Reform'd Wife* adheres closely to unity of action. Only in the Cleremont/Lady Dainty scenes does he leave the main action. Even these scenes are tied into the main action as they contribute to the exposure of Sir Solomon's character. Cleremont comes to him for advice on how to gain Lady Dainty, who happens to be an acquaintance of Astrea. A great variety of action appears to have been foreign to Burnaby's abilities, and here as in *Love*

Betray'd, the main reason for his inclusion of a subplot seems to have been to prove that he was not confined by the rules which, in fact, he had great difficulty in escaping.

The premise on which Burnaby bases his *Ladies' Visiting Day* ensures that all the action, if not one and entire, will at least be very closely linked. The title, in effect, unifies the action by emphasizing the play's setting on a visiting day in which any number of visitors and incidents is possible. The play opens at the beginning of Lady Dolt's visiting day with Polidore sending her a letter by his man Ned. He rather enigmatically instructs Ned to see that Sir Testy Dolt intercept the letter and hurries him on his way. Courtine, one of Polidore's friends, enters as Ned is leaving and stops him to discover the object of his mission. Rather intrigued to find that the letter is addressed to Flora, Lady Dainty's maid, Courtine asks Polidore for an explanation. Polidore tells him that Fulvia, Lady Dolt's niece, is actually the intended recipient of the letter, but since Sir Testy throws Polidore and Lady Dolt (who has a *tendre* for Polidore) together, he is attempting by means of this letter to make him jealous. The visiting day is about to commence back at Sir Testy's house, as he complains to his man Supple that this one will absolutely be the last he will allow since they make intrigues too easy. Instead, he slyly informs Supple that he will allow Polidore to visit as he has "such an Evidence of his Modesty . . . as is not to be question'd"[14] locked in his trunk. The first visitors of the day enter at this point to entertain Fulvia and the audience with their various humours and eccentricities while Lady Dolt and Polidore meet at the park. Lady Dolt assures Polidore that the way is clear for them to enjoy their "vertuous Inclinations" (*LVD* 210), but he warns her about the letter on its way. Shocked, she runs out to prevent Sir Testy from discovering it. Courtine and Friendly enter with Courtine's raptures over Lady Lovetoy and

---

[14]William Burnaby, *The Ladies' Visiting Day*, in *The Complete Dramatic Works of William Burnaby*, ed. F. E. Budd (London: E. Partridge, The Scholartis Press, 1931), p. 205. Future references to this play are from this edition and will be noted in the text in the following

his decision to marry her even though she is an "eminent Fool" (*LVD* 212) as the first act comes to a close.

As the second act begins, Fulvia is visiting Lady Lovetoy who is regaling her with the reasons she despises Englishmen. Fulvia counters with good sense and practicality to no avail when Lettice announces the arrival of the tradesmen downstairs. As Lovetoy is viewing their exotic wares, a Turkish boy comes in with a letter from Courtine who tells her that he will come to her that night in any design she desires. The boy then serenades her with some of Courtine's own compositions. The scene shifts to Sir Testy's house to show him informing his wife that nothing good could have persuaded her to go out so early in the day. The letter arrives, and he reads it aloud to her and Flora, but then discovers it is addressed to Flora. Flora is afraid, on cue, then asks Sir Testy to write her response. Since he conveniently commands Lady Dolt to do the honors, she reciprocates by composing the letter as well. In another part of the house the young Fulvia and Polidore are conducting an on-again, off-again courtship. The act closes as they reluctantly admit their love for each other and decide to seek Sir Testy's approval.

Sir Testy comes in from Lady Lovetoy's house jangled by the women's noise to find Lady Dolt playing cards with Polidore. Unobserved, he listens to their talk and sees Polidore kiss Lady Dolt's hand as he consoles himself with the recollection that Polidore is not physically able to carry the intrigue to its natural conclusion. He watches Lady Dolt's advances and sees how Polidore puts her off with his talk of "honor" and his refusal to talk her out of the "little Conflicts" which she feels must separate them. Sir Testy's voyeurism is interrupted when Supple comes in to inform him that the parlour chimney is on fire. Lady Dolt continues to lure Polidore into seducing her when Supple tells them of the fire, and they leave the room. When the fire is put out, Fulvia arrives and harasses her

manner, *LVD* page number.

uncle for not letting her have a husband of her own choosing. She informs him that she does not know "how far the pleasure of Plaguing" him "may carry her" (*LVD* 231) if he does not relent. She leaves as the despondent Sir Testy relates to Supple how moving to this fashionable side of town has ruined his life. The visiting day progresses when Fulvia reenters with Lady Lovetoy and the Turk. As Lady Dolt is at prayers, they discuss religion, manteau makers, men, ladies' fashion, country ladies, and modesty. Courtine enters, but Lovetoy abjures him to leave, since she will accept only an exotic lover. When she admits to him that she liked Prince Alexander of Russia who had visited London in the recent past, Courtine conveniently remembers that his tailor has a suit of the Prince's. He leaves, victoriously informing Lovetoy that he is off on foreign travels. Sir Testy interrupts the ladies' visit to attempt to sell Lady Lovetoy some wines but is disappointed even in this endeavor and stays around long enough to learn that his wife has gone out with the Bawd and to be subjected to another plea from Fulvia to be allowed to marry. He exits scorning his cuckoldry.

Lady Dolt and Mrs. Junket, the Bawd, are discussing Sir Testy's jealousy as they prepare to enter the house when Flora comes to tell them how angry Sir Testy is. At this point, Sir Testy enters, and Lady Dolt tells him they have been buying china, a ruse he does not believe until the china arrives to further his confusion. Totally baffled, he can only leave. Courtine arrives at Sir Testy's dressed as a Muscovite and is, naturally, followed by Lady Lovetoy who cannot wait to see the exotic Prince Alexander. The "Prince," whom the Tsar supposedly has sent to England to learn shipbuilding, sweeps her off her feet with his luxurious, exotic apparel and the information that he has loved her since his previous trip but only waited to learn enough English to "adore" her in. After he leaves, Lovetoy decides to marry him, but Lady Dolt reminds her Courtine will ask Prince Alexander to meet him on the duelling grounds if she does. This news only serves to delight Lovetoy. As they leave, Sir Testy comes in and decides to accept five hundred pounds from Polidore for giving his blessing to his marriage with Fulvia. He secretly plans to let them divorce after she discovers Polidore's secret and thereby get even more money from her second husband. Captain Strut, another of Fulvia's suitors, challenges Sir Testy to a duel when Polidore enters and beats him. Sir Testy then informs Polidore of his decision and sends Lady Dolt in to Polidore to entertain him while he is gone.

Polidore is confused at some of the things that Sir Testy says but realizes that he must have obtained a letter Polidore once sent his father which claimed that he had met with an accident making an arranged marriage impossible. Believing that Sir Testy is offering her to the highest bidder, Fulvia disguises herself as a suitor and, in front of Polidore, offers Sir Testy a thousand pounds for her hand. Unlike her uncle, Fulvia's lover Polidore passes his test by becoming incensed with the suitor and Sir Testy and challenging this new rival to fight for Fulvia's love. The final scene moves away from the escapades of the lovers and would-be lovers and shows Lady Dolt entertaining her friends Lady Lovetoy, Lady Drawle, and Mrs. Triffle.

Coming after an entire act filled with challenges and possible challenges, the fifth act quite suitably ends with a duel. Fulvia, who is in disguise, and Polidore are on the duelling grounds where Fulvia tells Polidore that she has "lain" with Fulvia a hundred times. Enraged, Polidore exchanges swords with her and reaches into his scabbard to draw only a hilt from its folds. Polidore informs her she will have to kill him to get Fulvia, but instead she embraces him. At this point, she reveals her identity to Polidore and tells him to go to Sir Testy with the news that he has killed his rival. Before he is able to do so, Supple informs Polidore that Sir Testy has received another offer for Fulvia, so the lovers decide to elope. When Sir Testy enters, Supple tells him that the boy suitor has been killed and his devious master decides to blackmail Polidore to keep silent. In the final scene of the play, all the visitors have departed and Lady Dolt is expressing her relief at being alone when Lady Autumn comes in to wish that she too had a jealous husband. They begin to talk about that notorious hypocrite Lady Olivia who then enters much to their joy. Supple brings in Lady Weepwell and Lady Sobmuch, two widows who grieve intensely before they leave. Lady Dolt's day is not quite finished, however, for Mrs. Ruffly is entertaining her with tales of Old Fops and his young wife when Sir Testy comes in bringing Polidore and Fulvia to announce to Fulvia and the others that she is to be married to a fox hunter who has written to offer for her. She refuses to agree to marry anyone but Polidore and cruelly ruins Sir Testy's scheme by revealing that she was the "boy" who was "killed" in the duel. Sir Testy, though set back by this news, is not quite at a loss, for he pulls out the letter Polidore had written his father. The women are angered by the letter, but Polidore denies its contents and asserts that he wrote it only to escape an undesirable marriage. He and Fulvia are reunited, much to Sir Testy's dismay. At this point, the newly wedded Lady Lovetoy and Prince Alexander enter and she wishes aloud that Courtine were there to see her victory. The "Prince" regrets this impossibility as he asserts that he has killed Courtine only to have Lady Lovetoy affirm that she is glad at the circumstance. Courtine reveals himself nonetheless to his indignant wife who feels cheated but agrees to the marriage as long as he will dress in this manner for a month. The fiddlers come in to celebrate the nuptials as Sir Testy leaves to get a divorce.

The action of *The Ladies' Visiting Day* is more closely knit than that of either of Burnaby's other two plays; Hume calls it "beautifully modelled, even overwrought"[15] while Burnaby's contemporary Crites found it "a lose [*sic*] unjoynted huddle of Intrigue and Description."[16] The Courtine/Lovetoy plot could be viewed as a subplot in the manner of the Cleremont/Lady Dainty strain in *The Reform'd Wife*; however, it comprises a much larger part of the action and is more closely wedded to the main action as Fulvia and Lady Lovetoy are obviously close friends whereas Lady Dainty appears to be a mere acquaintance

[15]Hume, p. 437.

[16]Gildon, *Comparison*, p. 181.

of Astrea and Clarinda. This closer association results in much more interaction between the couples so that elements of the Courtine/Lovetoy plot actually serve to further the Sir Testy/Lady Dolt/Polidore/Fulvia plot. The only incidents in the play which detract from unity of action, in fact, are the scenes which depict the "visiting day" itself. Although Lady Dolt's conversations with Lady Sobmuch, Lady Weepwell, and Mrs. Triffle capture the essence of a visiting day and expose various popular eccentricities, these segments, interspersed as they are with the main action, would tend to detract from the unity of action if they were not provided for in the expository material in the first act as well as in the title of the play.

Granville's Jew of Venice and The She-Gallants

George Granville made fewer material alterations to Shakespeare's *Merchant of Venice* than did Burnaby or Gildon. *The Jew of Venice*, according to George Odell, is one of the adaptations which "had a long life of fifty years or more, driving the original for all that time from the stage." [17] With the exception of the masque of *Peleus and Thetis*, Granville's *Jew* differs only minimally from Shakespeare's play. The few changes effected by Lord Lansdowne serve essentially to unify the plot more than that of the original. In Granville's first act, he eliminates the characters Salanio and Salerio and the discussion of Antonio's mysterious melancholy along with Salanio's forboding guess that Antonio's "mind is tossing on the ocean" [18] engrossed in the idea that everything he possesses

---

[17]Odell, vol. 1, p. 87. For a complete look at the dates on which these adaptations (as well as the adapters' original plays) were performed, the length of time they supplanted Shakespeare's plays on the stage, and other details relevant to performance, see the appropriate volumes of William Van Lennep, et. al., *The London Stage, 1660-1800* (Carbondale, Ill.: University of Southern Illinois Press, 1960-69).

[18]William Shakespeare, *The Merchant of Venice*, in *The Norton Shakespeare*, ed. Stephen Greenblatt, et. al. (New York: W. W. Norton and Company, 1997), p. 1090. Future references to this play are from this edition and will be noted in the text in the following manner,

could be lost as all his worldly goods have been entrusted to ships at sea. Granville instead moves directly to the conversation between Antonio and Bassanio, and establishes Bassanio's need for money and his love for Portia. Only after Bassanio applies to Antonio for money does Antonio mention that his "present Fortunes are . . . at sea" and that he will have to borrow money himself in order to satisfy Bassanio's needs. The elimination of the exchange between Antonio, Salerio, and Salanio thereby focuses the attention on the romantic plot between Bassanio and Portia, lessens the play's preoccupation with Antonio, and, all in all, enables Granville to entitle the play *The Jew of Venice* by pitting Shylock against Portia and Bassanio even more than in the original version by Shakespeare. The next scene in both versions of the play centers on Portia and Nerissa. Granville makes few alterations in this scene and is content to modernize the language, extensively cut the descriptions of the suitors, and omit Portia's mention of Bassanio which Shakespeare includes in act one, scene two, lines 112-121:

> Nerissa: Do you not remember, lady, in your father's time, a Venetian, a scholar and a soldier, that came hither in company of the Marquis of Montserrat?
>
> Portia: Yes, yes, it was Bassanio – as I think, so was he call'd.
>
> Nerissa: True, madam. He of all the men that ever my foolish eyes looked upon was the best deserving a fair lady.
>
> Portia: I remember him well, and I remember him worthy of thy praise. (*MV* 1.3.94-99)

Why Granville chooses to omit this open avowal of Portia's regard for Bassanio in favor of the comic descriptions of the suitors is not clear. In the following scene, he remains true to Shakespeare's plotting and changes only minor details. He shortens Shylock's "Jacob/Laban" dialogue and has him consider taking an eye or a nose as his bond before settling on the pound of flesh. He also

---

MV act.scene.line number.

adds a final speech by Antonio on the joy of giving. After Bassanio's assertion in
The Jew, similar to the one he makes in *The Merchant*, that "A Villain, when he
most seems kind,/Is most to be suspected" [19] Granville's Antonio is not content
to let the matter drop by reminding Bassanio that his ships will be home a month
before the bond comes due. He closes the act by asserting that he would give his
"whole Body, every Drop of Blood,/To purchase" his "Friend's Quiet!" (*JV* 9)
and then shows the goodness of God to those who give and the joy inherent in the
act of giving itself.

After having been relatively faithful to the final scene of Shakespeare's
first act, Granville begins the second act of *The Jew of Venice* by removing the
scene in which Portia delineates the terms her suitors must accept to win her hand
as well as the comic exchange between the runaway Lancelot Gobbo and his blind
father who does not recognize him. The elimination of these scenes does not
affect the basic plot line. Portia reinforces the theme of appearance versus reality
in her assertion to the Prince that his dark complexion will not cause her to dislike
him, for, as she says, "In terms of choice I am not solely led/By nice direction of a
maiden's eyes" (*MV* 2.1.13-14), thus providing both him and the audience with a
nice clue as to the location of her portrait. Granville does not use this
opportunity to make his play rich in meaning, but cuts this scene and the next in
favor of getting right to the conflict of Shylock with Bassanio and Antonio. He
begins his second act with the return of Shylock to his home where he informs his
daughter Jessica that he will be dining with Christians that night, and that she
should make the house secure. Since Granville has omitted the initial appearance
of Jessica in which she has entrusted Lancelot with a letter for Lorenzo, the first
time Jessica comes on stage, she informs the audience that Lorenzo is going to
elope with her that night. At this point, Lorenzo enters with Gratiano. He and

[19]George Granville, *The Jew of Venice* (London: Ber Lintott, 1701; reprint ed.,
London: Cornmarket Press, 1969), p. 9. Future references to this play are from this edition and
will be noted in the text in the following manner, *JV* page number.

Jessica prepare to leave when Antonio comes to bring Gratiano to the feast. The scene changes and moves to Antonio, Gratiano, Bassanio, and Shylock who are toasting each other as well as love, friendship, money and women when Bassanio expounds to his friend on the power of music. The "Mask of Peleus and Thetis" suddenly interrupts to entertain the company and audience. Antonio, greatly pleased with the entertainment, thanks his "noble minded Brother" for treating his company "with such an Air of true Magnificence" (*JV* 9) when Bassanio is called to the ship to sail for Belmont.

Granville has not only cut the first two scenes of *The Merchant of Venice* in order to include the masque, but he has also eliminated at least half of Shakespeare's original act two. Missing from Granville's version are Bassanio's agreement to take Lancelot Gobbo into his service, and Gratiano's plea to accompany Bassanio to Belmont (he goes in Granville's version, too, but the reason is never made clear). Jessica's escape from her father's house is much more dramatically effective in Shakespeare as well, for here, dressed as a boy, she returns to the house to rob her father of more money before she leaves with Lorenzo. Shakespeare also shifts back to Belmont in act two to see the Prince of Morocco mistakenly choose the gold casket and then moves to Venice again to show Salerio and Solanio reviewing the events of the night and hinting at Antonio's future misfortunes in their discussion of a lost ship which they fear to be his. In the final scene, Shakespeare once more takes the action to Belmont where the Prince of Aragon chooses the silver casket much to his dismay and to Portia's delight. And, more significant in terms of the plot, she hears that a fair suitor, who Nerissa hopes is Bassanio, has just alighted to try his fortune.

In act three, Granville once again cuts the initial scenes and goes directly to Bassanio's choice of the caskets. He sacrifices the opening scene in which Salerio and Solanio, discussing the ruin of yet another of Antonio's ships, are accosted by Shylock, who berates them for knowing of Jessica's elopement beforehand and avenges himself by informing them he will foreclose on Antonio's bond. Granville also omits Tubal's report on Jessica's whereabouts and his information on further losses for Antonio's ships. The third act of *The Jew of Venice* begins instead with Portia's trying to convince Bassanio "to defer a Month or two" (*JV* 21) before choosing so they can have a month of friendship before losing each other forever. In both versions, Bassanio proceeds despite Portia's pleas, chooses successfully, and receives Portia's ring, vowing never to part with it. At this point, Granville departs slightly from the original as he has Gratiano and Nerissa bickering over their own wedding plans while in the original they have been planning to marry all along contingent on Bassanio's success.

Another change in the action occurs when Bassanio, overjoyed by the outcome, plans to send word to Antonio that he will pay his bond and all will be well. The festivities are interrupted in both versions when Jessica and Lorenzo bring Salerio in with a letter from Antonio telling of his ruined fortunes and of Shylock's plaguing insistence on justice. Portia offers to pay the debt doubled and trebled and twenty times over. After sending Bassanio to rescue his friend in Granville's version, Portia and Nerissa leave for the home of her kinsman Bellario to devise a plan to rescue Antonio. In *The Merchant*, Portia and Bassanio's farewell is followed by a prison scene in which Shylock taunts Antonio. Granville places this scene last in his act, inserts the "Has not a Jew eyes?" speech from act three scene one and has Shylock accuse Antonio of prior knowledge of Jessica's elopement thereby adding a more tangible motive for revenge than Shakespeare does with Shylock's "So can I give no reason, nor I will not;/More than a lodg'd hate, and a certain loathing/I bear Antonio" (*MV* 4.1.59-60). Shylock's accusation also ties Jessica and Lorenzo's elopement more fully into the main action of the play and thus heightens the unity of action. The final scenes of Shakespeare's third act consist of Portia's informing Nerissa of her plan, and the discussion between Lorenzo and Jessica concerning the visitation of the sins of the fathers on the children and their praise of Portia's goodness, scenes which provide commentary, but do not further the action appreciably.

Granville's fourth act represents a truncated version of Shakespeare's with few superficial changes and no real alterations to the plot. He adds, for instance, Bassanio's offer to die for Antonio with Shylock's subsequent refusal on the grounds that Bassanio will probably hang himself after Antonio dies and thus serve Shylock's purpose even better. He has the Duke seize Shylock in anger, and, in his version, Portia and Nerissa reenter the court for the "ring" episode. Other than these minor changes, both versions proceed in the same manner. The Duke reluctantly calls Antonio in to judgment since Shylock will not relent. Bassanio comes and attempts to pay double the debt to no effect. Portia saves Bassanio's friend by appearing in the guise of Balthazar, a lawyer sent by Bellario, who deems that Shylock can exact his bond only if he does not take one jot of blood. Shylock asks for the money instead, but it is denied him and he is imprisoned for seeking the life of Antonio. To compensate Antonio for his troubles, the court grants him half of Shylock's money which he keeps in trust for Lorenzo and Jessica, and to further punish the Jew, the Duke "condemns" him to become a Christian. Both plays end act four with the exchange of rings between Bassanio and Portia and their counterparts.

Granville makes even fewer changes in act five, which opens with Lorenzo and Jessica mooning over the beauties of the night as they learn of Portia's and Bassanio's imminent arrivals. As the plays conclude, Portia and Nerissa tell their husbands how they really obtained the rings again, and Portia gives Bassanio the happy news that Antonio has three ships safe while Nerissa transfers the deed to Shylock's goods to Lorenzo and Jessica. Granville edits Shakespeare's final act, keeping the main plot intact and altering only the specific language.

Like his predecessors, Granville adds a masque to the action of the play, but in all other regards, the only changes he made in the plot of the play serve to unify the action. The elimination of Lancelot Gobbo, the Prince of Morocco, and the Prince of Aragon tightens the plot and keeps the emphasis on the main characters although much expository material and many of the comic scenes are excluded in the process. Further, Shylock's claim that Antonio aided his daughter to elope with Lorenzo provides a more technically "adequate" basis for the inclusion of the elopement scenes.

Even though it does not contain a masque, the action of Lansdowne's *She-Gallants* is not as unified as his *Jew of Venice*, an odd circumstance considering the French source Granville drew on for this play, but perhaps accounted for by the character-driven nature of Restoration comedy. The action begins as Constantia and Angelica, walking about the Mall in men's apparel, marvel that their success as men has surpassed their success as women. Angelica has conquered Lady Dorimen whose niece Lucinda is to marry Angelica's lover, Bellamour, so that she can "get into her Ladyship's Family, and have some Power over her Inclinations . . . to find an Expedient to break off a Match." [20] Constantia admits that she is helping Angelica in order to discover if Frederick, the man Constantia loves and whom she therefore has treated execrably, loves her truly. To gain this knowledge, she has become Frederick's friend by posing as her brother Courtall. The result thus far is that Frederick has proposed to Constantia and offered Courtall/Constantia the choice of his four sisters in a "cross Match" (*SG* 3), and all four have courted her shamelessly. As Constantia and Angelica admire each other's counterfeit masculinity, Sir Toby enters with good news of their conquests. Sir Toby, Angelica's father who has not seen her since she was ten years old, is now trying to help these two young gallants win their ladies. Soon the Mall is filled with ladies and gentlemen. Angelica and Sir Toby follow Lady Dorimen offstage as the four sisters of Frederick taunt Courtall about his inconstancy. Then Lucinda and Placket come on stage, and Lucinda asks if her note to Bellamour has been delivered. She is tired of him since he has become so sure of himself and also because her old lover Philabel has returned. As she

---

[20]George Granville, *The She-Gallants* (London: Henry Playford, 1696; Three Centuries of English Drama, 1642-1700, TC-II-569), p. 2. Future references to the play are from this edition and will be noted in the text in the following manner, *SG*, page number.

informs Placket, "If my old Lover had not return'd, I might have made my new one the happy Man; but since I hear Philabel came last night to Town, I find my self more inclin'd to my first Promise than my last, and in this have only acted like a Woman of the Age; if one Lover had fail'd, I entertain'd another in case of necessity" (*SG* 8). When her aunt returns, Lucinda tells her that she is not sure she wants to marry Bellamour, and that gentleman, who has just come within earshot, rebukes Lucinda for her insincerity and infidelity. He reads her letter to him aloud and attempts to "clear" his "Innocence" with her. She will not abide his presence and sends him away. Upon his dismissal, he goes to her maid to bribe her into telling him who his rival is.

The second act begins with Frederick and his four sisters discussing love. The sisters all claim "'tis impossible for a Woman to be in Love" (*SG* 15), but they all quibble over who is to get Courtall and rush home when the servant arrives to tell them of Courtall's presence there. Vaunter and Sir John Aery come on the scene at this point to discuss their rival claims to Lucinda but quickly change their stories when Bellamour enters with Angelica, still dressed as a man, who is trying unsuccessfully to persuade him to meet her cousin Angelica again. As Vaunter and Sir John rail at the concept of marriage, Sir Toby saunters down the mall informing Philabel of the changes in morals and manners since he has been away at war. Philabel will not agree with Sir Toby's cynical view of women unless "*Lucinda* has been false" in which case he "will then turn Railer, ... and conclude the worst of 'em all" (*SG* 26). On cue, Placket enters and delivers Lucinda's note to Philabel which warns him to disregard any rumors he may hear concerning her activities. Angelica is overjoyed to discover Lucinda's love for another, but now must turn Lady Dorimen against Bellamour. The act closes as Philabel goes to woo his lady.

As the third act opens, Angelica arrives to sway Lady Dorimen against Bellamour. The scene then shifts to Courtall and the four sisters as he tries to decide which to wed. Courtall gives all four notes, one of which supposedly contains his choice; then he tells each that she is his choice. They leave the stage to "proceed to Election" (*SG* 36), and the curtain rises on Lady Dorimen, Angelica, Lucinda, and Philabel all listening to a song in Dialogue, the closest thing to a masque in this play. After the song is finished, they digress on the topic of wits, writing plays, and obscenity when Angelica tells Sir Toby he should be angry at Bellamour since he made pretensions to his daughter in the past and was even privately contracted to her. Bellamour denies the allegation, but Lady Dorimen orders him out to Lucinda's delight. Before he leaves, Bellamour hints at a "meeting" on the duelling grounds with Angelica, then wonders if Philabel is his rival for Lucinda's heart. As the others leave to "Play a Pool" (*SG* 45), he curses them and all womankind.

As the fourth act commences, Frederick is opening his sisters' notes only to find that "this is all a Trick" (*SG* 47), as every note declares for a different sister. Frederick is justifiably angry, and they leave to teach Courtall a lesson. Angelica and Constantia, on the other hand, are ecstatic as they muse about Bellamour's downfall. Sir Toby brings Angelica a note from Lady Dorimen whom she then goes to visit. Downstairs, Bellamour is taking leave of Lucinda when Vaunter and Sir John come in berating her for sending for them and then making them "wait Three Hours in the Dark" (*SG* 55) as Lady Dorimen has had them secured in a closet. Bellamour pities her for having to stoop to their company but is rebuked in turn when they say he set the assignation himself. As he leaves, Bellamour notes that his "broken Vows" to Angelica "are well Reveng'd" (*SG* 57), and Lucinda has Placket tie the two braggarts up until they "discover upon what Errant they came hither" (*SG* 58).

By the fifth act everyone is in a quandary. Angelica reads the challenge she has received from Bellamour to her friend Constantia, who does not know what will be the outcome. Angelica has had enough sense to bring her look-alike brother, Courtall, into the action so that he can settle the matter. They pass Lady Dorimen's door which is opening, and as they go off, she exits the house. Soon all the principal actors are on stage. Frederick draws on Courtall and Constantia, not knowing which has wronged his sisters. Luckily for him, Bellamour appears at this time and agrees to help him fight the two. As they advance, Constantia reveals her true identity. The scene moves to Sir John and Vaunter tied in chairs discussing the ills they have suffered in the name of love. Placket comes in to see if they have repented and will no longer spread lies about their conquests. She forces Aery into promising to marry her before she releases them. Next, Angelica appears on stage in woman's apparel for the first time. Bellamour enters from the opposite side and sees the masked lady, who entreats him to leave in order to spare her honor. He begins to change for the duel, which is to take place "on this very spot" (*SG* 67), and agrees to depart only if she will remove her mask. She taunts him with the wrong he has done to her sex and wonders that he is "not afraid to be torn to peices after so known a Treachery to Angelica" (*SG* 67). Then she unmasks to show him the face of the "Enemy" he "expected" (*SG* 68). Shamed and still in love with her, Bellamour asks for her forgiveness. She agrees to love him and forgive him, but she can never quite trust him again.

As they reunite and the others come on stage, Placket recognizes Angelica as Lady Dorimen's "little spark in Petticoats" (*SG* 70) after which Angelica reveals herself to her father, Sir Toby. Delighted to have such a resourceful child, Sir Toby agrees to treble her fortune. Bellamour begs everyone's pardon, and since repentance is in the air Lucinda sends Placket for Sir John Aery and Vaunter in order to force them to ask forgiveness. Unfortunately, they have not been chastised enough and come in attempting to boast again when Philabel puts an end to their blustering. As in almost every traditional comedy, all the couples decide to marry at the end, and, infected by their spirit, Vaunter and Sir John also decide to marry *someone*. As Sir John is about to be forced to settle for Placket, Courtall runs in brandishing his sword before him in an attempt to fend off Frederick and his four sisters. Constantia, with her wig off, is being angrily attacked by the four sisters when Courtall agrees to pay for his sister's errors. Proposing an exchange of prisoners, Frederick takes Constantia into his protection as she "thrusts her Brother" (*SG* 75) at her lover's sisters. Vaunter and Sir John take what Courtall leaves, and the play comes to a halt as Lady Dorimen ponders the remarkable resemblance between Courtall and his sister and, as a result, on appearances in general. The victorious Angelica brings down the curtain as she reflects on the effect of constancy in love.

The She-Gallants is entitled with reference to the disguises Angelica and Constantia take on, and all the events in the play hinge on the escapades of these two in their masquerade. Although both are given equal credit in the title, Angelica's story line tends to dominate the play, perhaps because Bellamour is a stronger character than Constantia's love, Frederick. Another possibility for the dominance of Angelica's plot line is that her situation has been the impetus of their masquerade. Two interrelated stories nonetheless make up the play, and all the incidents in the play have a direct bearing or more or less depend on the actions of these two ladies. Even the actions of the most expendable characters, Vaunter and Sir John Aery, are tied into the main plot and, in fact, bring the two plots together as both court Lucinda (Angelica plot line) and end by courting Frederick's sisters (Constantia plot line). The double plot here is not the one prescribed by Aristotle for comedy in which one situation ends happily while the other fails, and it is certainly not the classically unified plot Granville achieves in his *Jew of Venice* or Burnaby in his *Love Betray'd*. The French original may account for the classical flavor which nevertheless pervades the play.

Dennis' The Comical Gallant and A Plot and No Plot

According to Leo Salingar, *The Merry Wives of Windsor* shows "Shakespeare exploiting the methods of the Italian double plot to the uttermost,"[21] and Dryden also noted its classical regularity in at least two

---

[21]Salingar, p. 238.

different essays, "The Grounds of Criticism in Tragedy" and "Of Dramatic Poesy"[22] for the Anne Page-Fenton affair comes to fruition while Falstaff's escapades lead him to disgrace. Nicer in his definition of unity than most, in his "Large Account of Taste in Poetry, and the Causes of the Degeneracy of It" (1702), Dennis discovered in it "no less than three Actions . . . independent of one another, which divide and distract the minds of an Audience" as well as "more than one insignificant Scene which has nothing to do with any other part of the Play" which is therefore "enough to obstruct and stifle the Action."[23] Despite the problems he discovered in the play, Dennis undertook the task of revising it since it was "not despicable" primarily because "it had pleased one of the greatest Queens that ever was in the World, great not only for her Wisdom in the Arts of Government," but also for "her nice taste of the Drama, for such a taste we may be sure she had, by the relish she had of the Ancients" (279).

Like Granville before him, Dennis structures his play so that every bit of dialogue and every incident relate to the main conflicts and point to the climax. In the first act of *The Comical Gallant*, he begins with Fenton obtaining the services of the Host of the Garter as go-between in his affair with Anne Page, whereas Shakespeare begins with a discussion between Shallow, Slender, and Evans on Shallow's quarrel with Falstaff during which time Evans brings up the remarkable eligibility of Mistress Anne Page because of her dowry of seven hundred pounds. The dramatic impact of Dennis' version may be initially greater; however, Shakespeare's subtle use of verisimilitude in allowing the situation to arise from the interaction of the characters rather than using the characters to further the action draws the audience in and gives necessary information at the same time. In this aspect, the first scene is representative of the basic differences throughout the

[22]Dryden, GCT, p. 247; ODP, p. 66.

[23]Dennis, LATP, p. 280.

two versions. Dennis continues by moving straightway to the intrigue as Anne enters and Fenton uncovers his plot to preoccupy her parents so they can elope. He has persuaded Sir John Falstaff that Mrs. Ford and Mrs. Page are in love with him, and he has deviously "prevail'd upon a couple of Falstaff's men to betray their Master's design both to Mr. Ford" and Mr. Page.[24] At this point, Shallow, Slender, Evans, and Simple enter in time for Slender to see Anne and decide that his friends are trying to persuade him to marry the right girl after all. Falstaff and his men come down the street, and when the others leave, he announces to Pistol and Nym that he will woo Mrs. Ford since "The report goes, she hath all the rule of her Husband's purse, she hath a legend of Angels" (*CG* 4), an exchange taken from Shakespeare's second act, scene two. His men rebel against his unsavory plans, and in league with the Host decide to inform the husbands what is afoot. As they leave, Caius enters and the Host attempts to stir him against Shallow and Slender, his rivals for Anne's hand. The scene shifts then to Shakespeare's act two, scene two in which Mrs. Page and Mrs. Ford are discussing the love letters they have received from a gallant. Upon comparing notes, they discover that Falstaff has been wooing them both and decide to wreak vengeance upon him. Mrs. Ford will also use the stratagem to break her husband of this jealous nature as well as to help her nephew Fenton obtain Anne Page. The action returns to the street as Pistol informs Ford of Falstaff's plan. When Page enters to tell Ford of the duel between Caius and Slender, Ford tells him of Falstaff's plans and a comic scene, a variation on Shakespeare's act two scene two, in which Page refers to the duel while Ford speaks of Falstaff, shows the basic differences in each character. The first act ends when Ford decides to bribe the Host to let him disguise himself to learn the truth from Falstaff, Shakespeare's first scene of act two.

The basic changes Dennis has made in the action of the first act focus the

[24]John Dennis, *The Comical Gallant* (London: A. Baldwin, 1702; Three Centuries of English Drama, TCD-E-1546), p. 3. Future references are from this microprint and will be noted in the text in the following manner, *CG*, page number.

attention on Fenton's plot to elope with Anne Page. He eliminates the controversy between Falstaff and Shallow as well as Slender's accusation that Pistol stole his purse. Also omitted are the attention to Slender's appetite, shifted to the last lines of act four, the character of Mistress Quickly, whose function is, to a certain extent, taken over by the Host of the Garter and Doll Tearsheet, and the minor characters, Bardolph and Robin. Another notable change is the increased emphasis Dennis places on Fenton.

Dennis uses many of the incidents from Shakespeare's act two in his first act and is content to rearrange the remainder of Shakespeare's second act in his corresponding act. He begins with Caius awaiting Evans on the duelling grounds, Shakespeare's 2.3, and then moves to Ford, disguised as Broom, who is meeting with Falstaff to discover the truth of his wife's infidelity (*MW* 2.2). Doll Tearsheet, the bawd, enters with news from Mrs. Ford that she hates her husband and will gladly meet Falstaff between three and four at the Pyed Bull. He returns to Broom/Ford and feeds his suspicions unwittingly by promising Broom he shall lie with Mrs. Ford that night to pave the way for him and then feeds his passions by informing Broom that he chose Mrs. Ford only because he wanted to get money from her. The act ends by showing Evans and Simple waiting in the Park for Caius in preparation for the duel, a variation on *Merry Wives* 3.3.

Act three contains the most changes Dennis made in *The Comical Gallant*. In the opening scene, he shows Mrs. Ford and the Host preparing the buckbasket for Falstaff when he enters. He woos her extravagantly and believes he has won Mrs. Ford, but she accuses him of loving Mrs. Page as well. As he tries to convince her otherwise, a servant announces Captain Dingboy, and he runs off to hide behind a screen. Mrs. Page enters dressed as Captain Dingboy and attempts to seduce Mrs. Ford. They set an assignation, and as Mrs. Page leaves, she asks whom Mrs. Ford is expecting. When Mrs. Ford mentions Falstaff's name, Dingboy enumerates the ridiculous escapades the "perpetual Jest" has taken part in lately. Falstaff comes out ripping and roaring, ready to fight Dingboy, when a servant conveniently comes in to announce that the last man Dingboy met in a duel has just died. Mrs. Ford heightens Falstaff's fears by informing him that Dingboy has killed his man each of the four times he has fought. Dingboy shoots at Falstaff who falls down, then scrambles around in an attempt to escape. While Falstaff is in her power, Mrs. Ford tells Dingboy that Falstaff is only a farce in bed and actually gets him to admit it. A servant comes in with news of Mr. Ford's approach, so she makes Falstaff stand sentry while she and Dingboy go into the next room. To avenge himself, Falstaff creeps downstairs to expose his rival to the constable. Before he can leave, a servant comes up and tells him Ford wishes to speak with him. He calls Mrs. Ford out, and she decides to put him in a laundry basket to hide. Ford enters in a rage which he takes out on Dingboy when he cannot discover Falstaff. Dingboy sets two men on him to beat him, but Ford still comes at "him" as he tries to convince him that his wife is "a Virtuous Wife, and a civil, obliging, sweet tempered Creature" (*CG* 28). He makes a sudden leap for Dingboy, and Mrs. Page's hat and wig come off as she escapes. Ford exits seething with rage.

In order to make room for these interpolated incidents, Dennis omits several scenes from Shakespeare's third act and moves others either to act two or act four. The actual meeting between Caius and Evans, which Shakespeare presents as the first scene of act three, is Dennis' final scene in act two. Dennis eliminates Shakespeare's second scene, which sees Ford amazed at Page's blindness to his wife's infidelity and the Host's attempt to sway Page to hear Fenton's suit, as well as the fourth scene, in which Fenton and Anne, who are discussing their problems, are interrupted by Slender and Shallow, who come to court Anne. Dennis' version also moves the fifth scene of act five to the first scene of act four.

After some new dialogue between the Host and Ford, Dennis shows Falstaff, enraged over his mistreatment, recounting his tale to the Host (Mrs. Quickly in *MW*) and then Mr. Ford. Dennis alters the scene to include references to Captain Dingboy and has the Host reassure Mr. Ford that he helped deceive Falstaff in the matter. The Host then tells him that Falstaff and Mrs. Ford are to meet that night at Hern the Hunter's Oak, and they decide to dress Ford up as the Hunter, in which guise Falstaff is to appear, and have him meet his wife before Sir John arrives so that he "may make a plain discover" whether he wears the horns in earnest or not (*CG* 35). Fenton and Anne enter and decide to elope that night during the confusion of the masquerade; the last scene is devoted to the color Anne is to wear to the masque and Slender's scanty appetite.

A quick glance at the action in Shakespeare's fourth act shows that Dennis eliminates most of the incidents and replaces them with ones of his own making. Shakespeare's fourth act presents several vignettes not directly related to the main action. The opening scene, after a brief mention of Mr. Ford's choler, depicts Evans putting young William Page through his "accidence"[25] as Mrs. Page and Mrs. Quickly listen. Following this scene, Shakespeare has Falstaff, once again with Mrs. Ford, forced to dress as "mother Prat," the "witch of Brainford," who is cursed and beaten by Mr. Ford. A short scene interposes to reveal the gulling of the Host by the Germans. Then Shakespeare has the wives revealing the truth to their husbands and devising the meeting with Falstaff that night along with the Pages' decision to dupe each other and bestow their daughter on Caius (Mrs. Page) and Slender (Mr. Page) in the turmoil of the masquerade. He once again leaves the main action in the fifth scene which plays on Falstaff's disguise as Prat and shows him revelling in the Host's cozenage by the three Germans. Or, as he says, "'I would all the world might be cozen'd, for I have been cozen'd and beaten too" (*MW* 4.5.93-94). In the final scene of the fourth act of *The Merry Wives*, Fenton bribes the Host to get a Vicar to marry him and Anne that night.

---

[25]William Shakespeare, *The Merry Wives of Windsor*, in *The Norton Shakespeare*, ed. Stephen Greenblatt, et. al. (New York: W. W. Norton and Company, 1997), p. 1272. Future references to this play are from this edition and will be noted in the text in the following manner, *MW* act.scene.line.

In his revision of *The Merry Wives'* fifth act, Dennis has skipped the first scene, which contains a dialogue between Ford/Broom and Falstaff as well as the second and third scenes, which have Page and Mrs. Page directing their chosen sons-in-law on how to identify their daughter before their arrival at Hern's Oak. The fifth act of *The Comical Gallant* picks up with Page, Mrs. Page, and Mrs. Ford at Hern's Oak informing the various interested parties as to how Anne Page is attired. Falstaff enters as Hern the Hunter when suddenly a horrendous noise bursts forth and the maskers begin to chase Falstaff. As they run off the stage in Dennis' adaptation, they lose sight of the real Falstaff and return cudgelling Ford who also is dressed as the Hunter. Mrs. Page steps up to him and asks how he likes Windsor wives now when the Host approaches with Falstaff unmasked. Shocked, they unmask Ford who, though he is "maim'd . . . crippled forever" (*CG* 45), heartily thanks his wife for having made him wise enough so that he will never again distrust her. Falstaff has learned his lesson, too, and supposedly will be cured of his lechery. The company taunts Falstaff, but Page invites him home to supper where they can laugh at Mrs. Page for having been outsmarted when Slender eloped with Anne. While Page gloats over his success, a Parson enters with Slender and Caius, both masked and dressed in women's clothes, walking hand in hand. (In *MW*, they "married" a "great lubberly boy" [*MW* 5.5.170] and "*un garçon*, a boy, *un paysan*" [*MW* 5.5.187], respectively.) When Fenton and Anne arrive unmasked, the two defeated suitors discover their folly much to their dismay and the amusement of the company. At this point in *The Merry Wives*, Anne and Fenton announce their marriage. In *The Comical Gallant*, Anne tells her parents, as they accuse her of disobedience, that she and Fenton are not yet married, but Fenton arranged this episode so that the parents would realize how "preposterous" (*CG* 47) the husbands they had chosen for Anne are. He releases her from her contract to him, as he will never teach her to be disobedient to them. Upon Fenton's master stroke, the play ends happily as the Pages give him leave to marry Anne, and the Fords inform their friends that Fenton is their heir.

Dennis' *Comical Gallant* conforms more stringently to the classical rule of unity of action than the original *Merry Wives*. Dennis keeps most of Shakespeare's plot intact and eliminates what could be seen as extraneous scenes, such as the drilling of little William by Evans and the scam by the Germans. Dennis' addition to the plot, Captain Dingboy, on the other hand, is in keeping with the main action of gulling Falstaff; in fact, this incident supersedes the second trick on Falstaff in *Merry Wives* in which he is dressed as Mother Prat. *The Comical Gallant* contains no extraneous scenes and actually contains few scenes in which some aspect of the plot is not further developed. The result, however, is that the characterization is more flat and the audience, hurled through the plot, does not understand the motivation behind the events as fully.

Dennis' *A Plot and No Plot* is also designed along classical lines. As the title suggests, it has the requisite "double plot" of comedy, one of which ends successfully and the other which fails dismally. Rambler in *A Comparison of the Two Stages* refers to it as "very regular,"[26] while Gerard Langbaine praises it as "exactly regular."[27] Belvil, who is being coerced by his rich banker uncle, Bull, to marry Justice Dowdy's daughter, has engaged the services of an actor friend, Baldernoe, to help him out of the marriage. Instead, he wishes to marry Sylvia who is promised to Batt Bull, his cousin. When Bull comes to prod Belvil into marrying on the next day, his man Rumour enters to inform him of the arrival of an English countess and her daughter from the continent. These noble ladies are actually Frowsy and Friskit, two ladies of doubtful reputation whom Belvil has employed to help him carry out his plans. Momentarily sidetracked but not swayed from his purposes, Uncle Bull leaves with a reminder to his nephew to

---

[26]Gildon, *CTS* 29.

[27]Gerard Langbaine, *An Account of the English Dramatick Poets* (London: by L. L. for George West and Henry Clements, 1691; Ann Arbor, Mich.: University Microfilms, TC-II-358), p. 38.

think on his "Father's last Will and Tremble."[28] After he leaves, Belvil explains to Baldernoe that he is setting his uncle up, aided by people his uncle has cheated, in order to retrieve their fortunes and make his own.

Act two begins at the theater as Frowsy and Friskit look over the audience wondering where Belvil is and searching for possible "lovers." Belvil tells her of his plan, but she is not convinced that it is worth her while since she is heading for Flanders with more recruits the next morning. Sylvia appears in her box, and Belvil goes to her to inform her about the man she is to marry the next day. Bull, Jr., enters, and Sylvia quickly discerns that he is a "Fop and a Monkey" (*PNP* 24) who treats people, in Belvil's words, "with a surprising familiarity" (*PNP* 25). Batt Bull, who does not realize the identity of the lady, ingratiates himself with his future bride by showing her a billet doux from a duchess and boasting of his amorous encounters. Belvil tricks him into asserting that he would marry any woman; in fact, he claims that as "all Wives are hideous alike," he would as soon marry the woman he "hat'd most" as any other (*PNP* 28). After Bull leaves, Sylvia tells her love that Bull is handsome enough, but she will marry Belvil if he can obtain his uncle's consent in the next two hours. Belvil plots vengeance on his uncle and cousin for the many wrongs they have done him, and the most proper revenge he can think of is to marry Batt Bull to Friskit, "For so extravagant a Drab and so extraordinary a Fop are tallies to one another" (*PNP* 30).

The third act has Frowsy and Friskit at Bull's house where young Bull, calling himself Dorant, approaches them as Friskit falls into a counterfeit swoon. The "Countess" makes Batt believe that he courted her daughter in Paris, all the time denying a previous acquaintance herself. She lays the blame for her daughter's fit on the fact that she had fallen in love with him on the continent "before she was sure of his heart" (*PNP* 37). By playing on Batt's pretensions,

[28] John Dennis, *A Plot and No Plot* (London: for A. Parker, 1697; Three Centuries of English Drama, TCD-852), p. 11. Future references are from this microprint and will be noted in the text in the following manner, *PNP* page number.

Frowsy convinces him to offer to marry Friskit immediately. As they are discussing his heritage, the servant comes in to prepare them for the arrival of a very tipsy Bull, Sr. Frowsy is upset, for "If the old man staid but a quarter of an hour longer, in all likelihood Friskit had been coupled, and the Fop had been sped" (*PNP* 43). She consoles herself with the thought that she has also begun her plan to deceive the father even as she tells him of his son's alliance.

Having convinced Bull, Sr., that she is a countess, Frowsy tells him the tale of Dorant. As they talk, Bull, Jr., slips away to be followed by his lady, but Frowsy "discovers" him in the process. Bull, Sr., explodes and beats him both for this escapade and for affronting Sylvia. Never completely at a loss, Bull, Jr., stops his father by informing him that "the young Lady who lies in" his "house to night, has taken a fancy to this Son of a Whore's person" (*PNP* 49) whereupon Bull immediately drops his stick but still demands to know why he calls himself Dorant. Satisfied that Dorant sounds more like a viscount's name than Bull, the father reconciles with his son as Frowsy returns to laugh at them for having "consented to have carried this cheat on against themselves" (*PNP* 50). Friskit goes out "to take the air" as Frowsy asks Bull, Sr., to "break this business" to Dorant's father. At this time, a knock sounds on the door, and Greg tells his master that a half a score "surly, snarling, sowre look'd fellows" (*PNP* 53) are looking for a French marquis, and even worse, officers are searching a house down the street with the intention of coming to Bull's house next. Baldernoe chooses this most appropriate moment to enter "In a chair, Singing and whimsically drest," attended by fiddlers and dancers. He, of course, is the French Marquis, a notorious political "Plotter." The servants breathlessly announce the officers and Constable Bungy as Baldernoe and his men rush offstage to attire themselves as other officers. When Bungy attempts to search the house, Baldernoe insists that he has already searched it and discovered nothing suspicious. They exchange blows, and Bungy insists on emptying everything in the cellar "for fear there should be Gun-powder or Fire-arms hid there" (*PNP* 60). Baldernoe instead suggests that old man Bull "have de look . . . of de ver dam Rogue" and tells Bungy to take him and Frowsy into custody. Some of the officers carry them away as Baldernoe and Bungy engage in a drinking song composed by Wycherley. Bungy begins to worry about the consequences of their sham conspiracy, but Baldernoe reassures him that "'twill be in our sham Plot, as 'tis often in real Conspiracies./Where poor Rogues 'scape, who first the Plot begin,/And the rich Sots are swing'd, who are drawn in" (*PNP* 62).

As the curtain goes up on the final act, Belvil is praising Baldernoe as "the very Genius and power of Cheating" (*PNP* 63) for carrying the plot through successfully. Baldernoe fills Belvil in on the details. His men have driven Bull around town to confuse him and then brought him back home, making him believe that he was going to Newgate. Baldernoe gloats at how everything has contributed to further his uncle's alarm. For even as the chair men brought him home, "Hawkers roar'd out a Proclamation just published, for the apprehension of Conspirators" and Baldernoe paid one of the hawkers to "bellow out" Bull's name. While they are speaking, Bull, Sr., arrives at the door and complains about the room, only to be told that many men have been "hang'd out of this Room" (*PNP* 65). Bull, Sr., is not impressed; in fact, the totally confused man exclaims, "This is the only Jayl in Town that I have not yet been in. But I dont like coming to this Newgate a jot" (*PNP* 65). As he has experienced several bad omens since arriving, Bull asks for pen and paper that he can turn "Evidence" before the night is over. Being neither trustworthy nor terribly honest, Bull tells the jailer that he will "produce Traytors" to save himself, and will, in fact, "take the first persons" he "can light of" (*PNP* 65) without regard to their guilt or innocence. The jailer angrily informs him that he would load him down with irons were it not for his obligations to Bull's nephew, Belvil. Bull grasps at this opportunity to bribe the jailer and decides to exchange Belvil's right to marry for his freedom. Rumour comes in to tell him the Marquis informed on Bull and adds that Bull should have patience since he will be out by Friday when he will probably be hanged.

As Bull is despairing again, Belvil and Sylvia arrive. Bull is so happy with them that he releases both from his guardianship, and then Belvil tells him that he has arranged his escape for the paltry sum of five thousand pounds. Bull reluctantly gives them access to the money, and they leave as Batt Bull and Friskit approach. Bull, Sr., has been expecting his son's capture, so he is not surprised to see him. Bull, Jr., wonders momentarily why his father is in the "Devil's Apartment" which has been nailed shut for twenty years. After all, Batt comments, "Yesterday he was afraid to pass by the very door" (*PNP* 69); however, he keeps his thoughts to himself and only reinforces his father's beliefs when he confirms that he and Friskit are indeed "Prisoners! Ay, prisoners for life" (*PNP* 69). Bull, Jr. decides his father is mad and humors him long enough to send for Belvil to convince him he is in Bedlam. Belvil returns after having married Sylvia, and he and Batt catechize Bull, telling him he is a Bethlemite and repeating the truth to him about Frowsy and Friskit until he believes that he has been moved to Bedlam. When he realizes that he has been holding commerce with drabs and rogues, Bull breaks loose, runs and looks out the door, discovers that he has "been all this while" in his "own house," and rails at his companions for having so "grossly impos'd upon" (*PNP* 76) him. Belvil reconciles Bull to his fate, promising to pay back the five thousand pounds if he approves his marriage and informing him that Batt and Friskit were married by a bogus magistrate. His grateful Uncle Bull acknowledges Belvil's success in humbling his pride and opening his eyes to his own weaknesses as the curtain drops.

Like *The Comical Gallant, A Plot and No Plot* contains the double plot acceptable in classical comedy. Dennis does not adhere as closely to unity of action in this play as he does in his adaptation of *The Merry Wives*. In that play, he rejects every scene included purely for comic effect or exposition, whereas in this play he includes several scenes which do not further the action. The scene at the theater, for instance, in which Friskit attempts to lure a Beau as Frowsy and Belvil discuss his plan in the background does not have any real bearing on the main plot except, perhaps, in making Batt look more ridiculous as he takes this "drab" for his wife. The overall effect of the play, nonetheless, is unified as every scene promotes in some way the gulling of Bull, Sr., and the union of Belvil and Sylvia.

Summary of Unity of Action

In action, as in the matters of time and place, the adaptations by these four playwrights conform to the law of unity more rigidly than the original versions by Shakespeare. The interpolated masques in three of the plays, though they do not contribute to the working out of the plots, are sanctioned by no less an authority than Aristotle himself. None of the authors includes a masque in his original play. This point may suggest that they were added to the alterations merely to give the author a chance to exert his own creative powers more fully and add interest in the form of musical entertainment to a plot which he felt was already too well known to attract a large audience.

The masques aside, several characteristics mark the plot changes devised by all four of these men. Each excludes scenes which Shakespeare included purely for comic effect as well as those scenes which, though they add to the play's meaning by either reemphasizing a trait of character or a particular theme, are not essential to the working out of the conflict. Dennis, for example, excludes William Page's lesson; Gildon excises the scene in which Pompey and Abhorson attempt to execute Bernardine; Burnaby fuses Sir Andrew Aguecheek and Malvolio into Taquilet and, thus, eliminates several scenes played primarily for comic effect; and Granville also omits a comic exchange between Lancelot Gobbo and his blind father. Granville likewise does not include the comic and thematically significant scenes in which the Princes of Morocco and Aragon incorrectly choose the gold and silver caskets by trusting in appearances rather than in the good sense outlined in their verses. Pompey's day in court does not appear in Gildon's version of *Measure for Measure* to contrast the unjust system which sends Claudio to his death while it deals leniently with the pimp. Burnaby excludes Olivia's exchange with the fool; and, finally, Dennis omits the cozening of the Host by the Germans.

In addition to, and perhaps even more significant than the omission of incidents not necessary to the main plot, at least three of these playwrights achieve greater unity of action through a refocusing of action and a rearrangement of scenes so that almost every dialogue and every action point toward the climax. Gildon plunges the audience into Angelo's dilemma and postpones the expository scenes which detail the Duke's reasons for leaving Vienna until the second act. Granville rearranges the events of the third act so that Bassanio and Portia part immediately after he learns of Antonio's troubles rather than after the prison scene which interposes in Shakespeare's version.

Of all three playwrights, Dennis reorganizes the play the most. Practically his entire first act consists of Shakespeare's second act, and he moves several lines, at least, from Shakespeare's first act to his fourth act, notably the attention to Slender's appetite. Only Burnaby, admittedly the least concerned with the unities, does not rearrange Shakespeare's plot. The changes made by Dennis and the others lead to more straightforward plot lines in which scenes dealing with the "happy" plot are usually grouped together within an act and are separate from those pertaining to the "gulling" plot. Shakespeare, on the other hand, intersperses these scenes so they reinforce each other thematically and also provide added interest by building suspense in the audience. The unity achieved by these four playwrights in respect to time, place, and action adheres more closely to the letter of the laws. In this instance, as is usual, the "letter" kills while the "spirit" of classical comedy which shines in Shakespeare's original plays gives abundant life. As John Dennis remarks in the Dedication to *The Invader of his Country* (1720), "'tis an eternal general Rule, that a Copy has neither the free Spirit, nor easy Grace of an Original."[29] Although he might not affirm that

---

[29]John Dennis, Dedication to *The Invader of his Country*, in *The Critical Works of*

application of the unities contributes to the lack of grace which characterizes these adaptations, this methodical plotting surely robs the plays of much of their vigor.

John Dennis, ed. Edward Niles Hooker, vol. 1 (Baltimore: The Johns Hopkins University Press, 1939), p. 178.

"Nor durst they look into the Muses Well,
Lest the cleer Spring their ugliness should tell;
Affrighted with the shadow of their Rage;
They broke the Mirror of the times, the Stage."
> William Davenant, Prologue to Ben Jonson's *The Silent Woman*,
> the first play presented at court after the Restoration.

CHAPTER III

THE ADAPTERS AND THE REFINEMENT OF MANNERS AND MORALS

Having survived the Commonwealth's fiery attempt to destroy it, the English theatre arose from the embers confident that it had been "refined" by the tribulations undergone and furthermore convinced that it reflected the refinement of morals and manners that characterized the Englishman of the late seventeenth century. This refinement of manners and morals led the dramatists of the Restoration to believe that Shakespeare's plays would not suit the more elite audience who now were the only segment of the populace with enough money to frequent the theatre; similarly, the opposition presented by the Puritan faction forced the playwright to avoid scrupulously all manner of oaths, profanities, obscenities and to reform the morals of the plays by punishing vice, rewarding virtue, and virtually eliminating moral ambiguity. As an example of man's progression upward on the spiritual/intellectual plane, Restoration drama, the "Mirror of the times," continually had to parry the blows of two strong opponents, the idea of the immorality of the stage and what was seen as the vulgarity of style characteristic of the preceding age.

Although primarily describing the alterations Davenant made in his version of *Hamlet*, Arthur Nethercot pinpoints the modifications representative of most Restoration adaptations. According to Nethercot, Davenant:

lopped off many lyrical and sententious passages and stressed the
dramatic; he made various "improvements" in the language and
style; in accordance with his contracted promise to free the plays
under his surveillance from scurrility and profaneness, he diluted or
deleted all possible oaths. Without altering the original structure or
plot, he changed close to three hundred passages, in the cause of
greater clarity and greater elegance for a new age.[1]

Nethercot thus considers the essence of Davenant's alterations as the
clarification and supposed polishing of style, the heightening of dramatic import,
and the excision of offensive language. Clarity, above all, seems to have been
Davenant's watchword, a legacy he left to those who followed him. For the
critical writings as well as the plays of Granville, Gildon, Burnaby, and Dennis
evidence a supreme concern not only for lucidity of style but for clearly delineated
morality as well.

Davenant's Prologue to the King quoted above also set the tone of
dramatic criticism in regards to the morality of the theatre for the entire Augustan
period. Instead of the "theoretical speculation" as to "what drama *should* be and
how it could be improved" typical of the past ages, Restoration criticism, Robert
Hume asserts, "is very full of apologies and justifications, arguments that drama is
not so very wicked, or need not be, and ought not to be suppressed."[2]   Hume
contends that the critic/dramatists of the Restoration merely "pay lip service to
inherited moral platitudes," platitudes which the same men largely "disregard in

[1]Arthur Nethercot, *Sir William Davenant: Poet Laureate   and Playwright Manager*
(New York: Russell and Russell, 1966), p. 383.

[2] Hume, p. 489.

practice" as playwrights.[3]   Hume's statement appears valid on the surface,
considering the risque subjects and "warm" situations exhibited in the plays of the
Wycherleys and Congreves, plays whose morality may be obscured by what
Bernard Grebanier calls the "pervading heartlessness and cynicism" typical of "all
Restoration comedy."[4]   Restoration critics nonetheless continually affirm the
moral efficacy of their drama. Indeed, the adapters of Shakespearean comedy did
attempt to "clean up" the plays, not by deleting sexual innuendo and expunging
wicked characters, but instead by showing rather unrealistically the workings of
poetic justice which ordains that evil fails while goodness prospers and likewise
by making absolutely certain that the audience understands who is good and who
is evil.

Gildon and The Refinement of Morals

One of Shakespeare's "problem plays," *Measure for Measure*, is formed,
according to David L. Stevenson, "somewhat after the fashion of a Donne poem,
made up of a series of intricately interrelated moral ironies and reverses, held
together by the twin themes of mercy and justice, and resolved by a final balancing
out of paradox."[5] The complex web of motive and action, idealism and humanity
presented by the play obviously would not accord with the Restoration's
preference for clearly defined moral issues and consistently drawn characters. In
adapting *Measure for Measure* Charles Gildon therefore resolved the ambiguities
of the situation and, in doing so, simplified the characters so that each is either

[3] Ibid., p. 32.

[4] Bernard Grebanier, *Then Came Each Actor* (New York: David McKay Company,
Inc., 1975), p. 26.

[5] David L. Stevenson, "Design and Structure in *Measure for Measure*," *English
Literary History* 23 (December 1956):262.

wholly admirable or contemptible.

Gildon, in Bernard Levison's opinion, "cleans up" the entire atmosphere of *Measure for Measure*. Shakespeare's original "is permeated with an aura of corruption that envelops Vienna, from the sleazy bawdy of Mistress Overdone and her pimp Pompey to the arbitrary and hypocritical 'justice' distributed by Angelo."[6] Levison later notes that although Gildon eliminates the bawds and the pimps from his version of the play, *Measure for Measure, or, Beauty, the Best Advocate*, in fact, strikes the audience as a much more "prurient" play than the original. To prove his point, he quotes the passage in act four scene one in which Angelo tempts Isabella with jewels and "treats" the audience "to the spectacle of a nun pretending to sell her virginity for a 'Cabinet of gems.'" Such passages "contain neither the healthy delight in sexuality . . . nor the frank bawdiness of the low-life characters in Shakespeare's *Measure for Measure*."[7] Though Levison is right in terms of the overall effect of the alterations, Gildon did make some changes which, when viewed discretely, clarify the moral position.

In removing the scenes with the "low" characters from the play, Gildon eliminates the superficially offensive material, but even more significantly, he heightens the workings of poetic justice in the play. In Shakespeare's version the scenes containing Mistress Overdone, Pompey, and Lucio expose a world in which "Liberty plucks Justice by the nose,/ The baby beats the nurse, and quite athwart/Goes all decorum"(*MM* 1.3.29-31). Although Pompey, the pimp, is in custody by act two scene one, a comic scene that in Levison's words shows "'justice going nowhere' which is what happens at all levels of society in the

6 Levison, p. 41.

7 Ibid., p. 107.

play,"[8] he is released by Escalus. His "punishment" at this point consists solely of a warning to leave his way of life or he will be "whipped" (*MM* 2.1.223).

Pompey is apprehended again in the second scene of act three as is Mistress Overdone. The fate of "Madam Mitigation," a "bawd of eleven years' continuance," (*MM* 3.1.425) is never known to the audience although she goes off to prison attempting to plea bargain by supplying information on Lucio. Gildon for some reason also abbreviates the role of Lucio, a "lewd fellow" (*MM* 5.1.503) in Shakespeare, who, as Levison notes, is the only character in the play not pardoned by the Duke.[9] Pompey ironically gets the chance to shorten his imprisonment by participating in the execution of Claudio, a man whose only crime is that he is married to Julietta legally but without the sanction of the church.

Claudio's words to the Provost who carries him to prison adequately express the fickleness of justice which has inflicted the ultimate punishment on him while allowing worse transgressors to escape unscathed:

> Thus can the demigod Authority;
>
> Make us pay down for our offense by weight
>
> The words of heaven: on whom it will, it will;
>
> On whom it will not, so; yet still 'tis just.

(MM 1.2.100-103)

Gildon's Claudio echoes these words in act two scene three but with two major differences. This play, first of all, contains no graphic examples of justice gone awry to contrast with Claudio's situation, while the major portion of Shakespeare's play builds up to this speech by the introduction of Lucio,

[8] Ibid., p. 42.

[9] Ibid., p. 77.

Mistress Overdone, and Pompey. Even more important, when Claudio responds to the "Friar" who is attempting to comfort him, he assures him that he realizes "Heaven is merciful; Because 'tis wise and just, and knows our sorrows:/But," he adds, "Man by ignorance jealous of our Hearts,/Or else by his own Passions, led from Goodness, Still deviates from the beauteous Paths of Mercy,/And seldom keeps the noble Tracks of Justice" (*BBA* 18), thus placing the blame for the inconsistencies of justice on the imperfect rule of man rather than on any failure of heaven. Shakespeare's Angelo, like his Claudio, realistically concedes to Escalus that justice does not always prevail when he admits that "The jury passing on the prisoner's life/May in the sworn twelve have a thief or two/Guiltier than him they try" (*MM* 2. 1. 19-20). Gildon excises these and the following lines from Angelo's speech so that the audience does not have to doubt that Providence parcels out justice with a steady hand, and, he reinforces this idea in the final scene of the masque as well as in the Duke's closing words:

> With equal hand to all I'll Justice do;
>
> Favour shan't blind my Reason, but Reward
>
> And punishment shall wait on Guilt and Merit;
>
> Impartial Justice, Kings shou'd mind alone,
>
> For that 'tis still perpetuates best a Throne. (*BBA* 48)

Gildon also achieves an increased sense of poetic justice in his play by altering the marital status of Claudio and Julietta and that of Angelo and Mariana. While in Shakespeare's version Claudio and Julietta are married legally but not acceptably by the church, in Gildon's a clandestine religious ceremony has been performed as well. Claudio calls "all Heav'n to witness" that he and Julietta were married. He tells the Duke/Friar, "A Father of your Order joyn'd our Hands," adding that "'Twas Father *Pierre*, not long/Return'd to *France* to his own Monastery" (*BBA* 19). Since the couple's marriage is now sanctioned by both legal and religious authorities, Gildon has no trepidation in freeing Claudio in the final scene of the play. In Shakespeare's version, Claudio's release stems from the application of mercy to the law; in Gildon's, it results from the eventual revelation that he has been unjustly accused. Angelo's position in Shakespeare's version is similar to Claudio's in that he, too, is guilty of fornication with his affianced wife but is pardoned by the Duke at the end of the play. Gildon cannot countenance this state of affairs and, as with Claudio and Julietta, he makes Angelo and Mariana already married. In some ways, Angelo does not receive poetic justice even at the close of Gildon's play, for his situation differs from Claudio's in intention, if not in fact, and the fate he ordains himself at the beginning of the play, "Yet, when I fail so, let me be Sentenc'd" (*BBA* 3), is not carried out. The moral ambiguity of Angelo's motive versus his action apparently did not bother Gildon. Mechanically, at least, *Measure for Measure, or, Beauty, the Best Advocate* therefore presents a world in which justice always prevails.

Paradoxes of character, disliked by the Restoration stage, are dealt with summarily in Gildon's version of *Measure for Measure* so that, in Levison's words, Angelo is "made the unquestioned villain" of the play while the Duke and Claudio, "both of whom have rather unsavory characteristics in Shakespeare, emerge unsullied."[10] Gildon probably makes more changes in the role of Angelo than in any other character in the play. Shakespeare introduces Angelo as a virtuous man. In delegating authority to Angelo, the Duke praises his character and his virtues:

---

[10] Ibid., p. 70.

> There is a kind of character in thy life
>
> That to th'observer doth thy history
>
> Fully unfold. Thyself and thy belongings
>
> Are not thine own so proper as to waste
>
> Thyself upon thy virtues, they on thee. (*MM* 1.1.28-32)

The first time Angelo appears in Gildon's version the audience sees him in action as the cold dispenser of arbitrary justice. Even this early in the play, Angelo's duplicity in Claudio's conviction becomes evident. When Escalus begs him to spare Claudio's life, because he has "perform'd most Noble Deeds/To serve his Country, and declares he's married," Angelo responds that "passion" rather than "virtue" most frequently inspires young men to distinguish themselves in war and that, as far as his "vain Pretence of Marriage" is concerned, "'tis/An Old, a Common Trick, t'evade the Laws:/Or, it 'twere true, it was so Clandestine,/That it deserves the fate He now shall meet" (*BBA* 3). Angelo not only knows that Claudio is not guilty and practically confesses his knowledge to Escalus and the audience, but he also admits that even if Claudio is married, he will still suffer the full punishment of the law. Although Angelo proclaims that he only wants justice served, in this case he is not dispensing justice any more than he is dispensing mercy. He completes his speech by wondering how he could face Julietta's "Friends" if he were to pardon Claudio. Escalus quickly retorts that Julietta's friends are more interested in her dowry than in her honor, and Angelo's real reason for condemning Claudio becomes apparent.

The change in Angelo's motivation greatly simplifies his character. For, the audience no longer has to deal with a man who, though he is "precise,/Stands at a guard with envy, scarce confesses/That his blood flows, or that his appetite/Is more to bread than stone" (*MM* 1.3. 50-53), at least believes himself to be administering justice. The Angelo of Gildon's version, on the other hand, appears to realize from the outset that he may be convicting an innocent man.[11] This speech of Angelo's is too diplomatic and too brief to malign his character to any great extent up to this point in Gildon's play. By the time Isabella goes to plead her brother's case with him, Angelo's hypocrisy becomes clearly evident. Though Shakespeare's Angelo only tells Isabella to "be gone" (*MM* 2.2.69) when she asks him to put himself in Claudio's place, Gildon's Angelo adds, "Ha! my Soul! how near she strikes on the Truth" (*BBA* 5) and then, later, "Ha! She speaks such pointed Truths, that wounds/My guilty Soul" (*BBA* 6). The audience now knows that Angelo has committed a crime similar to the one for which he has condemned Claudio to death, and Angelo's villainy is established once and for all. In Levison's opinion Gildon's abridgement of Angelo's final speech in Shakespeare's corresponding scene further darkens Angelo's character.[12] While Shakespeare's Angelo is consumed by self-doubt, "What dost thou, or what art thou, Angelo?/Dost thou desire her foully for those things/That make her good?" (*MM* 2.2.177-79), Gildon's Angelo merely wonders that virtue should so tempt him and then decides to "think no more on't, but with Musick chase/Away the Guilty Image" (*BBA* 7).

Angelo does not succeed in banishing his desire for Isabella in either play. In Shakespeare's version of the play Angelo's attempt to seduce Isabella consists of the passionate threats of a man maddened by love. Gildon adds a scene that casts Angelo in the role of what Levison calls "the conventional vile seducer."[13]

11 Ibid., 75.

12 Ibid., p. 72.

13 Ibid., p. 73.

In this scene Angelo, aware that Isabella will not sell herself in order to save her brother's life, nonetheless tempts her with a cabinet filled with jewels, informing her that "Wealth draws a Curtain o're the face of shame,/Restores lost Beauty, and recovers Fame" (*BBA* 29) and in so doing, loses the last bit of respect the audience may have had for him. Levison sums up the differences between Shakespeare's and Gildon's versions of Angelo when he comments, "Where Shakespeare emphasizes Angelo's internal conflict between responsibility to the law and his own passion for Isabella, Gildon devotes more space to the machinations the Deputy goes through to engineer a union with her."[14] Shakespeare's Angelo is the essentially good man who struggles with, but fails to overcome temptation, while Gildon's is the hypocritical villain from start to finish.

As Gildon makes Angelo a more accomplished villain than Shakespeare does, he also resolves any uncertainty the audience may have about both the Duke and Claudio. Shakespeare's Duke opens *Measure for Measure* and appears from the beginning to be a benevolent ruler who is leaving Vienna in the hands of his most able deputy. By the next time he comes on stage, the Duke explains that he has handed over the rule of his city to Angelo because for the past fourteen (or nineteen, there is some inconsistency here) years, he has not enforced the laws stringently enough and all decorum has gone "athwart" (*MM* 1.3.30). Gildon's Duke makes his first stage appearance with this speech, and like Shakespeare's Duke acknowledges that he wants to witness the effect Angelo's severe administration of the rules will have on the people. Gildon omits the final lines in which Shakespeare's Duke admits another reason for his temporary abdication:

[14] Ibid., pp. 106-7.

> ... More reasons for this action
>
> At our more leisure shall I render you.
>
> Only this one: Lord Angelo is precise,
>
> Stands at a guard with envy, scarce confesses
>
> That his blood flows, or that his appetite
>
> Is more to bread than stone. Hence shall we see
>
> If power change purpose, what our seemers be. (*MM* 1.3.43-54)

Unlike Shakespeare's Duke, Gildon's does not seem to have had any intention of "testing" Angelo by investing him with the rule of Vienna. In Gildon's version, this speech leads to Friar Thomas' observation that the Duke has "already found how" he has "been mistaken/In *Angelo*" whom he had "so long thought a Saint" (*BBA* 17). The Duke's disguise as a friar loses some of its questionable character as he now has a good reason to examine Angelo's behavior surreptitiously. This revelation about Angelo also persuades the Duke that perhaps his deputy has accused Claudio unjustly. By masquerading as a friar, the Duke thus will be able to delve into the case and discover the truth objectively and to his own satisfaction.

When Shakespeare's Duke first visits the prison in the guise of a friar in act two scene three, he gives no indication that his objective in coming has been to speak alone with Claudio and Julietta to determine whether or not they have been unfairly accused. Julietta happens by as the "Friar" tells the Provost that he has "come to visit the afflicted spirits/Here in prison" (*MM* 2.3.4-5). The Duke's visit with Claudio in act three scene one of Shakespeare's play–he sees Claudio immediately before Julietta in Gildon's–is tarnished by his eavesdropping on the conversation between the convicted man and his sister, who enters as the Duke is leaving. Although Gildon's Duke tells Isabella that he has "overheard" (*BBA* 24) her tell Claudio of Angelo's proposition, the audience does not witness the Duke's command to the Provost, "Bring me to hear them speak where I may be concealed" (*MM* 3.1.52). The Duke's "eavesdropping" appears unintentional in Gildon's play, although he does make a similar request before Claudio and Julietta are united, as they believe, for the last time in act four scene three. The circumstance is vastly different here, for the Duke asks the Provost, who has sworn an oath against it, to allow the two to meet and the Duke and Friar Thomas "take all the guilt" for the meeting on themselves. Since they are responsible for engineering the meeting, their interest in it does not disturb the audience quite as much as Shakespeare's Duke's intentional "overhearing" of Claudio and Julietta's meeting.

The change in Angelo's marital status also affects the characterization of the Duke. Shakespeare's Duke feels no scruples in suggesting that Mariana take the place of Isabella in the garden even though he knows that she and Angelo have not undergone the actual marriage ceremony. He reassures Mariana, "He is your husband on a pre-contract./To bring you thus together 'tis no sin"(*MM* 4.1.72-73). Gildon's Duke, on the other hand, is able to appease even the most puritanical audience as he reassures Mariana, "He is your Husband, and it is no Sin/To bring you thus together" (*BBA* 32).[15]

Gildon's reduction of Lucio's part in the play further contributes to the simplification and idealization of the Duke's character. He totally eliminates from both act three scene two and act five scene one Lucio's observations that the Duke not only has been, in Levison's words, "negligent of his duty in leaving his realm" but that he has a "penchant for intrigue" as well. By this time, the audience knows

---

[15] Levison mentions the effect Angelo's marriage has on several characters in the play. Not only does it absolve the Duke of blame for making an "immoral suggestion" and keep Mariana from prostituting herself, but it also prevents Isabella from "condoning an act that she would not herself commit" (71).

that Lucio is not the pattern of respectability himself; yet, the aspersions he casts on the Duke still produce some ambiguity surrounding his true character, ambiguity which the Duke has actually helped foster by his "desire to manipulate others." Levison also notes the commentary Lucio provides "in a more serious mood" when he tells Isabella her brother would have lived "If the old fantastical Duke of dark corners had been at home" (*MM* 4.3.146-47). Levison remarks that although Lucio is "not by any means Shakespeare's spokesman" he does bring up "questions about the Duke's motives." "The Duke does, after all," he continues, "cause Claudio, Isabella, and Julietta to suffer needlessly. Gildon's Duke also creates needless suffering, but in the adaptation, where Lucio is relegated to providing introductory exposition, no one seems to notice."[16]

The Duke's final actions towards Lucio in Shakespeare's version of the play also detract from the overall effect of his character. After having pardoned everybody in the play at Isabella's request, the merciful Duke pronounces a heavy sentence on Lucio, first decreeing that he marry "any woman wronged" and the "nuptial finished,/Let him be whipped and hanged" (*MM* 5.1.503-507). Lucio, instead of asking the Duke for his life, rather pleads to be pardoned from marrying the whore. Shakespeare's Duke must inwardly chuckle at this request and obviously expects it, for he revokes the rest of the punishment commanding only that Lucio marry Kate Keepdown, a fate Lucio bemoans, for "Marrying a punk . . . is pressing to death, whipping, and hanging" (*MM* 5.1.515-16). The Duke, although he has previously forgiven Lucio's transgressions, retorts that "Slandering a prince deserves it" (*MM* 5.1.517). This scene is admittedly for comic effect; nonetheless, the Duke seems unduly incensed by Lucio's unjust

[16] Ibid., pp. 76-77.

criticism. A Duke, who professedly does not "think the man of safe discretion," who bows to the "loud applause and *aves* vehement" of the people (*MM* 1.1.70-71), should similarly be able to take the unjust criticism levelled at him without being overly upset by it. After all, Lucio tells him that he "spoke it but according to the trick" (*MM* 5.1.498), and the people of Vienna probably did assume that the Duke countenanced their licentiousness because he was a partner in their deeds. Coming virtually at the end of the play, this exchange makes the Duke appear slightly childish and pettish. Gildon's Duke appears in sharp contrast to Shakespeare's, particularly in this final scene. Without a Lucio to punish, the Duke spends the entire final scene not only dispensing a painless justice but reflecting on it as well.

Gildon ennobles his Claudio almost as much as he does the Duke. The most obvious change he makes in Claudio is in the fact that he and Julietta are actually married and not simply affianced as is the case in Shakespeare. From the very beginning, Gildon's Claudio is introduced as a more ideal character than Shakespeare's. The first time the audience hears of Claudio in *Measure for Measure*, he is being led through the streets on his way to prison. When Mistress Overdone extols him to Lucio and the other gentlemen as being "worth five thousand of you all" (*MM* 1.1.55), her glowing praise is somewhat shadowed by the character of the speaker who happens to be a bawd. Gildon, on the other hand, introduces Claudio in Lucio's commendation, "Claudio, so fam'd for every Noble Virtue,/That proves him worthy his Illustrious Race; /Young, Brave, and Learned, tho' he is a Noble Man" (*BBA* 2); and, in this instance, since the speaker himself is a respectable character, the praise seems more credible.

Claudio's acceptance of blame differs in the two versions of the play as well. In *Measure for Measure*, Claudio acknowledges that he and Julietta have committed a crime in not exchanging religious vows so that they could obtain her dowry, but he does not feel that his crime deserves the punishment it has elicited. Though actually married to Julietta in Gildon's version, a conscience-stricken Claudio laments that although he has not committed the sin for which he is being punished, "yet it was a Sin to wish for ought/Beyond Possession of so pure a Virtue." He continues, "For oh! a Lady's Honour/And lost for me, is a more cruel Murther,/Than if I'd ta'ne [sic] her Life" (*BBA* 18).[17] Gildon adds another dialogue in act four scene three which heightens Claudio's nobility. In this scene, primarily added as a sentimental love scene, Claudio and Julietta, as Levison comments, "argue at length the question of who is to take full blame,"[18] both affirming that they have lost each other because they sought worldly goods.

In accepting guilt based not on an actual crime, but on a very fine moral distinction, Claudio becomes a more dignified character. Gildon adds the primary distinction to Claudio's character in the exchange between him and his sister Isabella. For rather than asking his sister to surrender to Angelo to save his life, Claudio ponders the unwelcome thought of death and expresses his desire to live. When the shocked Isabella exclaims, as in Shakespeare, that she cannot believe her brother would be "made a Man out of . . . [her] Vice," Claudio cuts her short. He explains:

> Your over-nicety of Honour feeds

---

[17] Levison also comments on Julietta's apotheosis in Gildon's version. Since she appears only once in Shakespeare, when she confesses to the Duke/Friar, Gildon has little ambiguity to resolve in her character. Virtually his own creation, Gildon's Julietta is simply and consistently drawn.

[18] Ibid., p. 76.

> Your fancy with strange ugly forms,
>
> That have no real Existence;
>
> But by excess of Vertue you offend.
>
> I said indeed, that I wou'd Live, what then?
>
> Is't not the Voice of Nature that abhors
>
> The fatal Separation? Then where's the Crime? (*BBA* 24)

Claudio continues to explain to her that he was merely thinking of Julietta when he spoke and that the only thing he desires from Isabella is that she "take the tender Mourner" to her "Bosome,/And comfort her sad Soul" (*BBA* 24). Although the request made by Shakespeare's Claudio is entirely human, it evidences a complex character, which, though basically good and noble, is not always altruistic. The nobility of Gildon's Claudio, like the justness of his Duke and the villainy of his Angelo, is constant.

In *The Lives of the Poets* Gerard Langbaine refers to the "moral" of *The Roman Bride's Revenge* as "one of the most noble of any of our Modern Plays, it being to give us an Example in the Punishment of *Martian*, that no Consideration in the World, ought to make us delay the Service of our Country."[19] As Langbaine's comment proves, Gildon's first play, a tragedy, exhibits a similar emphasis on poetic justice and consistent characterization as his altered form of *Measure for Measure*.

A superficial examination of *The Roman Bride's Revenge* may lead the audience or reader to believe that, although the Emperor, Perennius, and Lætus deserve their violent deaths, the suicides of Portia and Martian do not represent poetic justice. Both characters are, after all, noble and good, and neither has

---

[19] Langbaine, p. 176.

committed any crime worthy of death. Aurelian, Portia's brother and Martian's best friend, gives the first clue that Martian bears some guilt towards Rome and therefore merits his fate. Before the marriage rites take place, when Martian feels a strange foreboding course through him, he proclaims that the "Gods are angry" at his "Happiness." Aurelian responds, "Have they not Reason think you?" He continues by explaining that Martian should fear the wrath of the gods for "amidst all this Hurricane of Nature,/And all th' expiring Gasps of falling *Rome*," he is "Deaf to their Calls, . . . lost in lazy Loves" (*RBR* 5). Martian quickly answers the call of his country and declares that he will no longer neglect its service but go off to defend Rome immediately following the wedding ceremony.

When the Emperor interrupts the wedding by having Martian arrested for treason, Martian confesses an even greater guilt, a guilt he bears for fighting to keep the Emperor in power:

> Oh! the just Gods! . . . but I deserve it all!
>
> For if I am a Traytor 'tis to *Rome*.
>
> To let this purple Monster lay her wast.
>
> For she derives her Sufferings all from me,
>
> Her Widow'd Matron's Pangs, her Orphan's Tears,
>
> Her ravish'd Virgins, and her murthered Fathers.
>
> For 'twas from me she took thee for her Lord. (*RBR* 8)

By the end of the play, Martian has attempted to redeem himself for his negligence. As he commits suicide, he proves the justice of his action in his lament for doubting Aurelian, but most importantly, Portia. Aurelian offers another explanation at the close of the play when he sees Martian's spirit hovering above on its way to reunion with Portia. "Methinks I hear him thunder out aloud/To all the listning World this Godlike Maxim," Aurelian continues, "Learn from my

Fate, that Tyes of Love or Blood,/Are of no Force against the Public Good" (*RBR* 52). Martian's suicide does represent poetic justice in that it reunites him with Portia, whom he loves more than honour and country. Furthermore, since he had forsaken his country, though only briefly, he cannot be allowed to live to rule it.

Aurelian's fate is similarly suitable. Torn by grief as Martian dies, Aurelian considers suicide. Spurred by his friend's final assertion that the gods demand Aurelian's life as ruler of Rome, he agrees and lives to rule. Although Martian has been the "favorite" of the people throughout the play, Aurelian has been more faithful to his country. At Martian's wedding Aurelian chides his friend for taking time out from the service of Rome to marry Portia. And, while he recognizes the "honour" Martian bestows on his sister, Aurelian adds that he himself "must prefer" his "Country/To all, to every Good, that's meerly mine" (*RBR* 5). Aurelian's loyalty to his country and his friend remains steadfast. Once the Emperor's villainy is established, Aurelian's dissimulation–he appears to be pandering to the Emperor while actually raising an army to take Rome and avenge Martian–proves him to be fighting for rather than against his country in an effort to depose a vile ruler.

Portia's case presents more difficulty. Portia, in Martian's words, "all fair, all white, without one Spot" (*RBR* 49), commits no crime throughout the play, sins against no one, and only technically merits her punishment for wreaking vengeance on the Emperor by poisoning him and herself in their "Bridal Bowl." Absolved even of Martian's fault of loving her more than he does his country, Portia vows to him, "I swear, I love thee more than Health, or Life,/Than Liberty, or wish'd for Peace of Mind/Next to my Countrys good, and my own Honour!" (*RBR* 15) Portia, the prototypical sentimental heroine, faithfully faints through five acts as she loses her husband to exile and must fight the advances of both the

Emperor and Perennius. Despite her "Immortal Virtue" (*RBR* 16), or perhaps because of it, she is not able to rid Rome of the Emperor without paying with her own life. All the time she plots her death, she believes that Martian also is, or will soon be, dead and that her brother Aurelian has been false to them both. Nothing remains to hold her fast to life. After she has drunk the poison, a living Martian and a faithful Aurelian appear, and she helplessly mourns over the "malignant Influence" of her "stars" which has brought them both back, "yet left no Hopes of Happiness" to her (*RBR* 47). Portia must find justice after death where "are Joys above, for suff'ring Virtue" (*RBR* 37). Her final words affirm the justness of her fate, a fate which, as she says, "gives my *Martian* to my Arms for ever . . . 'tis Heav'n–all beamy Joy" (*RBR* 49). Portia could ask for nothing better.[20]

Although ultimately the recipients of poetic justice, in at least two places in the play both Portia and Martian question whether or not justice exists. When Cleander tries to persuade Martian to return to the army and lead them in a coup against the Emperor, Martian sees the case as hopeless:

> . . . 'twill be in vain, for Knaves will still be uppermost;
>
> They float aloft, like Chaff upon the Water,
>
> Which though by moving you a while disperse,
>
> Soon as the ruffl'd Element's settl'd,
>
> They gather all a top again. (*RBR* 12)

Portia, rather than wondering why the evil and incompetent receive more than their due, ponders why she and Martian must be made to suffer. She grieves, "O!

---

[20] The Empress' fate is an entirely different matter. Her only crime is in loving her husband too much, yet she is the first character in the play to take her own life. Her plan to avenge herself on Portia cannot even account for her fate as she believes herself to be giving Portia to the safekeeping of the Vestal Virgins who will deliver her to Martian. She consider's Portia's feelings as she plots with Perennius and Lætus, "If she does love but half so well as I,/She will be swift to catch this blest occasion" (*RBR* 14).

all ye Heav'nly Powers! that fixt this World,/With the Cement of Universal Love/Why is such tender Passion not your Care?/Such Virtue, and such Truth by all forsaken?" Martian informs her to "Accuse not Heav'n" for his "Crimes alone" (*RBR* 12) have led to his unhappy fate. In *The Roman Bride's Revenge*, justice indeed triumphs.

Poetic justice easily prevails in the play primarily because of the consistency with which the characters are drawn. Martian, Portia, and Aurelian never falter in their ideals once the play has begun. Though they sometimes doubt each other, Portia and Aurelian both dissemble only to accomplish their goal of avenging Martian, and the audience always realizes that their honor and nobility are intact. Perennius similarly poses no complex problems for the audience as he begins the play a scheming flatterer with a lust for Portia as his ruling passion. Gildon never reveals the full import of Perennius' villainy with regards to the troubles Rome is having at the beginning of the play, but he does have Lætus advise Perennius to turn the Emperor from Martian by lies and deceptions. Perennius' lies pave the way for the downfall of Rome. This act, as it was goaded by his "love" for Portia, could still garner sympathy for Perennius were it not preceeded by other attempts to sway the Emperor. In giving his friend advice, Lætus condemns Perennius in the audience's eyes:

> Think of the Emperor; you know the ways
>
> To twist and wind him as your Interest leads:
>
> You feed his changeful Appetite with Pleasures;
>
> His Anger, and his Smiles are at your beck;
>
> If *Martian* like a Gyant stole your Heav'n,
>
> Make your fond *Slave* destroy him with his Bolts. (*RBR* 2)

In the end Perennius remains the deceiver he has been throughout not only by attempting to steal Portia away from the Emperor but by killing Lætus, who is helping him to remove suspicion from himself.

The Emperor is the only character who occasionally confuses the audience. Lætus describes the Emperor as a person whose own self is "the Center/To all the Motions of his Love, or Hate" (*RBR* 3), a description Martian reinforces and darkens as he rails at himself for keeping the lascivious, villainous Emperor in power only to be repaid by having his bride torn from his arms. The Emperor's licentiousness does not begin to account for his villainy. Martian attributes the Emperor's prowess in battle not to any zeal for his country but to a bloodthirsty streak which "Wanton'd in Goar," and he shows the Emperor's cruelty once and for all when he forbids Portia from asking him for justice. He informs his bride that she is pleading with a man who has no conception of justice whatsoever: "How can the source of daily Wrongs love Justice?/Or Honour move his mean degenerate Heart/That leaves his noble Father still in Bonds,/The shameful Footstool of the *Persian* King" (*RBR* 8).

His character established, the Emperor somehow manages a few surprises, particularly in his dealings with the Empress Valeria. When she begs him to return to her, he not only has to flee her presence to avoid surrendering to her wishes, but after she is gone, he suffers pangs of conscience, "It was not well to leave her in Despair;/I might have giv'n at least some doubtful Hope" (*RBR* 28). He even eventually persuades himself to give up all dreams of Portia for the "willing Charms that Court" him, but his admirable resolve falls by the wayside when Valeria's plot to remove Portia from his keeping surfaces. His pity for Valeria, based largely on her seductive charms, does little to alleviate the Emperor's dark character. Even as he dies, he craves "more Beauty, young Balmy Boys and

Girls," and, when he is denied pleasure for all times,wonders, "Why am I Emperor, but to have my Will?" Recounting a vivid picture of sin and death and feeling the intense heat and cold of hell, the Emperor expires. Ruled throughout by the lusts of the flesh, his only satisfaction in the end is in a delusion: "How I rejoice that Pleasure dies with me" (*RBR* 50).

Burnaby and The Refinement of Morals

William Burnaby's adaptation of *Twelfth Night*, *Love Betray'd*, does not show the same concern with poetic justice that Gildon's two plays exhibit. Since the incidents of this play are of less significance, poetic justice rests in the ridicule of folly and affection. He does explicitly state the "moral" at the end of *Love Betray'd*, a moral which suggests that justice not only punishes those who are foolish but rewards those who are good and honest. Moreno closes the play by announcing:

> . . . Now the Adventures of the Day are over;
>
> We may look back with pleasure on our Toils;
>
> And thro' the various turns this truth observe;
>
> That Honesty is still the care of Providence!
>
> By *Rodoregue*, we see that good will wait upon a
>
> worthy action–By *Sebastian*, that Fortune can't
>
> long stain an honest Friendship.
>
> *And here I find, that some kind Star above,*
>
> *Has still a Blessing left for Honest Love.* (*LB* 61)

Although clear from the resolution of the play, this doctrine does not always go unquestioned.[22]   Cæsario notes at the end of act two, "On this alone

---

[22] The stress placed on Rodoregue and Sebastian in this final speech is misleading; the

depends most human Bliss,/When kindly Heaven forbids us what we wish" (*LB* 24), and the agonies that Moreno goes through in his hopeless love for Villaretta and she in her infatuation for Cæsario give credence to Cæsario's words, not to mention the struggle that Cæsario encounters in an attempt to procure Moreno's affection. As in Shakespeare, the two receive faithful loves in Viola and Sebastian in return for their fidelity.

The circumstances surrounding the pairs of lovers differ in Burnaby, though. Villaretta in this instance is not a faithful sister grieving over the loss of a dear brother, but a widow rejoicing that she has been freed from the bondage of a husband she obviously did not love. "The greatest Happiness of our Lives," she informs Emilia, "is to have got free from the Mens Dominion very early" (*LB* 2). She receives the attentions of her suitors with haughty disdain and ridicule and feels that the only way to deal with men is to deceive them. Villaretta's unhappy experience with men has not only embittered her towards her own courtiers, but it has also made her resent any attempt by a man to court a woman. Her cousin Drances mentions the fact that one morning he had told her housemaid that he loved her "and she sent her to the Devil immediately" (*LB* 8) for he never saw the girl again. A true adversary of love, Villaretta tells Emilia that the only happy woman "is she that's a little Handsome; no Fool; and that never loves" (*LB* 18).

Shakespeare's Olivia differs extensively from Burnaby's Villaretta. Secluded from love in respect for her dead brother, rather than by a contemptuous scorn of men, Olivia deserves the true love she finds in Sebastian more than Villaretta does. Shakespeare's Olivia and Viola mourn for their lost brothers and

---

two play very minor parts in *Love Betray'd*. Rodoregue and Sebastian are no more consistent or deserving of their good fortune than their counterparts in Shakespeare. Rodoregue, in fact, comes off as a marauding pirate made noble only in his affection towards Sebastian. Sebastian's rough treatment of his man Pedro also darkens his image.

Sebastian for his lost sister. Burnaby's Villaretta is a widow; Viola has left home
to pursue her love for Moreno; and Sebastian alone believes himself bereft of a
sibling he adores. Although the balanced, symmetrical plot of Shakespeare's play
does not necessarily make the pairing of the lovers more just, it does make for a
conclusion that seems more poetically "right."

Pride accounts for the biggest contrast between Villaretta and Olivia. Olivia
does not disdain the Count; in fact, she has only praise for his character:

> Your lord does know my mind, I cannot love him,
>
> Yet I suppose him virtuous, know him noble,
>
> Of great estate, of fresh and stainless youth;
>
> In voices well divulg'd, free, learn'd, and valiant,
>
> And in dimension, and the shape of nature,
>
> A gracious person. But yet I cannot love him.
>
> He might have took his answer long ago (*LB* 258-63).

Olivia's refusal of the Count may not be founded solely on her seven years' vigil
for her brother, but, according to Sir Toby, may also be due to her unwillingness
to marry above her station. Villaretta's pride is the ruling feature of her character,
on the other hand. Unlike Olivia, who does everything in her power to turn
Orsino's attentions away from her, Villaretta keeps him hanging, "because," she
says, "it pleases me to govern him that governs *Venice*" (*LB* 3). Cæsario
pinpoints Villaretta's character: "She's a peevish Beauty,/That likes her self too
much" (*LB* 46), and, indeed, at this point, she does seem to be caught up in a self-
love which admits no rivals. Her pride may not be based totally on vanity,
though, for she has obviously been hurt in her first marriage. Villaretta's pride,
not Taquilet's, is also the stimulus for the subplot which Drances initiates to
"beat down her Pride, the grand Bulwark that defends more Women than Virtue"

(*LB* 10).[23] When confronted with the likeness of Sebastian in the enchanting
Cæsario this woman who claims immunity from the charms of men falls instantly
in love and is ready to be subject to man once again, a fitting "punishment" for one
violently opposed to love.

Burnaby's approach to *Twelfth Night* differs in characterization as well as
in the disposition of poetic justice. In his discussion of the play F. E. Budd
briefly notes the changes Burnaby introduced in the characters: "Olivia loses her
initial dignity, Orsino is less poetic in his subservience to love, and Viola is given
pertness as a substitute for charm."[24] Of the main characters in Burnaby's play,
Villaretta differs most from her prototype; however, both Viola and Moreno
occasionally diverge from the pattern Shakespeare created for them. Moreno, not
quite as saccharine as Orsino, indicates at least once that he recognizes Villaretta's
faults. Though he pines for her love, he would like to "tear the Tyrant" from his
heart, and he refers to her as "a true Merciless, Insolent–" but "Charming
Woman–!" (*LB* 7) even in the first act of the play. Orsino, on the other hand,
never has any cause to doubt Olivia's compassion or purity of heart until she
shows her preference for Cesario.

Other than his recognition of Villaretta's scornful nature, Moreno does not
substantially differ from Orsino. Both are inconstant in their love, if not
inconsistent in their characterizations. The quickness with which both turn their

---

[23] In *Twelfth Night*, the joke is on Malvolio, whom Sir Toby characterizes as "an
affected ass . . . so crammed, as he thinks, with excellencies, that it is his grounds of faith that
all that look on him love him" (*TN* 2.3.132-35). In making Villaretta the target of the jest,
Burnaby ties the subplot more closely to the main action. Taquilet, in fact, receives almost no
penalty for his pretensions to Villaretta whereas Malvolio suffers great humiliation. Shakespeare's
Malvolio deserves the embarrassment more than Burnaby's Taquilet. Malvolio proceeds with his
courtship despite Olivia's prophetic words to him in act one scene five, "O, you are sick of self-
love, Malvolio, and taste with a distempered appetite" (*TN* ll.77-78), while Drances must
persuade Taquilet that Olivia loves him despite their different stations in life.

affections from Olivia/Villaretta to Viola, though surprising, does not occur without some preparation in either play. *Twelfth Night* perhaps sets the stage for Orsino's change of heart better, as it hints several times that no man, Orsino included, can remain true. Orsino himself tells Cesario that the fancies of man "are more giddy and unfirm,/More longing, wavering, sooner lost and worn,/Than women's are" (*TN* 2.4.32-34). Feste accuses Orsino of bearing an equal share of man's fickleness, when he tells the Duke his "mind is a very opal" and he "would have men of such constancy put to sea, that their business might be everything and their intent everywhere, for that's it that always makes a good voyage of nothing" (*TN* 2.4.73-76). These clues as well as the Duke's overstatement of his fidelity to Olivia prepare the audience more adequately for his turnabout in the final act of the play.

Moreno seems to be a little more drawn to Cæsario throughout the play than does Orsino. As Moreno questions Cæsario about "his" own love life, he praises his manners, sense, and "soft insinuating ways." In response to Moreno's question as to whether Cæsario's love returned his affection, the youth replies, "She kist me often, and told me so, but did not love me" (*LB* 15-16). Orsino's questioning is not as personal and flattering, although his affection for Cesario is evident. When faced with Cesario's apparent duplicity at the end of the play, Orsino avows his love more openly than Moreno. Maddened by jealousy, Moreno starts to stab Cæsario. Orsino first wants to strike at Olivia, then takes out his anger on Cesario, "whom," he says, "by heaven I swear, I tender dearly" (*TN* 5.1.122). Moreno, on the other hand, waits until Viola emerges to proclaim the love he bore for Cæsario. Moreno is different from Orsino, but he is probably neither a more or less consistent character, nor does he represent a more moral

[24] Budd, p. 76.

version of the Duke.

Burnaby's Cæsario, though not measurably different from Shakespeare's in consistency of character, seems to be slightly less moral. The interpolated scene in which Cæsario pretends to be Villaretta's physician in order to discover her true feelings about Moreno coarsens both Cæsario and Villaretta in the audience's eyes. Cæsario agrees to the deception only because she fears that Villaretta's disdain for the Duke is counterfeited in order to gain his affections more securely. Repaying a suspected fraud with another does little to enhance Cæsario's character. The circumstances surrounding Burnaby's Cæsario in some ways do serve to justify this action. Rather than the shipwrecked heroine who, by chance, lands in Illyria where she meets and falls in love with the Duke, Burnaby's heroine has purposefully come to court the favor of the man she has loved for two years. "Unable longer to endure the torture of my Wishes," she tells Emilia, "I left my Brother, and my House, and 6 Days since, without a Servant, landed here in *Venice–*" (*LB* 11-12). Since she has braved untold danger and deprivation in her attempt to win Moreno, Burnaby's Cæsario can be excused a slight breach of conduct and still merit "That noble Honour, and that matchless Truth" (*LB* 60), which is her "reward" for constancy in her love for Moreno.

In his edition of Burnaby's plays, F. E. Budd claims that Burnaby's greatest "virtue" as a playwright "is that he does not attempt to be virtuous." Burnaby reacted to the sentimental comedy prevalent in the late seventeenth century and refused "to pander to his audience by admitting to his *dénouements* the psychologically incredible moral conversions so popular with sentimental dramatists."[25] Not overtly moral in their depiction of life, Burnaby's plays

[25] Ibid., p. 103.

nonetheless instruct as well as delight the audience, though the instruction is aimed at improved manners and more prudent behavior rather than moral reformation.

Burnaby's original plays, as a result, were the object of a great deal of controversy. Crites in *A Comparison Between the Two Stages* declares that *The Ladies' Visiting Day* has "no Moral,"[26] and Budd notes that Restoration audiences "pretended to object to its morality, or lack of it, and more sincerely, winced under its ridicule."[27] Burnaby forecast the reception of *The Ladies' Visiting Day* in the play itself when he has Lady Dolt and her friends refer to it as "smutty" (*LB* 254). In *The Reform'd Wife*, Astrea expresses what must surely have been the common opinion about Burnaby's plays when she tells Sir Solomon that "the dishonest Liberties of the Stage are such, that we seldom hear any thing, that diverts without something that offends." When Clarinda replies that the moral of the play usually justifies the inclusion of offensive material, Astrea quickly retorts, "Nay there you are lost, *Clarinda*, for tell me a Play in which there is not for a Moral, if you Marry you're a Cuckold, and Woman's Virtue is a *Chimera*." Clarinda may answer for the playwright in her response:

> . . . The Licence is indeed too great, yet the fault is equal in the Town, and the Poet who only shows us the world a little too near, for, turn but your Eyes off the Stage, and you shall see that your agreeable Woman is a Coquet, and your agreeable Man an Atheist, and the first step to be very witty, is (it seems) to be very wicked. (*RW* 2)

If Burnaby does include some material that offended a certain segment of his audience, he, as did the poet Clarinda mentions, drew on that same audience for

[26] Gildon, p. 181.

[27] Budd, p. 84.

inspiration, and dealt with their foibles more justly than real life usually does.

Both *The Reform'd Wife* and *The Ladies' Visiting Day* portray jealous husbands, amorous wives (but not for their husbands), and two pairs of young lovers who have a difficult time getting together either because of a mercenary guardian or their own follies. Every character in both these plays receives his or her share of poetic justice, even though that justice is frequently tempered with mercy, especially in the cases of the husbands and wives. Sir Solomon Empty and his wife Astrea in *The Reform'd Wife* as well as Sir Testy Dolt and Lady Dolt in *The Ladies' Visiting Day* receive justice enough to frighten the husbands and reform the wives, but at the last moment each is spared the fate he or she fears the most. Sir Solomon, who is ready to assist in the cuckolding of any husband other than himself, certainly deserves to suffer cuckoldory himself. Because of the intervention of Clarinda, who is in love with Astrea's beau, he does not have to endure this indignity. Astrea is similarly saved from discovery by Clarinda. Though she has probably carried on such encounters before without Sir Solomon's knowledge, Astrea's hypocritical stance in pretending to hate men so that she is free to dally as she chooses merits some type of punishment. Though her deception never becomes apparent to Sir Solomon, Astrea comes close enough to discovery to be "convinc'd of the Folly, the Confusion, and the Adversity" of her actions and to speak the final words of the play: "*The Guilty still with anxious Cares are prest, /The truly Good alone are truly Blest*" (*RW* 45).

Sir Testy Dolt, unlike Sir Solomon Empty, does not advocate adultery for anyone. He does deserve to be taunted with the possibility of cuckoldry, since he continually throws his wife at young Polidore, whom he believes to be more suited for a "Querister" (*LVD* 267) than a lover. Polidore gets his revenge on Sir Testy in two ways. In the end, he is able to outsmart Sir Testy, the mercenary guardian of his love, and win the hand of Fulvia even as he unintentionally persuades the jealous old man that he has enjoyed Lady Dolt's favors. Sir Testy exits the play as he goes to obtain a divorce from Lady Dolt. Although she has been unsuccessful in seducing Polidore, Lady Dolt, like Astrea, a "*Matchiavil* in Love" (*LVD* 202), repents her philandering at the conclusion of the play only because of the trouble she has had to go to in order to keep her honor from being besmirched. Her final words, spoken in response to Lovetoy's assertion that she now is "sensible of" her "Folly," show the nature of her repentance: "And I of mine, so much, that I'll pursue it no longer; and now I am fully satisfy'd, that in doing Ill, tho' a Woman's conduct be ever so delicate, the short-lived Joy is still disturb'd.

And tho' our Vice behind it leave no sting,

The best Ill-Woman is a wretched thing " (*LVD* 270).

Much to her dismay, Lady Dolt's siege of Polidore yields her nothing. The lesson Lady Dolt has received may not have benefitted her. Her only regret is that she had not made Polidore "sure." The lesson is nonetheless passed on for the moral edification of the audience.

The other couples in both plays all receive their due as well, although Freeman seems less deserving of Clarinda than Polidore of Fulvia. Both lovers appear as interested in the financial holdings of their sweethearts as in the ladies themselves. Freeman takes Clarinda and forgets Astrea basically because he is foiled in his rendezvous with Astrea and Clarinda does, after all, have five hundred pounds a year. The whole plot of *The Ladies' Visiting Day* rests on Polidore's courtship of Fulvia, which he can carry on only under the cover of his friendship with Lady Dolt. Polidore never intends to cuckold Sir Testy; Freeman only lacks the opportunity. Polidore continually voices his amazement that Sir Testy "makes" him "play with his Wife" (*LVD* 202), and he provides a running commentary on the "vertues" of women, which consist solely in not having their intrigues discovered. His counterpart, Freeman, far from being the complete rake, has too many scruples to follow Sir Solomon's advice and make the husband of his Cœlia (Astrea) his friend. Claiming that "there's none so free of their Honour, as those that are very tender of it" (*RW* 14), Freeman, like Polidore, condemns the hypocrisy of women.

Neither of the women is under any illusions about the man she eventually marries.[28]   If they do not exactly deserve the husbands they get, Fulvia and Clarinda not only agree to accept Polidore and Freeman as they are, but each intervenes to make her chosen fate certain.   Clarinda knows in the end that in accepting blame for Freeman's presence in Sir Solomon's house she is preventing Astrea and Freeman from receiving their just deserts and that the husband she is taking is a rogue.   Luckier in her husband than Clarinda, Fulvia tests Polidore's love by pretending to be another suitor and assaulting her own honor which Polidore is ready to defend with his life.   The endings of the plays bring each a just fate as the cynical Freeman wins the realistic Clarinda and the slightly more romantic Polidore finally obtains the hand as well as the heart of Fulvia.

Although Freeman does not, by any means, strike the audience as a morally depraved character, his compunction in not wanting to befriend the husband of his lover represents the most divergence from consistent characterization in either of these plays.   Sir Solomon and Sir Testy are the quintessential jealous husbands throughout, and Astrea and Lady Dolt, the wives,

---

[28] A similar situation exists with the other pair of lovers in each play. Cleremont in *The Reform'd Wife* and Courtine in *The Ladies' Visiting Day* agree to tolerate the eccentricities of Lady Dainty, the noted hypochondriac, and Lady Lovetoy, who prefers everything foreign, in order to enjoy the ladies' sizeable fortunes.

are determined to evade the constant scrutiny of their husbands and fulfill their own desires. Freeman and Polidore represent the young men interested in both money and love; Clarinda and Fulvia, their ladies, are virtuous (so far), but wise to the ways of the world. Cleremont and Courtine as the best friends of the heroes are in love with ladies of affectation and immense fortunes. Lady Dainty and Lady Lovetoy, finally, are their too genteel inamoratas, personified in Lady Dainty's assertion, "I don't care what is offended, so my tast is not" (*RW* 13). Never straying from type, these characters pose no moral dilemmas for the audience, which knows to empathize with the young lovers less immured in vice, to despise the jealous husbands, and to dislike but pity the wives. None of Burnaby's characters are very bad, they are only very naughty; and, hoping that what never succeeds does not appear attractive, Burnaby exposes their naughtiness to the delight and instruction of the audience.

Granville and The Refinement of Morals

Granville's *Jew of Venice* closely follows the plot of Shakespeare's original and shows no extensive heightening or lessening of poetic justice. Granville does include more explicit statements of poetic justice at both the beginning and the ending of the play. The Prologue to *The Jew of Venice* clearly states the importance of poetic justice in the play and recognizes the disjunction between justice in a play and in real life,

> To day we punish a stock-jobbing Jew.
>
> A piece of Justice, terrible and strange;
>
> Which, if pursu'd, would make a thin Exchange
>
> The Law's Defect, the juster Muse supplies,
>
> Tis only we can make you Good or Wise,

Whom Heav'n spares, the Poet will chastise. (*JV* 1)

Poetic justice thus proceeds in *The Jew of Venice*. Surprised and gladdened by Shylock's terms, Granville's Antonio accepts the bond with a forfeiture of a pound of flesh in exchange for three thousand ducats as he asserts that "Heav'n still is good/To those who seek the Good of others" (*JV* 9); while Shakespeare's Antonio simply notes the Jew's kindness and reflects that he should have three times the value of the bond in his possession a month before it expires. Antonio and his friends have reason to doubt the goodness of heaven throughout the play as Shylock attempts to exact payment, but in the end, Portia, who saves the friend of her husband, informs Antonio that he has indeed been spared not only from certain death, but from penury as well. As she delivers the letters to him that disclose the safe harbor attained by all the ships he thought lost, she tells him, "Virtue like yours; such Patience in Adversity,/And in Prosperity such Goodness,/Is still the care of Providence" (*JV* 45). Shakespeare's Portia forgoes the commentary and merely announces the strange fortune that brought these welcome letters into her hand.

Granville's Portia overtly speaks of the justness of Providence in another instance as well. Although she attempts to dissuade Bassanio from immediately choosing, when he clearly has decided his course, she proclaims, "If Love be just, he'll teach you where to choose" (*JV* 22), and love, or fate, or Bassanio's own good character indeed leads him to select the lead casket over the showier silver and gold ones. The deletion of the scenes depicting the Moor and the Prince of Aragon as they incorrectly choose slightly lessens the effect of Bassanio's correct choice by not providing the contrast of two men who believe themselves more deserving than they really are with Bassanio who is ready to hazard all for the woman he loves.

Although he has been ready to sacrifice his own life for Antonio, the worthy Bassanio surprises the audience in the last scene of *The Jew of Venice*. When Portia declares that she has lain with the learned Daniel, he angrily lashes out at the merchant, "*Antonio*! This was your doing" (*JV* 44). Unlike Shakespeare's Bassanio, Granville's does not declare that he would sacrifice his wife for his friend; nonetheless, Bassanio's rage at Antonio seems misplaced and as strangely out of character as does Portia's extended taunting of her husband with her alleged infidelity.

Granville gives Shylock a few more damning lines throughout the play and changes the mercy he receives at Antonio's bidding in order to slightly intensify poetic justice in his case. In addition to his intense hatred of Antonio, Granville's Shylock also wishes to make Bassanio suffer and in this desire proves even more despicable than his prototype, who appears to bear no malice towards Bassanio. Shylock refuses to allow Bassanio to take the place of his friend, one of Granville's melodramatic additions to the plot, because, as he tells Bassanio, "When he has paid the Forfeit of his Bond,/Thou canst not chuse but hang thy self for being/The Cause: And so my ends are serv'd on both" (*JV* 35). The end Shylock himself receives differs in Granville's version. Granville's Antonio does not require him to become a Christian as does Shakespeare's merchant but only takes half the Jew's fortune in keeping for his daughter and son-in-law. Whether this change exhibits less or more poetic justice depends on the person viewing it. To a probably anti-Semitic Restoration audience, it would have represented a more just ending for Shylock since he is bereft of everything of value and denied the possibility of Christian salvation. Shylock, on the other hand, would have found this the more merciful, or as he would probably phrase it, the more just ending.

In his Prologue to *The She-Gallants*, Granville proclaims his intention "to strike" a "Stroke" at "Vice," the "Motly Beast" which has overtaken London in order "to Correct" the manners and morals of those who see the play. Granville's play indeed includes many moral reflections, though, as he mentions in the prologue, it also contains several warm passages inserted, he claims, purely for moral edification. Throughout the play, characters comment on the wickedness of the age characterized by rampant homosexuality (*SG* 2); hypocrisy, or as Frederick's sister Diana says, "the Virtues of Mankind are all but Vices in disguise" (*SG* 7); malicious gossip, "the Town is always ready to believe any ill that's said of a Woman" (*SG* 19); the confused morals of a town which "abhors Modesty and Vertue" and whose "inseparable Companions" are "Impudence and Vice" (*SG* 33); the *preciosité* of language and manners espoused by the same women whose scruples are not offended when they engage in multiple affairs (*SG* 39); and, finally, marriages based on avarice, ambition, or passion rather than the sound foundation of lasting love (*SG* 73). Not content with the mere exhibition of vice, Granville ends his play with a moral discourse on the content arising from a clear conscience. As Bellamour says, "They who are Rich by indirect means, or Great by Evil Practices, or enjoy forbidden Loves, are all miserable at the bottom," and Philabel affirms, "Innocence is the foundation of true Joy, and without it all Possessions are imperfect" (*SG* 73).

The driving force of Granville's play, love, rather than intrigue, propels the action, forcing Angelica into the habit of a man in order to regain Bellamour's affections by turning Lucinda's aunt against him. Constantia similarly takes up her masquerade so that she can discover if Frederick truly loves her and "is a Man of Honour" (*SG* 3). In carrying on the masquerade, Angelica and Constantia occasionally sully their own honor; however, as they deceive the people about them in the cause of true love and no real ill effects result, both deserve to win the men they love. Angelica's love for Bellamour has been constant although she has not seen him in the past two years and he has ignored all her attempts to contact him. Her attempt to sway his affections from Lucinda does not detract from her worthiness either. Lucinda has only entertained Bellamour as a suitor during the absence of her own love, Philabel. Now that Philabel has returned, Lucinda resolves "Not absolutely to break" with Bellamour until she knows "how *Philabel* continues inclin'd" (*SG* 9). Lucinda's fickleness sharply contrasts with Angelica's constancy which obliterates most of the blemish arising from her deception.

Angelica is more than worthy of Bellamour, who shows a similar inconstancy to Lucinda's. When Angelica in her disguise as a gallant broaches the subject of why Bellamour broke faith with her, he responds breezily, "it was my fortune to see *Angelica* and to love her. It was my fortune to be absent from her, and to forget her." Though he agrees that she is beautiful and witty and wishes her all the best, he asserts that the "Luck which over-rules all" often ordains that "the deserving are not always the successful." He continues his discourse on fate by adding: "The Children of this World have all different Portions; some have Wit, others Beauty: But where there is no Merit to be found, those have Fortune which is the Cordial Drop prescrib'd by Providence to comfort 'em, for the severity and unkindness of Nature" (*SG* 20).[29]   No matter how accurate

---

[29] The third and fourth stanzas of the song in dialogue reinforce Bellamour's ideas on fate:

> Thirsis. *Mysterious Guide of Inclination,*
> *Tell me Tyrant, why am I*
> *With equal Merit, equal Passion,*
> *Thus the Victim chosen to dye?*
> *Why am I*
> *The Victim chosen to dye?*

> Delia. *On Fate alone depends Success,*

Bellamour's ideas on fate may be in real life, they do not turn out to be entirely true in this case. Bellamour deserves one part of his fate: his constant love for Lucinda merits rejection. Lucinda openly rejects him–she has already done so secretly, pending the disclosure of Philabel's constancy to her–after she discovers his broken vows to Angelica, whom he had cast off for no good cause. Because of the determined intervention of Angelica, fortune does not leave the undeserving Bellamour stranded, and he and Angelica are reunited.

Granville doles out poetic justice more capriciously to other characters who are even more consistently drawn. That notable pimp, Sir Toby Cusifle, receives no justice other than the temporary blow to his honor as he learns of Bellamour's treatment of Angelica. The other gallant, Constantia, escapes the fury of Frederick and his four "wronged" sisters when her brother, the real Courtall, appears on the scene to take her place in the duel and marry one of the sisters.[30] The braggarts, Sir John Aery and Vaunter, are mocked in several ways. They are imprisoned in a closet, humiliated by being forced to recant their fantastic boasts of amorous adventures, and degraded through Sir John's forced engagement to Plackett, Lady Dorimen's maid. Then, strangely enough, they are rewarded with their choices of Frederick's four sisters as brides. Poetic justice deals most appropriately, on the other hand, with Lady Dorimen, whose situation teaches her to "trust not in appearances" (*SG* 75) and leaves her without a suitor at the end of the play as well as with the mortifying realization that she has attempted to seduce a woman in breeches.

> *And Fancy Reason over-rules;*
> *Or why should Virtue ever miss*
> *Reward, so often given to Fools?*

[30] Constantia proves herself worthy of the *deus ex machina* and will not allow her brother to fight the battle alone, but takes part in it herself as well (61).

Dennis and The Refinement of Morals

Moral instruction becomes the focus of John Dennis' version of *The Merry Wives of Windsor*, which he calls *The Comical Gallant*. Dennis uses Shakespeare's basic plot, but in changing only three or four points he makes the play more overtly didactic, not only ridiculing vain pretensions such as Falstaff's to Mrs. Ford and Mrs. Page, exhibiting the folly of unwarranted jealousy, and exposing to the Pages, Slender, and Caius "that a forced Marriage is but a lawful Rape," but also in having Fenton and Anne recognize "the curse that attends a clandestine Marriage" (*CG* 49). Although Shakespeare's play touches each of these issues, Dennis uses them more consciously, or perhaps more emphatically.

In Dennis' version every incident of the plot is the end result of the machinations of a character who wishes to teach someone else a lesson. Fenton initiates Falstaff's amours for Mrs. Ford and Mrs. Page to divert the Pages from his relationship with Anne. Shakespeare's Falstaff needs no convincing, but mistakenly believes them to be irresistibly drawn to him. Fenton only instigates the action though; Mrs. Ford directs it. After she and Mrs. Page receive their duplicate letters from Falstaff, Mrs. Ford sees the possibilities in the situation which she enumerates in an aside:

> ... now will I make treble use of what has happened. I will reclaim
> my Husband from his extravagant jealousie, my management shall
> be a Satyr upon those vain Fellows, who scandalously interpret a
> Womans innocent freedom, and I will take care that my Nephew
> shall stalk under this fat Beast, till he arrives at your Daughter.
> (*CG* 8)

Shakespeare's Mrs. Ford merely wishes that her husband could see the letter, which, she says, "would give eternal food to his jealousy" (*MW* 2.1.88-89). In

The Comical Gallant Mrs. Ford leaves nothing to chance and virtually becomes the arbiter of justice, or, as she tells Falstaff at their first assignation, "I pretend to bestow no favours on you, but only to do you Justice" (*CG* 21).

Shakespeare's Falstaff is treated to being carried in a basket and dumped in the mud and dressing as the old woman of Brentford in return for his lasciviousness. Dennis includes the first punishment in his version of the play, but instead of putting Falstaff to the indignity of dressing as an old woman and giving him a much deserved beating from Mr. Ford, he makes him undergo the supreme blow to his ego by forcing him to stand guard while his prey, Mrs. Ford, ridicules him and apparently makes love to another suitor, a mere "Stripling." He rails at the change in his fortune but reluctantly realizes that he deserves it:

> . . . what has happen'd looks like a Judgment upon me. For, what brought thee hither, ask thy self that question, old Jack? Why, Vanity, Covetousness and Letchery. And how hast thou been pepper'd in all three? At the very time that thou hast been yearning to be at performance, thou hast been forc'd in the very face of the party to make a Libel upon thy Impotence. There's for thy Vanity, a plaguy Mortification! And at the very moment that thou wer't going to dig for the Oar, a Rakehell in Red, before thy very eyes, came and took possession of the Mine. There's for thy Covetousness. A jerker i'faith. And in the Height and Rage of thy own Desire, thou art here standing very foolishly, and holding the Door for another. Another Devilish Mortification. They are at it, I warrant you, helter skelter by this time. (*CG* 26)

Dennis, interestingly, does not make Falstaff the victim of the mask as Shakespeare does. As a result, Falstaff does not have to bear the fairies' pinches and their appropriate chant, "Lust is but a bloody fire,/Kindled with unchaste desire,/Fed in heart, whose flames aspire,/As thoughts do blow them, higher and higher" (*MW* 5.5.92-95). The fate Dennis reserves for Falstaff is no more or no less appropriate than that Shakespeare dispenses, but it does elicit a stronger recognition of guilt by Falstaff himself. The only admission of guilt that Shakespeare's Falstaff makes is when he learns that the fairies were actually children from the village. He moans, "By the Lord, I was three or four times in the thought they were not fairies, and yet the guiltiness of my mind, the sudden surprise of my powers, drove the grossness of the foppery into a received belief— in despite of the teeth of all rhyme and reason–that they were fairies" (*MW* 5.5.117-22), but he does not explicitly note the justice of his punishment as Dennis' Falstaff does.

Though Mrs. Ford also intends justice for her husband, she merely sets the stage for his cure and does not actually effect it herself. The justice Mr. Ford receives is more painful and more appropriate in Dennis' version than in the original. In *The Merry Wives*, Falstaff informs him that he has a rendezvous with Mrs. Ford at ten or eleven that night. In *The Comical Gallant*, he must hear an exchange between Falstaff and Doll Tearsheet, the bawd, as they arrange the meeting, and his dialogue with Falstaff in which the old pimp draws the prospective customer a tantalizing picture of an amorous Mrs. Ford is trebled at the very least. Shakespeare's Ford is continually taunted with the possibility of his wife's wantonness, but he receives no retribution for his groundless, insane jealousy. Mr. Ford, who exclaims at one point that "Folly must have due its Chastisement" (*CG* 28), promptly receives his own in *The Comical Gallant* when he goes to the inn where Falstaff and Mrs. Ford were supposed to meet. Although he cannot find Falstaff, he discovers "Captain Dingboy," who accosts him with, "You are jealous, you Blockhead! Sirrah, your Wife's a Virtuous Wife, and a civil, obliging, sweet tempered Creature" (*CG* 28) upon which she strikes him, loses her wig and runs away. Ford not only believes himself cuckolded by a fool, but "cudgell'd by a Woman" (*CG* 28) as well.

Ford's encounter with Dingboy does nothing to lessen his suspicions and he must be subjected to greater ignominy before he realizes that his wife is faithful. His brother-in-law, the Host of the Garter, who knows of the prank designed for Falstaff at the mask that night, arranges for Ford to take his place. He tells Ford, "You shall lie conceal'd here till twelve, and then we will dress you to Fain Falstaff's shape which is luckily drying below at the Fire, and putting a pair of Horns on your head, send you to Hern's Oak, before Falstaff's time is come, and there you may make a plain discovery whether you wear them or no" (*CG* 35). Ford has to bear the taunts and pinches of the fairies at the mask, but wearing the horns of Hern the hunter turns out to be the best medicine for him. Though he is "maim'd," and "crippl'd for ever," he finally realizes that he has been an "Ass" and has "so vilely wrong'd the best of Women" (*CG* 44). Dennis thus greatly increases poetic justice in Ford's case.

The cases of Slender and Caius are slightly different in the two versions as well. Shakespeare has them take two lusty boys for wives in *The Merry Wives*, but Dennis ordains a more fitting fate for them by having the two rivals for Anne Page's hand "marry" each other. When Mrs. Ford tells Slender how to know Anne at the mask that night, she warns him to be very careful because Caius will be near, and Slender responds, "He near me! If I do not play him such a Prank, that all Windsor shall laugh at him; Then say, that Slender's a Fool" (*CG* 41). Both parts of Slender's prophecy come true, for when they return from the ceremony and see Anne Page at Hern's Oak with Fenton, Caius exclaims, "Begar

I vill see vat damn Bish I ha married." Much to his surprise, when the lady unmasks, she turns out to be "dat Jackanape Slender" (*CG* 46), and the two men appear even more ridiculous than in Shakespeare's play.

Fenton and Anne Page are worthy characters in both versions of the play, but, in eliminating the actual elopement from his play, Dennis makes their situation more instructive for the audience. In the end of *The Merry Wives*, Fenton explains away any blame attached to their marriage:

> Th' offence is holy that she hath committed,
>
> And this deceit loses the name of craft,
>
> Of disobedience, or unduteous title,
>
> Since therein she doth evitate [i.e., avoid] and shun
>
> A thousand irreligious cursèd hours
>
> Which forcèd marriage would have brought upon her. (*MW* 5.5.202-207)

Mr. and Mrs. Page are forced to embrace "What cannot be eschewed" (*MW* 5.5.214). In *The Comical Gallant*, on the other hand, Fenton does not marry Anne, but takes part in the confusion at the mask in order to expose "what preposterous choices" Slender and Caius were for Anne Page. He does not rebuke them for their folly, but, in fact, knows that "in the match each had provided for her" they had "designed her Happiness, her Interest, and her Honour." The true gentleman, Fenton releases Anne from "any obligation" as he claims he has "so truely considered of the terrible consequences which attend the just displeasure of a Parent, that I am resolv'd either to owe my happiness to you, or not to be happy at all, and I will never teach her to be undutiful to me, by perswading her first to be disobedient to you" (*CG* 48), and she has recoiled at the thought of disobedience from the outset of the play. Fenton would have had to persuade

Anne to be disobedient, for when he tells her he will have the Reverend Prebend waiting to marry them that night, she responds, "Will he have the face to pretend 'tis a Duty to disobey my Parents?" (*CG* 37) Since he waits for the Pages' blessing to marry, Dennis' Fenton is rewarded not only with a loving wife and an obedient one as well but also with the promise of inheriting the estate of his uncle and aunt, the Fords.

Although each receives his just rewards in *The Comical Gallant*, the characterization in some instances is not as consistent as in *The Merry Wives.* Shakespeare's Mrs. Ford and Mrs. Page want only to show Falstaff that "Wives may be merry, and yet honest, too" (*MW* 4.2.89) As Mrs. Ford tells Mrs. Page, "I will consent to act any villainy against him that may not sully the chariness of our honesty" (*MW* 2.1.86-87), and the tricks they play on Falstaff are simply harmless pranks. Dennis' inclusion of the Captain Dingboy episode blemishes the characters of Mrs. Page and Mrs. Ford as Mrs. Ford pretends to engage in an adulterous liaison. Even though Mrs. Ford's suitor is none other than her good friend, Mrs. Page, this joke makes the two characters a little less admirable in the audience's eyes.

Dennis' Mrs. Ford bears some blame for manipulating events to suit her purposes. She knows that she and her husband are planning to make Fenton heir to their rather sizeable estate, and she no doubt realizes that this move would do much to reconcile the Pages to the match. She nonetheless maintains the secret until Fenton receives the blessing of the Pages, thereby keeping Fenton and Anne in a turmoil over their decision so that they do not know what is the greatest evil, disobeying her parents and eloping or risking a forced marriage for Anne. Because she thinks Anne's parents absolutely fixed in their choices of Caius and Slender, but even more because she wants her nephew to "owe his success to his Wit, and not to his Money" (*CG* 49), Mrs. Page does not divulge her plans for Fenton's inheritance. In a way, Mrs. Page's machinations here are in keeping with her character, for had she revealed everything, this merry wife would have missed out on a great deal of honest fun. John Dennis would also have been left with only half a plot.

Another character whose actions are occasionally inconsistent in Dennis' play is Mr. Page. Page seems to be a good-natured, level-headed character in both versions of the play. When Ford is consumed with jealousy over Falstaff's courtship of his wife, Mr. Page trusts his own wife implicitly and can laugh at the whole situation. Yet this same man in *The Comical Gallant* for no good reason prefers to marry his daughter to an utter simpleton rather than to Fenton. Shakespeare resolves this problem by having Mr. Page refuse the alliance between Fenton and Anne because he believes that Fenton, who is above Anne in birth and has lived a wasteful, riotous life so far, wants to marry her only for her money. His concern for Anne's financial well-being does not quite compensate for his desire to marry her to Simple, but it does prevent Mr. Page from inconsistently committing himself to an absurd notion for no reason whatsoever.

The entire plot of *A Plot and No Plot*, Dennis' original play, is absurd; yet, like *The Comical Gallant*, it is structured to teach a lesson. Young Belvil, in love with Sylvia but prevented from marrying her by Bull, his uncle and her guardian, designs a scheme to obtain his uncle's blessing for his marriage as well as the five thousand pounds Bull owes his friend Colonel Medley while simultaneously showing the old man the folly of conspiring against the government as well as the vanity of his son Batt's pretensions to wealth and station. Belvil discloses the full extent of his good intentions to Baldernoe when he claims that exposing his uncle's foibles "would therefore be just and instructive Satyr upon Mankind in general, and would plainly show us how easily we believe what we eagerly desire; and what a constant *Cully* reason is to Passion" (*PNP* 12) thereby delineating the moral of the play.

A Plot and No Plot fulfills Belvil's prophecy admirably as it shows Bull, the notorious plotter, drawn into a sham conspiracy swiftly and completely. The old tightwad who stingily holds onto the five thousand pounds he owes his friend Medley, in Belvil's words, "refuses to pay his old friend, and one of the warmest of his own party, one hundred pounds, though he has all his fortune by him" (*PNP* 2). This same man suffers no qualms in giving a thousand pounds to a total stranger in order to help further the plot against the government. He receives his comeuppance for his avarice and his gullibility, when as he is led to believe that he has been arrested for his part in the conspiracy. Taken for a meandering ride, Bull believes himself to be in Newgate, where he will stay until Friday when he supposedly will hang. This hard old codger had been dedicated when he and Macfleer had discussed the coming invasion. He even capered about merrily when Macfleer detailed the horrors that would accompany the takeover, "Then you will behold this City flowing with human gore, your Virgins ravish'd, your Matrons violated, and your Widows–well diverted" (*PNP* 11). Bull is not dedicated enough to any plot to give up his life for it. As soon as he is incarcerated, Bull asks for pen and paper on which to write a narrative. As he tells Joe the jailor, "I must produce Traytors to save my self, and Gadsbud I'll take the first persons I can light of: I'll give my self as little trouble as I can" (*PNP* 65). When he discovers that his execution apparently is fixed, he readily gives Belvil five thousand pounds in order to effect his escape.

Old Bull is also foiled in his marriage plans for Belvil and Sylvia. Having planned a marriage for Belvil[31] with Justice Dowdy's daughter and reserving Sylvia and her fortune for his son, Batt, Bull readily accedes to Batt's wish to marry the daughter of the Countess instead. His chosen daughter-in-law proves to be a prostitute, and his pretensions have thus been adequately rewarded. At the end, he realizes the result of his machinations, "Was ever man serv'd as I have been? I have been us'd like a Bartholomew Cokes; I have been cheated of five thousand pound, have been made to pass for a mad man: And my Son in all likelihood is marry'd to the worst of Drabs" (*PNP* 76).[32] Taken to the brink of disaster, Bull receives a reprieve when Belvil informs him that not only have the imprisonment and the conspiracy been shams, but so has the marriage. Furthermore, in exchange for Bull's blessing on his marriage to Sylvia, Belvil promises to repay Bull the five thousand pounds he cozened from him and to pay Colonel Medley the same sum. Bull has received adequate ridicule, but the ridicule has not been gratuitous. Belvil, rather, planned the whole "to assuage" Bull's "itch of Caballing, and correct" his "Credulity," so that he will be "secure from more dangerous attempts." Belvil's reflections on Bull's self-deception end the play:

> Few tricking Rogues would be believ'd,
>
> Unless their Sotts by Self-conceit,
>
> Were accessaries in the cheat,

---

[31] The terms of his father's will state that if Belvil marries without Bull's approval he must forfeit half his fortune.

[32] After Bull beats Batt for pretending to be Viscount Dorant, he agrees that the daughter of the Countess would be more impressed with that name than Bull and similarly that her daughter would make a more appropriate wife for Batt than Sylvia would have. As Frowsy, the "Countess," returns to the room, she reflects, "I suppose by this time they may have consented to have carried this cheat on against themselves" (*PNP* 47), which is indeed what Bull does throughout the play.

And by themselves were first deceiv'd. (*PNP*
79)

Bull's lesson has been painful, but it has also proven beneficial, and, in the end, he receives mercy rather than stringent justice.

Old Bull is not the only character in *A Plot and No Plot* whose follies merit ridicule. His son Batt is as full of vanity and pretensions as he is, and Batt's foolishness actually accounts for a large part of Bull's punishment. He reveals himself to be an easy target for Belvil's plans as soon as he opens his mouth to proclaim, "I hope my judgment may be taken for a foolish thing as soon as another mans," a point on which Belvil will capitalize adequately. Batt's judgment seems to rest on the idea that money and position equal merit. He tells Belvil that he "always treat[s] people *De haut en bas*, who have not a great deal of money" and rebukes his cousin for behaving "so gently to all sorts of people" (*PNP* 24) so that he must be ashamed of him.

Not content with showing Sylvia what a conceited fop Batt is, thus making her decide that she cannot marry him after all, Belvil decides that Batt "must smart too," and he discloses his plan to avenge himself on his uncle Bull by punishing his son. "Since I have depriv'd him of the Wife design'd for him," he says, "I will put very fair for providing another for him." Then, he reveals the perfect justice of his scheme as well as its moral efficacy: "In Friskit I have made a proper choice for him. For so extravagant a Drab and so extraordinary a Fop are tallies to one another; so surprizing a Match may be very instructive, and show the ridiculous vanity of some Coxcombs who are now in my Eye" (*PNP* 29). Just as Belvil expects, Batt readily convinces himself that he knew and loved Friskit in France, jumps at the chance to marry her, and when the truth is revealed, believes it to be a jest. By the time Batt realizes that he has married a whore, Belvil has finished with his lesson and tells them that the marriage was a sham. Batt's penance, as a result, is brief, relatively painless, and, for all practical purposes, lost on the dimwitted Batt.

Belvil doles out justice and mercy in the play and receives his own due reward in the meantime. A worthy young man, he has had no difficulty in persuading his friends and servants to help in his plot to cozen his uncle. As the servant says, "Mr. Belvil is so honest, so worth, so liberal a Gentleman, that we have all engag'd to run through fire and water for him" (*PNP* 31). Frowsy interprets the situation a little differently when she speaks of the virtue of the young man who has "oblig'd them [the servants] all along by the goodness of his humour, and by the mildness of his carriage towards them, has distributed fifty pounds among them this morning" (*PNP* 32). Nothing in Belvil's character makes him unworthy of the hand of Sylvia. His close association with such disreputable characters as Frowsy, Friskit, and Baldernoe hints at some indiscretion in the past but does not appear to have had any lasting effect on his character. Like Fenton in *The Comical Gallant*, his sense of honor is strong enough to convince him to wait to marry his lady until he has received the approval of her guardian. Belvil may indeed be too good for Sylvia, whose character remains very sketchy throughout. At the beginning of the play, she fully plans to marry her guardian's son solely because he has bidden her to, and when Belvil asks if she will marry him contingent upon his receiving Bull's approval within the next two hours, her response is lukewarm and cynical. "Upon that condition," she says, "I may promise anything, and run no risque of performance" (*PNP* 29), but she seems willing enough to fulfill her part of the bargain once Bull bestows his blessing on the match. Belvil, likewise, deals honorably with his uncle and his cousin. Though he has had the perfect chance to ruin them and they have tried to ruin him in the past, he stops short of inflicting revenge and contents himself with "opening" their "Eyes" in order, as he tells them, "to prevent your being cheated for the future, and consequently to prevent your real misfortunes and your future Infamy" (*PNP* 78). Satisfied that Sylvia can now be his bride, Belvil can also be happy in the possession of a family who will no longer be gulls to any cozeners who happen along.

Moral instruction given through didactic speeches, artificially heightened poetic justice, and a resolution of ambiguity in character proves to be a hallmark of these Restoration adaptations as in the plays original to the adapters. Although the moral element appears most clearly in Charles Gildon's *Measure for Measure, or Beauty the Best Advocate*, the other plays nonetheless exhibit at the very least an overt statement of morality as in Granville's *Jew of Venice*. Seemingly more important to the Restoration than morality, what the adapters saw as an attempt at the refinement of style and what the modern audience sees as the elimination of poetry, also characterize all four of these adaptations.

The Refinement of Style

Aside from Shakespeare's disregard for the unities, Restoration critics spent more time in attacking Shakespeare's use, or misuse, of language than any other point. Hooker encapsulates the problems for which Dryden criticizes Shakespeare's expression, "its flatness, insipidity, play on words, bombast, solecism, coarseness, lack of grammar, obscurity, and affectation due to excessive use of figures of speech and unintelligibility."[33] When he notes "the tongue in general is so much refined since Shakespeare's time, that many of his words, and

[33]Hooker, vol. 2, p. 425.

more of his phrases are scarce intelligible," Dryden shows an implicit recognition of what he believes to be Shakespeare's handicap, but he stumbles onto the real situation more accurately in "Of Dramatic Poesy":

> I cannot say he is everywhere alike; were he so, I should do him injury to compare him with the greatest of mankind. He is many times, flat, insipid; his comic wit degenerating into clenches, his serious swelling into bombast. But he is always great, when some great occasion is presented to him; no man can say he ever had a fit subject for his wit, and did not then raise himself . . . high above the rest of the poets. (I.80)

Dryden recognizes Shakespeare's brilliance of style when he is dealing with lofty subjects; however, he does not appear to realize that what he sees as a "degeneration" of style may be intentional on Shakespeare's part.

Two hundred years later Herewood T. Price noted Shakespeare's conscious manipulation of style. After quoting the first twenty-three lines of *Twelfth Night*, Price comments that "Shakespeare's technique is obvious." He expands by adding that "when he [Shakespeare] wants to suggest crudeness, triviality, or insincerity, he adopts the artifices of Elizabethan convention. By indirection he reveals that he considers certain tricks of style to be cheap and flimsy." Price then focuses on the problem uppermost in the Restoration adapter's mind as he notes, "Critics often attack him for being intricate where it was so easy to be simple. These men forget that Shakespeare the dramatist sometimes imposed a duty on Shakespeare the poet, at which the latter must have groaned."[34]

---

[34]Herewood T. Price, "Shakespeare as Critic," *Philological Quarterly* 20 (July 1941):392.

Both Hazleton Spencer and George Odell have adequately shown the ludicrous changes in style made by the adapters. What they did not show are the changes that clarify and simplify the language so that it actually is more intelligible, though obviously less poetic. The adapters' commitment to clarity and simplicity probably accounts for their dislike of wordplay and figurative language. Although none of the adapters totally eliminate metaphors and similes from the altered versions, they do restrict the figures to one interpretation, denying the numerous possibilities Shakespeare's language invites.[35]   The Restoration's disapproval of wordplay shows up in these plays as well. Many of the puns in Shakespeare appear in the "low" comedy which is virtually eliminated by the adapters; even the density of language achieved in such lines as Portia's "In both my eyes he doubly sees himself,/In each eye, one. Swear by your double self,/And there's an oath of credit" (*MV* 5.1.244-46) fell into disrepute with the adapters and was virtually obliterated in the alterations.[36] Numerous passages occur throughout the adaptations, but the following representative examples show the basic direction in which the adapters moved the style.

Gildon and The Refinement of Style

In his version of *Measure for Measure*, Charles Gildon exhibits the adapters' concern with simplicity and clarity. Isabella's speech on man's pride exemplifies the types of changes Gildon makes throughout the play.   In Shakespeare, the speech appears as follows:

---

[35]Some of the adapters, Burnaby, for instance, add metaphors and similes.   See his version of "If Musick be the Food of Love" in which he deletes the analogies of music and the bank of violets as well as that of the sea and love in favor of his own contrast of the porcupine which uses its arrows on his enemy with the lover who directs his darts on himself.

[36]Burnaby includes at least one pun in his *Ladies' Visiting Day* and vaunts its presence

> Could great men thunder
>
> As Jove himself does, Jove would never be quiet,
>
> For every pelting petty officer
>
> Would use his heaven for thunder, nothing but
>
> thunder. Merciful heaven,
>
> Thou rather with thy sharp and sulphurous bolt
>
> Split'st the unwedgeable and gnarlèd oak
>
> Than the soft myrtle. But man, proud man,
>
> Dressed in a little brief authority,
>
> Most ignorant of what he's most assured,
>
> His glassy essence, like an angry ape
>
> Plays such fantastic tricks before high heaven
>
> As makes the angels weep, who, with our spleens,
>
> Would all themselves laugh mortal. (*MV* 2.2.113-
>
> 126)

Gildon makes a few alterations in the language so that the passage reads:

> If men cou'd Thunder
>
> As great *Jove* does, we ne'r shou'd be at quiet,
>
> For ever Cholerik petty Officer
>
> Wou'd use the Magazeen of Heaven for Thunder;
>
> Nothing but Thunder: Oh! Merciful Heav'n!
>
> Thou rather with thy sharp and Sulphurous Bolt,
>
> Dost split the Knotty and Obdurat *Oak*,
>
> Than the soft *Mirtle*. Oh! but Man, Proud Man,
>
> (Dress'd in a little *Breef* Authority,

in his preface, and Dennis retains many of Falstaff's puns in *The Comical Gallant*.

Most ignorant of what he thinks himself

Assur'd) In his frail Glassy Essence, like

An Angry *Ape*, plays such Fantastick Tricks,

Before High Heav'n, as wou'd make Angels laugh,

If they were Mortal, and had Spleens like us. (*BBA* 6)

Gildon has not substantially altered the basic import of this passage; yet, he has made several of its expressions easier to understand, albeit less eloquent. The first line indicates his trend as he moves from "Could great men Thunder" to the more modern "If men could Thunder." He continues the changes in that line by altering "Jove would never be quiet" which makes little sense on first reading as it seems to indicate that if great men could thunder like Jove, Jove would never *be* quiet, rather than that he would never *have* quiet, to the clearer "we ne'r should be at quiet." Other changes he makes in the passage include the move from the alliterative "pelting, petty officer" to the more substantive "Cholerik petty Officer"; and from the concrete imagery of "the unwedgeable and gnarled oak" to the more pointed "Knotty and Obdurat *Oak*." He changes the final lines of the passage considerably to make the image more lucid. The intent of Shakespeare's final lines is obscure and ambiguous, indicating either that though the angels weep over man's proud tricks, if they had spleens and could laugh at him, they would, or if they had spleens they would laugh until they became mortal. Gildon chooses the first interpretation of Shakespeare's lines so that the speech ends without ambiguity: "but Man, Proud Man . . . plays such Fantastick Tricks,/Before High Heav'n, as wou'd make Angels laugh,/If they were Mortal, and had Spleens like us." Gildon has robbed the passage of much of its beauty and eliminated the possibility for various interpretation; nonetheless, he has attained a more readily intelligible and more modern style both in this passage and throughout the play.

Burnaby and The Refinement of Style

While Gildon retains much of the form of Shakespeare's language, William Burnaby rewrites most of the dialogue, placing the few remnants of Shakespeare's verse in quotation marks. He makes significant changes even in the few verses he retains.   One of the longest passages that he repeats from Shakespeare is Rodoregue's testimony which he changes to:

> A Witchcraft drew me hither;
>
> That most ungrateful Youth there by your side.
>
> From you rude Seas, enrag'd and foamy mouth
>
> Did I redeem, a Wretch past hope! –For whose
>
> > sole sake,
>
> Known as I was, a publick Foe to *Venice* :
>
> I lay'd aside the cares of my own safety,
>
> And here expos'd me to this adverse Town,
>
> Where not an hour ago beset with Villains;
>
> I drew my ready Sword in his defence,
>
> And sav'd a second time his Life:
>
> But soon as the publick Officers had seiz'd me,
>
> And I became the Wreck of Fortune's spite,
>
> And in my turn his doubtless succour needed!
>
> Instead of drawing to relieve his Friend;
>
> He grew a stranger to my very Name!
>
> And basely vow'd he saw me not before;
>
> Deny'd me my own Purse with pitty, for his fate
>
> Had made me recommend this morning to his use. (*LB* 54-55)

Burnaby deletes some of the background information Antonio supplies concerning the depth of his affection for Cæsario, "His life I gave him, and did thereto add/My love without retention or restraint,/All in his dedication" (*TN* 5.1.74-76). In order to clarify the reasons for Rodoregue's danger and emphasize the risks he has taken, on the other hand, Burnaby adds, "Known as I was, a publick Foe to *Venice*:/I lay'd aside the cares of my own safety" where Shakespeare merely has Antonio say, "For his sake/Did I expose myself, pure for his love/Into the danger of this adverse town" (*TN* 5.1.82-84). Burnaby totally rewrites the next few lines. They read as follows in *Twelfth Night*:

> Drew to defend him when he was beset;
>
> Where being apprehended, his false cunning–
>
> Not meaning to partake with me in danger–
>
> Taught him to face me out of his acquaintance,
>
> And grew a twenty years' removèd thing
>
> While one could wink, denied me mine own purse,
>
> Which I had recommended to his use
>
> Not half an hour before. (*TN* 5.1.79-86)

Antonio's speech is picturesque and effective; however, Burnaby takes several of the more difficult sentence constructions and makes them more readily intelligible to his audience. In one instance, he changes "Where being apprehended, his false cunning/–Not meaning to partake with me in danger–/Taught him to face me out of his acquaintance,/And grew a twenty years removèd thing" to the more direct "Instead of a stretch'd out Arm to save me,/Instead of drawing to relieve his Friend;/He grew a stranger to my very Name!/And basely vow'd he saw me not before." Characteristically, Burnaby obscures almost as many lines in the passage as he clarifies, taking, for example, Shakespeare's simple "denied me my own purse,/Which I had recommended to his use/Not half an hour before" and turning it into the jumbled "Deny'd me my own Purse with pitty, for his fate/Had made me recommend this morning to his use." The whole of Burnaby's style nonetheless represents a simplification, clarification, and modernization of Shakespeare.

Granville and The Refinement of Style

Granville contrasts Burnaby in utilizing many of Shakespeare's lines from *The Merchant of Venice* in his version and setting off his additions, and, occasionally, Shakespeare's original words, in inverted commas. Granville's changes to Shakespeare's verse consist primarily of abridging certain passages and expanding others to make his point abundantly clear. He also modernizes some words, but, on the whole, adheres faithfully to Shakespeare's original words. An early speech by Nerissa shows the type of expansion Granville employs to connect a particular act to an abstraction, in this case relating the choice of the casket to the role that fortune always exerts in love. In *The Merchant of Venice* Nerissa speaks, "therefore the lottery that he hath devised in these three chests of gold, silver, and lead, whereof who chooses his meaning chooses you, will no doubt never be chosen by any rightly but one who you shall rightly love" (*MV* 1.2.25-28). Granville chooses to illuminate the audience further when he has Nerissa add:

> I have Superstition
> Enough to believe the Benefit Lot is destin'd for
> The best Deserver.
> Love is at best, but a Lottery to all,
> Your Case looks different, but is in Effect the same
> With the rest of the World: For it is Fortune that
> Always decides. (*JV* 4)

Granville chooses, on the other hand, to condense Portia's "quality of mercy" speech so that instead of Shakespeare's twenty-one lines, his version has only twelve. The only change he makes in it other than through abridgement is in changing "It is an attribute to God himself" (*MV* 4.1.190) to the slightly less concrete "It is the first of Sacred Attributes" (*JV* 33).

In altering Antonio's reflections on Shylock's obstinacy, Granville attempts clarification through the use of more modern, simpler words. Shakespeare's Antonio poetically compares the difficulty of persuading Shylock to have mercy with three impossible tasks:

> I pray you think you question with the Jew.
>
> You may as well go stand upon the beach
>
> And bid the main flood bate his usual height;
>
> You may as well use question with the wolf
>
> Why he hath made the ewe bleat for the lamb;
>
> You may as well forbid the mountain pines
>
> To wag their high tops and to make no noise
>
> When they are fretten with the gusts of heaven. (*MV* 4.1.69-76)

Although the gist of Antonio's speech appears in Granville's version, he does make a few significant alterations which make the sense of the passage more readily apparent:

> I pray you think you question with a Jew;
>
> You may as well expostulate with Wolves;
>
> You may as well go stand upon the Beach,
>
> And bid the Waves be still, and Winds be husht;
>
> You may as well forbid the Mountain pines
>
> To wag their Tops, and dance about their Leaves,

When the rude Gusts of Heav'n are whistling round. (*JV* 31)
Granville changes the three images here to read more easily. The first alteration he makes from "use question with the wolf" to "expostulate with Wolves" utilizes a more difficult verb, but the construction is more straightforward and easier to understand. The next image is much simpler in Granville as he changes it from "bid the main flood bate his usual height" to "bid the Waves be still," though the image is not precisely the same, moving as it does from the idea of the high tide to simple waves. In the final image of the passage, Granville, like Burnaby, simultaneously clarifies and obscures Shakespeare's passage as he alters "forbid the mountain pines/To wag their high tops and to make no noise/When they are fretten with the gusts of heaven" to "forbid the Mountain pines/To wag their Tops, and dance about their Leaves,/When the rude Gusts of Heav'n are whistling round." Although he replaces "fretten with the gusts of heaven" by the clearer "When the rude Gusts of Heav'n are whistling round," Granville also has the mountain pines "dance about their Leaves," a rather confusing and silly action.[37]

Dennis and The Refinement of Style

Like his predecessors, Dennis attempts to revise *The Merry Wives of Windsor* to make Shakespeare's language clearer and more modern. Dennis really does not alter much of the original language of the play, keeping the flavor and most of the original words of Falstaff's extravagant, blustering speech, including the puns,[38] the raging bombast of Ford, as well as the comic catachresis and

---

[37]Granville significantly does not clear up the ambiguity in Antonio's disposition of Shylock's goods (37 in *The Jew of Venice* and 4.1.381-85 in *The Merchant of Venice*), but utilizes Shakespeare's words verbatim.

[38] See for instance p. 3 in *The Comical Gallant* and 1.3.42-3 in *The Merry Wives*, which

dialect utilized by Caius and Dr. Evans. The major change Dennis makes, then, is in supplying what he calls a "free and easie" (Preface) dialogue for the lovers, Fenton and Anne Page.

Hazleton Spencer quotes some of the more awkward passages of Fenton's and Anne's dialogue in an attempt to show that Dennis has not improved on Shakespeare's language, and he is undoubtedly right, for the most part. Dennis does greatly expand the amount of dialogue between the lovers and changes it from blank verse into prose, which seems more natural since the bulk of the original play is in prose. A comparison of the dialogue between the lovers in both plays proves both Spencer and Dennis to be correct in their assertions; sometimes Dennis improves on the flow of the dialogue and makes it more natural, but just as frequently, he jumbles it and makes it difficult to follow.

The only exchange between the two lovers in Shakespeare's play shows their stilted, unnatural dialogue, especially in the part of Anne:

>*Fent.* I see I cannot get thy father's love;
>
>Therefore no more turn me to him, sweet Nan.
>
>*Anne.* Alas, how then?
>
>*Fent.* Why, thou must be thyself.
>
>He doth object I am too great of birth,
>
>And that, my state being galled with my expense,
>
>I seek to heal it only by his wealth.
>
>Besides these, other bars he lays before me–
>
>My riots past, my wild societies;
>
>And tells me 'tis a thing impossible
>
>I should love thee but as a property.

includes Falstaff's pun on waste/waist.

Anne. Maybe he tells you true.

Fent. No, heaven so speed me in my time to come!

Albeit I will confess thy father's wealth

Was the first motive that I wooed thee, Anne,

Yet, wooing thee, I found thee of more value

Than stamps in gold or sums in sealèd bags;

And 'tis the very riches of thyself

That now I aim at.

    Anne.   Gentle Master Fenton,

Yet seek my father's love, still seek it, sir.

If opportunity and humblest suit

Cannot attain it, why then–

          Hark you hither! (*MW* 3.4.1-22)

This excerpt from the first exchange between Dennis' Fenton and Anne shows Anne with a more realistic, if less saintly, reaction, which is stated more naturally, though still theatrically, and more in the manner of a Restoration heroine:

Fent. Can I then have the happiness to see you at last, unkind Mrs. Page?

Mrs. A. Well! Are you not the most ungrateful Man upon Earth, to upbraid me with unkindness, when I do and suffer so much as you? Have not both my Parents forbid me the very sight of you, upon pain of their mortal displeasure? And is it a small proof of my esteem for you, that I give you in disobeying their orders?

Fent. But have I not a greater right to you than either of your Parents can claim? Are you not mine by a Sacred Vow that was solemnly made, both in the Face of Earth and of Heav'n?

Mrs. A. The thought of that Vow distracts me.

Fent. Oh, Heavens, you repent of it then?

Mrs. A. Repent of it I can never: but I must always tremble when I think of the consequence.

Fent. How could you find it in your Heart to let me languish at Windsor three tedious days without seeing you?

Mrs. A. And can you ask? unjust Mr. Fenton! Has not my Maid inform'd you, how I have been watch'd perpetually? Has she not told you how I have been peltered both with Spiritual and Temporal Fools? Has she not acquainted you with the ridiculous notion that *Sir Hugh* has made to my Father? (*CG* 3)

Further in the play, Anne and Fenton have another conversation in which Fenton employs at least three gerunds (italicized below), awkward and clanging to the modern ear, in the space of a half page:

Fent. I obliged my Aunt Ford, in order to *the making me happy*, to perswade your Mother to this second meeting.

Mrs. A. You have made your self and me eternally miserable. My Mother would make use of this opportunity, to oblige me to marry Caius. They meet in masks it seems.

Fent. Yes, and Caius is to be there in Womens Apparel, in order to *the carrying you off* with the less suspicion.

Mrs. A. O Heavens! And is this too by your contrivance?

Fent. It is, I prevail'd upon Mrs Ford, to Propose this Stratagem to your Mother, as a sure expedient *for the joyning you and Caius.* (*CG* 36, italics mine)

Dennis obviously has not refined and clarified the style of *The Merry Wives of Windsor* to any appreciable extent in his *Comical Gallant*. All he has done is to add dialogue where none existed in order to clarify the moral positions of his characters, and, that dialogue is sometimes natural and clear but frequently jumbled and awkward.

Summary

As they endeavor to bring moral and stylistic clarity and simplicity to the plots, characters, and language of Shakespeare's plays, these adapters alternately fail and succeed within the confines of each play. Gildon's *Measure for Measure* fails in Angelo's bribery of Isabella with jewels when she is not tempted to submit in exchange for her brother's life. It succeeds in its didactic aim by disposing of the characters more justly in the end and in exhibiting Gildon's attempt to clarify and simplify some of Shakespeare's more ambiguous passages. Burnaby, who repeatedly avows his disregard for rules, occasionally clarifies and occasionally obscures the language of the play as he heightens the workings of poetic justice primarily by explicitly noting its presence and using it to punish, as in the case of Villaretta, rather than to reward characters, as is true for Shakespeare's Olivia. Like Burnaby, Granville's alteration of Shakespeare's *Merchant of Venice* consists mainly of a more overt acknowledgement of poetic justice and a largely unsuccessful effort every now and then to clarify Shakespeare's language. John Dennis takes the adaptations full circle to a more conscious rendering of poetic justice, though he errs in eliminating the reason for Page's dislike of Fenton and in including the prurient scene in which Mrs. Ford pretends to entertain two lovers at once. He fails dismally in giving his characters a "free and easie" speech and only succeeds in making them sound like stilted Restoration heroes and heroines.

All in all, the adapters' attempts to refine the morals and the style of Shakespeare's original plays, like their attempts to unify Shakespeare's plots, succeed only on the most superficial levels. The close attention paid to clarity and simplicity, desirable as it may be in prose, tends to reduce meaning and lessen the semblance to real life by obliterating the complexity Shakespeare captures with such facility and such beauty. Shakespeare's Angelo receives mercy at the hands of the Duke; Gildon's receives the less beautiful and less Christian justice. Shakespeare's Viola wins the heart of Olivia, Orsino, and the audience with her wit and charm; Burnaby's Cæsario attracts the audience but cannot win them with her manipulative pertness. Shakespeare's blank verse reverberates; Granville's echoes hollowly. Shakespeare's wives are merry but honest, too; Dennis' come close to passing over the line of honesty in their revenge. Refinement of Shakespeare was the goal of these four men in their versions of the plays. They failed to realize that Shakespeare's plays are quintessential like gold.

"She did not as most Bawds do, like a Novel, consist of Intreague
alone; but, like a Comedy, besides design, had wit, folly, and
humours in her."
    Belvil in Dennis' *A Plot and No Plot*

CHAPTER IV

THE ADAPTERS AND COMEDY

While the adapters were busy attempting to mold Shakespeare's canon
into well-wrought plays based on both classical and contemporary doctrine on the
unities, the architectonic end of poetry, and the superiority of clarity of language
over density and ambiguity, they were simultaneously attempting to reshape
individual tragedies and comedies so that they suited the Restoration conception
of each genre.[1] Though removing farcical elements, adding sentimental scenes and
heightening the importance of either wit or humour in the plays account for the
most significant changes made in these plays, the adapters also included diversions
in the forms of songs, dances, and spectacles, altered the nature of the trickery,
and, in at least one instance, lessened the role of nobility. Though none of the
adapters totally refashions Shakespeare's obviously Renaissance-Jacobean
comedy into a Restoration comedy, the flavor of the Restoration permeates each
alteration.

---

[1]Hazleton Spencer asserts repeatedly that Shakespeare's "fairy" way of writing comedy
did not accord at all with what the Restoration expected to see in a comedy. Hazleton Spencer,
Shakespeare Improv'd: The Restoration Versions in Quarto and on the Stage (New York:
Frederick Ungar Publishing Co., 1963). Some critics writing during the Restoration, including
Rymer and Malone, nevertheless, considered comedy to be his forte as well as his "chief delight"
(Hooker 433). The desire to better align Shakespeare's comedies with the Restoration ideal
nonetheless remained.

Songs, Revels, and Masques

The mechanical innovations of the late seventeenth century and the rise of the Italian opera influenced the adapters to provide extra entertainment in the midst of the plays. Leo Salingar notes the importance of songs, revels, and even masques in Shakespeare's original versions of the plays, as he comments:

> Moreover, in *Love's Labour Lost*, the *Dream*, *As You Like It*, and in *The Merry Wives* and *Twelfth Night*, such episodes are either made crucial to the unfolding of the plot, or set the tone of a large part of the play, or both. As a series of variations on the theme of the play within the play, these structural devices illustrate Shakespeare's interest in his own professional medium; at the same time, they illustrate his concern with the place of revels, pastime and comedy as such in the national life.

The inclusion of music, spectacle, and revelry does not apply to *The Merchant of Venice* and *Measure for Measure*. *The Merchant* has "scenes of revelry" which are only "marginal to the main plot, not central; while in *All's Well* and *Measure for Measure* there are no such scenes at all."[2]   In adapting three of the plays under consideration here, *Measure for Measure*, *Twelfth Night*, and *The Merchant of Venice*, Gildon, Burnaby, and Granville all add variety to the plot by including more songs and dances either by interspersing them throughout the play itself or by interrupting the action of the play in order to add a masque. John Dennis, who felt that its diversity was what made English comedy superior to classical comedy, significantly chose to adapt a Shakespearean play which already contained a spectacular masque, *The Merry Wives of Windsor*.

Charles Gildon, as usual, makes the most changes in his alteration of *Measure for Measure* as he adds "the Mask of Dido and Aeneas in four parts, a dialogue in song." Added to the play to provide diversity, the masque's inclusion

---

[2]Salingar, p. 301.

in the play is justified by Escalus who is hoping to melt Angelo's heart so that he will be merciful to Claudio, but, for Angelo, it becomes, interestingly enough, a possible diversion from the growing passion he feels for Isabella. Not content with catchy songs and sedate dances, as it mirrors the emotions raging in the bloodless deputy, Gildon's masque contains a "Dance of the Furies" at the end of which the "*Six* Furies *Sink*. *The four open the Cave fly up*" (*BBA* 16) in the second entertainment. The third entertainment makes use of extravagant machinery and has ships come on stage, undoubtedly to the wonder and awe of the audience. The fourth entertainment surpasses even that as "Phœbus Rises in his Chariot over the Sea. The Nereides Out of the Sea," followed by Venus who "descends in her Chariot," as "the Tritons rise out of the Sea" to perform what must have been an astonishing dance. The finale of the play, described only as a "grand dance" (*BBA* 48), must have exceeded all the other dances in vigor and excessive display. Shakespeare's *Measure for Measure* contrasts with only one song, "Take, O take those lips away" (*MM* 4.1.1-6), which a boy sings as Mariana comes onstage. Gildon includes the song in his play as well (*BBA* 31), with one minor change as Mariana's maid, rather than a boy, sings it.

Not as lucky in the production of his adaptation as Charles Gildon, William Burnaby wrote a masque for his version of *Twelfth Night*, which he called *Love Betray'd*, but, as he says in the Preface, "the House" neglected "to have it set to Musick," and the plans for the masque were abandoned. Without the masque, Burnaby's play actually contains less variety in the form of songs or dances than Shakespeare's original. Burnaby's, in fact, has only two songs, one when Cæsario sings "*If I hear* Orinda *swear*." (*LB* 14) and another as Emilia sings "Cloë *met Love for his Psiche in Fears* " (*LB* 21). In *Twelfth Night*, on the other hand, Shakespeare's clown sings four songs which serve as poetic commentary, "What is Love? 'Tis not hereafter" (*TN* 2.3.43-48), "Come away, come away death" (*TN* 2.4.50-65), "I am gone, sir" (*TN* 4.2.111-122), and "When that I was and a little tiny boy,/With a hey ho the wind and the rain" (*TN* 5.1. 376-395).

Burnaby nonetheless attempted to include more variety in his version of the play through the lost masque, which undoubtedly would have made extensive use of stage machinery, lush costumes, and fascinating dances. His own plays show his concern with diversity in comedy as his *Ladies' Visiting Day* not only has a boy sing "*Your Eyes*, Belinda, *you disarm*" (*LVD* 219), but the fourth act contains a dance by Moors, while a Bantam woman sings "*For mighty Love's unerring Dart.*" (*LVD* 250) followed in the fifth act by the song "Cloë *is divinely Fair*" (*LVD* 270). His earlier *Reform'd Wife*, not as diverse as far as entertainment is concerned, contains only a poem, "A Song upon a Sickly Lady" (*RW* 7), read by Cleremont and one song by Sylvia, "Fond Woman with mistaken Art" (*RW* 16). The nature of this play does not allow for as much extravagance, as the subplot deals with a hypochrondriac in this play whereas the one in *The Ladies' Visiting Day* deals with the necessarily flamboyant courtship of a woman who worships the exotic.

In *The Merchant of Venice*, the original entertainment was only minimally connected with the plot. Shakespeare's version includes one song, "Tell me where is fancy bred" (*MV* 3.2.63-72) and at Portia's return in the final scene the music which provides a backdrop for Jessica and Lorenzo's lovemaking, Granville alters the play by including an opulent spectacle in the form of a four-part masque of *Peleus and Thetis*. Not quite as extravagant as Gildon's masque, Granville's nonetheless shows Prometheus "chain'd to a Rock with the Vulture at his Breast" (*JV* 14) after which "the Vulture drops dead at the feet of *Prometheus*, his Chains fall off, and he is borne up to Heaven with *Jupiter.*" Both scenes are accompanied by "a loud Flourish of all the Instruments" (*JV* 19). In Granville's version the masque serves as Antonio's *bon voyage* entertainment to wish his friend Bassanio luck in his endeavor in Belmont. The masque also serves a dramatic purpose as it reflects a situation similar to Bassanio's by depicting the aid Proteus gives his friend Peleus in obtaining the favor of his love, Thetis, and the difficulties which arise from their union.

Though not as lavish as that in his *Jew of Venice*, Granville's *She-Gallants* also contains a variety of entertainment. The third act contains a song in dialogue composed by Angelica in her role as courtier to Lady Dorimen. Aside from diversion, the entertainment also provides commentary on Angelica's predicament with Philabel while it serves as the introduction to a discussion on wit in the following scene. Later in the act, she calls for the dancers who pirouette to the song, "*So well* Corinna *likes the Joy*" (*SG* 41).

Since the climax of *The Merry Wives of Windsor* is a masque, John Dennis was already provided with all the spectacle necessary to please even a Restoration audience. In his version of the play, therefore, he does not add any songs or dances. His own play, *A Plot and No Plot*, does evince his concern for variety in comedy. In the third act a boy enters and sings "When Cloë, I your Charms survey" (*PNP* 40-41) as Batt informs the "Countess" of his courtship of her daughter, and in the fourth act when Bull, Sr., is carried away by the officers, Baldernoe calls for the "Fiddles" so they can "rejoyce" over their "good success." A dance ensues followed by a drinking song composed by Wycherley, "A merry Cup, faith let me drink" (*PNP* 60-61). Like his predecessors, Dennis makes a half-hearted attempt to weave these songs and dances into the pattern of the play. No matter how hard the adapters try to integrate song, dance, and spectacle in their alterations, Shakespeare undoubtedly accomplishes the most successful incorporation of spectacle in any of these plays, an incorporation best exemplified in *The Merry Wives*, whose masque furnishes the climax to the play in addition to providing colorful songs and dances as well as the chance for pyrotechnics.

Mistaken Identity, Disguises, Trickery, and Errors

Never utterly dependent upon a variety of entertainment, comedy can exist apart from any songs, dances or spectacles whatsoever. Mistaken identities, disguises, trickery and errors, on the other hand, are virtually indispensable elements of sixteenth and seventeenth century comedy. Leo Salingar views

Shakespeare's comedies as an intermingling of the medieval, pastoral form of comedy[3] he had witnessed as a youth with plays based on "the fundamental classical notion of comedy as a matter of 'errors' due to trickery, disguise or fortune," adding that "these principles, with the latent awareness they carry of play-acting within the play, mark the distinctive feature of comedy in general, the difference between comedy and romance."

Each of the adapters, with the exclusion this time of Charles Gildon, chooses either to change the nature of the deception or trickery in the play or to carry the deception further than Shakespeare initially had in the main plot, and their own plays depend as extensively as Shakespeare's versions on deception and trickery in the unravelling of the story. Gildon removes most of the comic elements from his version of *Measure for Measure*, but the trickery which is an integral part of Shakespeare's play remains untouched in his version. In both plays, the Duke passes as a friar in order to observe the way in which Angelo administers the laws the Duke himself has allowed to fall into disuse, and Mariana is substituted for Isabella to trap Angelo into an acknowledgement of the necessity of mercy by forcing him into an admission of his own frailty.

Burnaby also retains the trickery Shakespeare provides in *Twelfth Night* but adds to it in his version of the play. Although her masquerade is forced upon her in *Twelfth Night* due to her shipwreck, Viola chooses to disguise herself as a boy in *Love Betray'd* so that she can be near the man she loves. The success of her disguise also is dependent in both cases on the existence of an identical twin brother. The cozening of Malvolio and Sir Toby's deception of Sir Andrew Aguecheek also remain a part of Burnaby's play but are changed in *Love Betray'd* by being combined and thereby receiving less emphasis in the plot, as Drances gulls Taquilet into believing Villaretta loves him. Burnaby increases the use of

---

[3]Ibid., p. 300. *The Second Shepherd's Play*, for example, certainly exhibits the importance of trickery and disguise in comedy.

trickery by having Viola take on an additional disguise when she pretends to be a physician so that she can delve into Villaretta's motive for consistently refusing Moreno.

Trickery and deception are also essential elements of Burnaby's *Reform'd Wife* and *Ladies' Visiting Day*. The main conflict of both depends entirely on deception. In *The Reform'd Wife*, Astrea pretends to hate men so she can carry on her intrigues without any interference from Sir Solomon, and in *The Ladies' Visiting Day*, Polidore pretends to court Lady Dolt to provide an opportunity for him to be near her jealously guarded niece, Fulvia. Burnaby uses trickery to an even greater extent in *The Ladies' Visiting Day*. As Polidore is deceiving Lady Dolt, Lady Dolt believes herself to be deceiving Sir Testy who, in turn, believes his wife to be safe as long as she is in the company of Polidore, whom he believes to be a eunuch. Even in the subplot of this play, Burnaby utilizes disguise in Courtine's masquerade as Prince Alexander, which so totally confounds Lady Lovetoy that she agrees to marry him almost as soon as he comes on stage.

The Merchant of Venice, like Shakespeare's other comedies, depends heavily on deception. Like Gildon, George Granville makes very few changes in the nature of the trickery in his version, *The Jew of Venice*. He does carry the deception on longer at the end of the play than Shakespeare does, as he has Portia and Nerissa further torture their husbands with the spectre of infidelity. In eliminating the role of Lancelot Gobbo, Granville, unlike either Burnaby or Gildon, removes a scene of deception, in this instance one in which the clown deceives his old, blind father.

The She-Gallants is proof that Granville nonetheless believed in the value of deception in comedy, as the entire play centers on the deception of Bellamour by Angelica and of Frederick by Constantia. In this play the two ladies pretend to be men so effectively that Angelica fools the lecherous Lady Dorimen into wooing her while Constantia receives the adulation of Frederick's four sisters. The errors which arise from the masquerades wreak havoc with the libidos as well as the hearts of the deceived ladies while they provide raucous entertainment for the audience.

John Dennis makes several changes in the kind of trickery employed in *The Comical Gallant*. The deception in his version of the play, first of all, is more conscious on the part of Fenton and Mrs. Ford. Shakespeare's merry wives decide more or less on the spur of the moment that they are going to avenge themselves on Falstaff by fooling him into believing Mrs. Ford is receptive of his attentions. Dennis' Fenton sets the whole plot in motion by informing Falstaff that Mrs. Ford and Mrs. Page are madly in love with him. The initial deception of Falstaff in Shakespeare's version is self-deception as he convinces himself that the ladies desire him. In both plays Mrs. Ford consciously deceives her husband in order to cure him of his jealousy. In Dennis' play she also deceives the Pages by aiding her nephew and Anne Page, a function performed by Mistress Quickly in *The Merry Wives*. The trickery of Caius and Slender both in the lapse of communication over the location of the duel as well as in the elopement is unchanged in Dennis, although he has the two "marry" each other rather than two young boys as is true in Shakespeare. A major change in Dennis' play is the disguise taken by Mrs. Page as Captain Dingboy which serves as the other punishment of Falstaff and takes the place of his masquerade as the old woman of Brentford in Shakespeare's version. In making this change, Dennis takes one of Shakespeare's few comedies in which a woman, interestingly enough, does not pretend to be a man, but in which at least five men dress up as women and adds a scene in which one of the female leads does disguise herself as a man.

A Plot and No Plot similarly revolves around deception. Belvil sets up a sham conspiracy to entangle his uncle Bull so that he can obtain Bull's approval to let him marry Sylvia. In the course of the play Belvil has Baldernoe, obviously a rogue and scoundrel, act the part of a French marquis; two prostitutes pretend to be an English countess and her daughter; and a host of other friends disguise themselves as officers of the law. He tricks Batt Bull into marrying one of the prostitutes and fools Bull, Sr., into believing that he is incarcerated first in Newgate, then in Bedlam.

The changes most of the adapters effect in the area of trickery and errors is in making the deception more conscious and voluntary, also the case in their own plays. The alteration may not necessarily result in a more classically correct comedy, though in the case of *The Comical Gallant* it does as Fenton's machinations unify the action in the play. Without exception it does result in a more manipulated play robbed of its spontaneity and natural exuberance.

Although classical comedies dealt exclusively with the common man, Restoration critics affirm the efficacy of using the upper classes and even nobility in their comedies since, in their opinion, the audience is more interested in those above them than those below them in social stature. According to Salingar, Shakespeare had begun this trend in his plays either by adding "a ruler in nearly every comedy" (with the exception of *The Merry Wives of Windsor* and *The Taming of the Shrew*), raising the rank of a ruler already included in the source, or giving the ruler "a much more active and prominent part."[4]

The adapters, despite the classical conventions, do not make extensive changes dealing with the role of nobility in the plays, but, interestingly, all four people their own plays with ordinary citizens. In altering *Measure for Measure*, which, in Salingar's words, "opens and continues as a play about government,"[5] Gildon, who generally aligns himself most closely with classical criticism, makes no attempt to lessen the role of the Duke, and the other characters, Isabella, Claudio, Julietta, and Angelo, are all wealthy and apparently of high rank in his version as well as in Shakespeare's. His tragedy *The Roman Bride's Revenge* deals specifically with nobility as it should according to classical rules and, in fact, contains no character of lower rank than Perennius and Lætus, cronies of the

---

[4]Ibid., p. 300; p. 253.

Emperor.

Burnaby also retains the noble rank of Moreno in his *Love Betray'd*;
however, in his *Reform'd Wife* and *Ladies' Visiting Day* he deals with the foibles
of the wealthy but not nobility.   In both instances some of the characters are
"cits," *nouveau riche*.   Sir Testy's origins are obvious in his change of address.
He bemoans this change from the merchant section to the fashionable side of
town, a change which signals a corresponding rise in society, "what a Pox made
me leave *Threadneedle street* ! Right Vertuous wou'd have it so; she must be near
St. James Park and *White's* Chocolate-house" (*RW* 233).   Others, members of the
upper classes, Philabel and Freeman, for instance, associate so closely with the
merchant classes represented in Sir Solomon and Sir Testy, that they must be on
the very fringes of the *haut ton*.

The same is true of Granville's adaptation, *The Jew of Venice*, and his own
play, *The She-Gallants*. Like Shakespeare, he includes the appearance of the Doge
in the trial scene. All Granville's characters are extremely wealthy, but evidently
not of the stature of Shakespeare's. Unlike her counterpart in *The Merchant of
Venice*, Granville's Portia does not number among her suitors the princes of
Morocco and Aragon but instead receives the unwelcome attentions of a mere
French count, English gentleman, and "*My Heer van Gutts*" a drunken Dutchman.
The lower class of Portia's suitors surely indicates a similar lower rank of the rest
of the characters.   The characters of *The She-Gallants*, Angelica, Bellamour,
Constantia, and Frederick, like Granville's Portia and Bassanio, are obviously
well-bred people, but by no means nobility, and in this play Granville includes no
one of higher rank than they are.

Once again, Dennis' choice of a play left him little to "correct." *The Merry
Wives of Windsor* is one of two Shakespearean plays without a ruler. Dennis
removes even the slightest reference to nobility in the play by not mentioning the
relationship between Fenton and Prince Hal as Page's major objection to his union

[5]Ibid.

with Anne and by eliminating the fairies' reference to the Queen and Windsor Castle in the masque. The characters in *A Plot and No Plot* are, once again, ordinary though wealthy citizens. Bull, Sr., made his fortune in trade, but his family are social climbers as is evident in Batt's pretensions to the woman he believes to be the daughter of a Countess. In his pose as Viscount Dorant, Batt exposes his father to the "Countess" as "a strange, humoursom, obstinate, old scoundrel and a paulltry Cit, the Devil take me to boot" (*PNP* 42). Sylvia and Belvil, a little more refined, more on the level of the Angelicas and Philabels in the other adapters' plays, are still obviously not nobility.

Measure for Measure becomes in Gildon's hands less of a comedy and more of a play in the heroic mode. The rank of the persons involved, also, is the very foundation of the play: without the moral dilemma posed to a man who wields great power, the play would not exist. Moreno, in Burnaby's *Love Betray'd*, is only incidentally royalty. No aspect of the plot really depends on his station in life. Here again Burnaby's disregard of classical edicts is apparent. Granville and Dennis make a slight attempt to bring their plays in line with classical conventions as Granville keeps the relatively unimportant appearance of the Doge, but changes Portia's suitors to minor nobility and mere gentlemen, and Dennis eliminates all explicit reference to nobility although his play is still situated in Windsor, near the castle.

The Preëminence of Humour over Wit

Diversity, trickery and errors, and low versus high characters all provided the matter of debate over comedy during the Restoration. The greatest question during that era remained the debate over the preëminence of wit or humour in comedy. Dryden, with his immense wisdom, eventually came to favor a melding of the two forms of comedy. Dennis, Gildon, Granville and Burnaby, in contrast, all avow the inherent superiority of humours comedy. Burnaby concisely states the majority opinion in a letter:

In Comedy also the chief Thing is the Fable, or Plot; the Excellence of which is to bring in such Characters and Incidents, as may naturally produce *Humour.* There will yet be room enough for *Wit;* but that Comick Poet, that makes *Wit* and (what we call) *Dialogue,* his chief Aim, ought to write nothing but Dialogues, for he can never obtain the Name of a Dramatick Writer, with the best Judges.[6]

Gildon's stand on the humour and wit controversy remains unclear even after close examination of his adaptation of *Measure for Measure* as he eliminates both equally from his play, replacing the comic with the sentimental. Deleted, for instance, are examples of wit such as the repartee of act one scene two as well as humours characters like Lucio, who has a penchant for creating and repeating gossip to belittle his superiors. Gildon's criticism also shows little or no concern with the superiority of humour over wit in comedy, as he focuses primarily on tragedy. In his *Complete Art of Poetry*, Gildon relegates humour to comedy and defines it as a "subordinate or weaker Passion." Practically the only other reference to humour in Gildon is his advice to the playwright: "Your characters must maintain the same *Humour*, Affectation, & c. thro' the whole Play, which they shew the Audience at the opening of the very first scene." [7] Since he revised *Measure for Measure* in the heroic mode, Gildon did not need to be overly concerned with the controversy.

William Burnaby was able to write, in F. E. Budd's words, "genuine wit," yet he "held wit in excess to be a blemish rather than an adornment."[8] His adaptation of *Twelfth Night* does not present a good example of Burnaby's views as it contains relatively little true wit and sacrifices the real humours characters Sir

[6]Burnaby, p. 459.

[7]Gildon, *Complete Art*, p. 265.

Toby Belch, Sir Andrew Aguecheek, and Malvolio for their pale imitations, Drances and Taquilet. Burnaby's introduction of Pedro, Sebastian's hungry malcontent servant, shows his attention to humour but does not exhibit any ability on his part to represent that humour faithfully. Burnaby's misbegotten attempts at witty dialogue in *Love Betray'd* may, in fact, tip the balance in favor of wit in this play. He expurgates Shakespeare's true wit, evident in such passages as Olivia's first appearance onstage:

> *Clo.* Wit, an't be thy will, put me into good fooling! Those wits that think they have thee do very oft prove fools, and I that am sure I lack thee may pass for a wise man. For what says Quinapalus?–'Better a witty fool than a foolish wit.' God bless thee, lady!
>
> *Oli.* Take the fool away.
>
> *Clo.* Do not you hear, fellows? Take away the lady.
>
> *Oli..* Go to, you are a dry fool. I'll no more of you. Besides, you grow dishonest.
>
> *Clo.* Two faults, madonna, that drink and good counsel will amend, for give the dry fool drink, then is the fool not dry; bid the dishonest man mend himself: if he mend, he is no longer dishonest; if he cannot, let the botcher mend him. Anything that's mended is but patched. Virtue that transgresses is but patched with sin, and sin that amends is but patched with virtue. If that this simple syllogism will serve, so. If it will not, what remedy? As there is no true cuckold but calamity, so beauty's a flower. The lady bade take away the fool, therefore I say again, take her away.

After this lengthy discussion of wit and foolishness, Feste proceeds to prove Olivia a fool:

[8]Budd, p. 102.

> *Clo.* Good madonna, why mournest thou?
>
> *Oli.* Good fool, for my brother's death.
>
> *Clo.* I think his soul is in hell, madonna.
>
> *Oli.* I know his soul is in heaven, fool.
>
> *Clo.* The more fool, madonna, to mourn for your brother's soul,
>
> being in heaven. Take away the fool, gentlemen. (*TN* 1.5.28-62)

Burnaby replaces this dialogue with his own idea of wit as Emilia and Villaretta
discuss Villaretta's widowhood.

> *Vill.* . . . . The greatest Happiness of our Lives, is to have got free
> from the Mens Dominion very early; they are all Tyrants–
>
> *Em.* If the Piece be as bad as your Pattern.
>
> *Vill.* It must be so; all Husbands are the same; Love makes 'em our
> Prisoners, and Jealousy our Goalers; so between these two, a poor
> Woman has no quiet–
>
> *Em.* Till they are dead.
>
> *Vill.* Ha! ha! right *Emilia*, the grave gives more people rest than
> those it holds–take care you don't want that comfort.
>
> *Em.* I fear it not–because you have burnt your Mouth, shan't keep
> me from tasting–I'll venture upon a Man, in spite of all the Terror
> upon him–in the Province of Italy, too.
>
> *Vill.* The worst Place in the World to marry in; if one wou'd be a
> Mistress, I shou'd choose *Italy*; If a Wife, *England*, but a Maid
> shou'd live in *France*, for there she may have all the Enjoyments of
> the other two and keep her character.
>
> *Em.* Upon such terms indeed one might live a Maid all ones life.
>
> *Vill.* Ha! ha! without repining at leading Apes hereafter. (*LB* 2-3)

The difference in these two passages is startling. Shakespeare's fool links his
metaphors subtly, moving from the "dry" fool to the "mending" metaphor
effortlessly, though he depends heavily on the wordplay Dryden disdains for

comic effect. Even in the puns Shakespeare is commenting on the very act of punning, and in so doing, Feste's nonsense becomes perfect sense, as he has told Olivia it will. Only in the final two metaphors does he throw in something totally unrelated and apparently senseless. In the very next exchange, he is easily able to show Olivia that she is mourning for her brother unreasonably. Burnaby's metaphors, on the other hand, are not only mixed unmercifully but consist primarily of clichés.

Humour does fare better in Burnaby's own plays, particularly in the characterizations of Sir Testy Dolt, the typically jealous husband who guards his wife from every man except the one he should fear the most, and Sir Solomon Empty, who gleefully advises Freeman on how to conduct his affair not knowing that Freeman's love is Sir Solomon's own wife, Astrea. Most of the minor characters in both *The Ladies' Visiting Day* and *The Reform'd Wife* are similarly humours characters. Their humours are fairly evident in their names: Captain Strut, Sir Thrifty Gripe, Saunter, Lady Weepwell, Lady Sobmuch, Lady Drawle, Lady Dainty, Careless, and Mrs. Friendlove.

The abundance of humour in Burnaby's *Ladies' Visiting Day* and *Reform'd Wife* does not denote an absence of wit. In these three plays, Burnaby is able to achieve a pleasing balance so that the wit either rises directly from the humour of the particular character or depends upon the humour of another. Careless' revelation of the character of women to Freeman is typical:

> *Car.* No Sir, but I never knew a Design fail where a Woman was the Ingineer–the Plots that don't succeed are made by Men.
>
> *Fre.* Ay, but there is more in it thanThou art aware of–how if it shake my Interest with the Fortune?
>
> *Car.* 'Tis impossible, for when once a Woman loves, nothing Cures her but Glutting.
>
> *Fre.* Yet a modest Woman will be startled at such Galantries.
>
> *Car.* In appearance she may, but a wild Man has always their

secret approbation, and every Woman has the Vanity to think she can keep him to her self.

Fre. Do'ye think so?

Car. And hope you'll find so–I never doubt a thing that depends on a Woman's Opinion of her self, for Nature has so order'd it that every one is prepar'd to believe whatever we can say of 'em.

Fre. Did you find her Maid of that Humour?

Car. She wou'd not listen to me because she did not like me (I pity her Judgment) but I never knew a Woman refuse a Man that she lik'd–when they don't Fancy, they are very Saucy and very Vertuous (*LVD* 33).

One feature that consistently characterizes Burnaby's successful use of wit is the avoidance of metaphor and figurative language.

George Granville's *Jew of Venice* takes its wit (much abridged) and humour directly from *The Merchant of Venice*. His Shylock is the same miser as Shakespeare's, drawn in slightly bolder strokes since much of the dialogue that elicits empathy for Shylock is cut. Almost all the comic moments in *The Jew of Venice*, few and far between though they be–even the comic account of Shylock's reaction to Jessica's elopement is axed–arise from Shylock's humour. About the only exception is the greatly shortened description of Portia's other suitors, witty in Shakespeare, abbreviated to two or three lines apiece so that only remnants of wit remain in Granville's version. With the excision of Launcelot Gobbo, Granville removes another source of wit from the play.

Granville's *She-Gallants* contains more humour and more wit than his *Jew of Venice*. Humour comes in the shape of several characters. Sir Toby Cusifle is the typical old pimp ever anxious to aid the young men in their amorous endeavors. Sir John Aery and Vaunter are the obnoxious braggarts, so full of their own self-importance that they mistake repulses by others as signs of encouragement. Sir John and Vaunter unwittingly reveal their true characters to the audience:

> *Sir J. Aery.* . . . Now I never take any thing for an Affront. If a Man calls me a Son of a Whore, Beged I always take it for a mark of familiarity and kindness. If any one kicks, or gives me a Box on the Ear, I take it all in good part. A very good Jest, i'faith, and I laugh till I hold my sides.
>
> *Vaun.* Thou'rt i'th' right, Beged; for why the Devil shou'd I suppose any Man would affront a Man of my Parts? Beged, 'tis a less'ning of one's self, and I thank thee, dear *Jecky*, from my Soul, for reforming me in this Error. (*SG* 17)

Witty dialogue also makes up a great part of the play, though it is integrated fairly well into the plot so that it does not seem to be merely a collection of epigrams as is true of Burnaby's *Love Betray'd*.

One of the major criticisms levelled at Dennis' *Comical Gallant* when it was first presented was that it did not contain "much Wit." Dennis countered the criticism by noting that if Wit is lacking in the play, "there is Humour every where," and humour is a commodity to be prized in a comedy since "the business of a Comick Poet is to shew his Characters and not himself." [9] Like Shakespeare in *The Merry Wives*, Dennis bases the play primarily on the humours of Sir John Falstaff, the quintessential braggart, and Mr. Ford, the jealous husband, and secondarily on the "cholerick" Dr. Caius, the foolish Slender, and that venerable wordsmith, Parson Evans. Dennis does delete the scene which has Evans giving William Page a lesson in Latin, a scene which derives its comedy from wordplay, frowned on by Restoration critics. Dennis also cuts a few witty observations, for instance, Falstaff's "I fear not Goliath with a weaver's beam, because I know also life is a shuttle" (*MW* 5.1.22-3) as well as Ford's "I will rather trust a Fleming

[9]Dennis, "Large Account," vol.1, p. 281.

with my butter, Parson Hugh the Welshman with my cheese, an Irishman with my aqua-vitae bottle, or a thief to walk my ambling gelding, than my wife with herself" (*MW* 2.2.265-268). Shakespeare's play, on the whole contains very little of what the Restoration critic saw as true wit, and it, like *The Comical Gallant*, is mainly dependent on the exposition of the humours of the characters to provide comedy.

The same is true of Dennis' *A Plot and No Plot*, which hinges on Bull, Sr.'s avarice and love of intrigue and Bull, Jr.'s self-importance. Any wit which arises comes directly from characterization, as in Belvil's assertion, made while reflecting on the paradoxical foolishness and gravity of his uncle, that "a Gown and Gravity frequently disguise a Blockhead. Folly has its Hypocrisie as well as Vice, and it is as common a thing to see a Sot grave, as a Villain Devout . . . . As if Wisdom maliciously sat on his outside on purpose to inform the world that he is an Ass within" (*PNP* 6). Dennis was not totally averse to the use of wit as is obvious in the repartee engaged in by Belvil and Sylvia which focuses on the difference between a wit and a fool:

> *Belv.* . . . An humble Fool is one of God's creatures and consequently very good; Ignorance and stupidity are Nature's follies, and Nature is always lovely; But Affectation is a Coxcomb's own.
>
> *Sylv.* Nay, we have certainly reason to bear with your downright Fool, for native Folly is a necessary foyl, and serves to set off the Brilliant [*sic*] of Wit, but Affectation is false and counterfeits it, to cheat us of our good opinions. (*PNP* 23)

Though Burnaby, Granville, and Dennis each may prefer humour over wit, none of them can avoid including wit in their own comedies. They seem to be more successful in excluding Shakespeare's wit or in tampering with it until it no longer resembles wit. Their goal of having virtually all the comedy emanating directly from characterization is, once again, best captured by Shakespeare himself in his

Merry Wives of Windsor.

The Elimination of Low Comedy and Farce

Although the Restoration critics preferred the exhibition of humour over wit in comedy, they were almost unanimous in disliking farce. This exclusion of farce from the alterations marks one of the most significant changes made by the adapters. Lane Cooper and Robert Hume, in fact, both see the removal of farcical elements from comedy in the Restoration as the feature which most distinguishes Restoration and Shakespearean comedy. Cooper contrasts "the broad humor of the Elizabethans and the innuendo of a Congreve."[10] Hume remarks that Shakespeare's comedy "reflected the whole of life–the serious, the romantic, the farcical. The comedy of manners, on the other hand, largely confined itself to the artificial gaiety of a fashionable coterie," and in so doing, it had "to pay a heavy price for cutting itself off from the rough business of ordinary life."[11] With the elimination of the lowest comedy from Shakespeare's plays, the adaptations, therefore, become more like Restoration comedies by undergoing the metamorphosis into comedies of manners.

Dryden once again provides the best argument against farce and low comedy in general in his Preface to *An Evening's Love.* He comments that "low comedy especially requires, on the writer's part, much of conversation with the vulgar: and much of ill nature in the observation of their follies," and he refers to farce as "forced humours, and unnatural events."[12] William Burnaby's letter to Congreve (1695) shows even greater distaste for low comedy and farce, in particular. Like Dryden, Burnaby calls farce "unnatural," and compares it to "sick Men's Dreams, compos'd of Parts that no man can reduce to one Body." His

[10]Cooper, p. 25.

[11]Hume, p. 278.

major complaint against farce is that it sacrifices realism and character development for the sake of what the modern playwright calls the "one-liner." Writers of farce, according to Burnaby, "run out of Nature to make you laugh; as if Comedy was only to make us laugh at the Folly of the Poet."[13]

The adapters apparently made little distinction between low comedy and farce, for they effectively rid the plays of both. Shakespeare's *Measure for Measure*, though it has a serious import and deals primarily with the ruling classes, also finds room for the horseplay, puns, and farce provided by Pompey, Justice Shallow, Elbow and Lucio. Gildon takes this play, removes the low characters and winds up with something that is not quite comedy, not quite tragedy, and not even sentimental comedy or tragicomedy. The following exchange from *Measure for Measure* contains the use of low characters, catachresis, and puns the Restoration playwright avoids:

> Angelo: How now, sir? What's your name? And what's the matter?
>
> Elbow: If it please your honour, I am the poor Duke's constable, and my name is Elbow. I do lean upon justice, sir; and do bring in here before your good honour two notorious benefactors.
>
> Angelo: Benefactors? Well! What benefactors are they? Are they not malefactors?
>
> Elbow: If it please your honour, I know not well what they are; but precise villains they are, that I am sure of, and void of all profanation in the world that good Christians ought to have.
>
> Escalus: This comes off well; here's a wise officer!
>
> Angelo: Go to, what quality are they of? Elbow is your name? Why dost thou not speak, Elbow?

[12]Dryden, *An Evening's*, vol.1, p. 145.

[13] Burnaby, Letter to Congreve, in *The Complete Dramatic Works of William Burnaby*, ed. F. E. Budd (London: E. Partridge; The Scholartis Press, 1931), pp. 458-59.

Pompey: He cannot, sir; he's out at elbow. (*MM* 2.1. 44-56)

Gildon eliminates this scene and all similar to it from his version of the play.

Low comedy is interspersed throughout *Twelfth Night*; the most notable instance perhaps is the cross-gartering scenes 2.3 and 3.4 in which Emilia and Sir Toby convince Malvolio to humiliate himself by dressing outlandishly in order to impress Olivia. Although Burnaby has Sir Toby's counterpart, Drances, convince Taquilet that Villaretta loves him, he eliminates most of the buffoonery accompanying the deception, retaining only the scene in which Taquilet and Drances attempt to duel with Cæsario. By replacing Malvolio as well as Sir Andrew Aguecheek with Taquilet, Burnaby in effect rids the play of its most comical moments.

Burnaby also eliminates the clown and the servant Fabian, but he adds Sebastian's servant Pedro, who can only think of his stomach. The following scene indicates Burnaby's idea of low comedy:

> Sebastian: Hold your grumbling, Rascal! you shall Eat presently.
>
> Pedro: Sir, you command me intirely–If I was a Woman at this time, that would stop my mouth–All my fear was Sir, that if I had dy'd here, the Serchers would a mistook, my Disease, and laid a Courtiers death to my charge; the Gout, or the merry Consumption! No body'd a thought of a Souldiers death, Starving! because I have Money in my Pocket, and a Shirt on.
>
> Sebastian: Hum! a very useful amusement!
>
> Pedro: Alas! Sir, 'twas worse than that for to divert my Spleen–
>
> Sebastian: Your Spleen Scoundrel!
>
> Pedro: My Hunger Sir, which is the same Distemper in Younger Brothers– . (*LB* 41)

A mercenary malcontent throughout the play, Pedro receives well-earned verbal and physical abuse from both Sebastian and Villaretta. A drunken Pedro comes staggering onstage in the final act. When Villaretta asks him which of the two "Cæsario's" is his master, he responds, "My Master Madam! Why you're the only Woman in *Venice*, by this time that don't know my Master" (*LB* 58) only to have her strike him when he continues to refer to his master's incontinence. The low comedy included in *Love Betray'd* differs from that of *Twelfth Night* in being more violent, more lewd, and more separated from the main action of the play.

Burnaby's only attempt at low comedy in *The Ladies' Visiting Day* is the beating Captain Strut receives from Polidore and Sir Testy. Polidore reacts violently when he realizes the true identity of his rival for Fulvia's hand. As he observes the braggadocio, Polidore asks him if he is not Captain Strut to which Strut responds, "Ay, Sir, and as good a Family— "Incensed by Strut's pretensions, Polidore exclaims, "As ever was caned Sirrah! was not you my Footman at the Revolution? I'll cool your Love," and then "(*Beats him.*)" (*LVD* 246). In Burnaby's earlier play, *The Reform'd Wife*, on the other hand, Mrs. Friendlove provides some low comedy, particularly when she comes onstage at the end of the play. Fully believing that Freeman is going to marry her, she prances in dressed in her wedding apparel to pronounce a curse upon the nuptials between Freeman and Clarinda:

> Friendlove: You false ungrateful Fellow, to serve a Woman of my Relations so. (*Aside*) But this damn'd Jade to make me wait so long: She was an hour looking for my false Teeth, if I had layn in 'em as I us'd to do at my Lady *Topers*, all had been well–I'll turn her away immediately–but first I wish you all jealous, when you have no reason, and secure when you have, and may every Body think your Wives Handsome, but your selves; and may your Children be as dull as if they were lawfully begot. (*RW* 44)

The courtship between Cleremont and Lady Dainty provides some physical comedy, especially when Cleremont finally takes charge and carries her off as she simultaneously struggles and embraces him (*RW* 35).

Like Gildon in *Measure for Measure*, Granville removes all the low comedy from his version of *The Merchant of Venice* by eliminating Launcelot Gobbo. The losses to the play include Launcelot's "confusions" of his blind father:

> Launcelot: [*Aside* .] O heavens, this is my true-begotten father
> who, being more than sand-blind–high gravel-blind–knows me not.
> I will try confusions with him.
>
> Gobbo: Master young gentleman, I pray you which is the way
> to Master Jew's?
>
> Launcelot: Turn up on your right hand at the next turning, but at
> the next turning of all on your left, marry at the very next turning,
> turn of no hand but turn down indirectly to the Jew's house.
>
> Gobbo: Be God's sonties, 'twill be a hard way to hit. Can you
> tell me whether one Launcelot that dwells with him dwell with him
> or no? (*MV* 2.2.28-39)

Other deletions include Lancelot's contorted reasoning concerning Jessica's legitimacy along with his assertion that Lorenzo should not have converted her because the conversion of Jews will raise the price of pork (*MV* 3.5.17-21). Serious in tone until the end when the couples quibble over the rings, Granville's version has no place for such tomfoolery.

Unlike his adaptation of *The Merchant of Venice*, Granville's *She-Gallants* contains at least one instance of low comedy in the midst of its witty dialogues. Always boasting of their numerous amorous encounters, Vaunter and Aery come to court Lucinda, but instead are treated to incarceration in a closet. The audience first learns of their imprisonment when the two are brought back on stage "*ty'd down in two Chairs*" as they bemoan their past lives in Sir John's parenthetical, "O *Vaunter, Vaunter*! What a miserable Life is a Whoremasters?" (*SG* 62) *The*

She-Gallants does not deal with any important topics such as the tension between justice and mercy, the tension which informs and gives shape to *The Jew of Venice*. Granville obviously had no trouble with including low comedy and farce in a play based upon the romantic relationships between two ordinary couples, an important topic, but not a weighty one, like the dispensing of justice.

John Dennis originally designed his own *Plot and No Plot* as a farce, but decided instead to write it as low comedy due to the significance of the subject. Although his version of *A Comical Gallant* does not have the serious impact that he seems to feel his own play does, Dennis nonetheless eliminated some of the broader comedy in the play in order to place more stress on the lesson Falstaff and Ford receive. Dennis eliminates, for instance, Falstaff's masquerade as the old woman of Brentford, in which guise he ironically encounters a much-deserved beating by Ford, the cozening of the Host by the Germans, Mistress Quickly's malapropisms, and the amusing lesson of William Page by Evans. Dennis retains, on the other hand, Falstaff's ludicrous escape in the buckbasket. The masque, hilarious in Shakespeare, becomes less funny in Dennis' version with Ford as the recipient of the pinches and taunts of the fairies but does provide physical comedy in both versions.

The importance of the story each play has to tell appears to determine whether the adapter excludes low comedy and farce from it. Each adaptation shows some reduction in the number of low characters as well as instances of broad or physical comedy. The more serious the topic, as in *The Jew of Venice* and *Measure for Measure*, the less low comedy the adapters include in their versions of the play. Unity of atmosphere seems to be the controlling factor in the exclusion or inclusion of farcical elements in the altered versions.

Tragicomedy and Sentimental Comedy

If the Restoration disliked farce, it paradoxically held tragicomedy and, especially, sentimental comedy in esteem. Perhaps initially a defense against

Jeremy Collier's attack on the theatre, sentimental comedy gave the playwright a chance to show ideal characters who were able to overcome great obstacles in their pursuit of happiness.

One of Shakespeare's problem plays, *Measure for Measure*, begins as tragicomedy which Gildon transforms by heightening the sentimental element. The brief scene in which Julietta appears is moving, but subtle rather than bathetic, as she willingly takes the larger share of the blame in the clandestine marriage. Julietta confesses that her "sin" was "of heavier kind than his"(*MM* 2.3.30), repents of it and takes "the shame with joy" (*MM* 2.3.38). The most emotional moment in her appearance onstage occurs after she learns that Claudio is to die the following day: "Must die tomorrow? O injurious law,/That respites me a life whose very comfort/Is still a dying horror!"(*MM* 2.3.39-41). Gildon's Isabella, not content with a simple expression of grief, goes into spasms:

> Must die to morrow! Oh, injurious Love!
>
> That dost the Life of my sad Life remove,
>
> Yet doom'st me still to agonizing Breath,
>
> And barr'st me from the sweet Retreat of Death!
>
> O, Heav'n! my *Claudio* to these Arms restore;
>
> Or when he dies, O let me be no more! (*BBA* 20)

Gildon also interpolates a scene between Claudio and Julietta to wring the last ounce of sentimentality from the situation. In this extremely maudlin scene, each attempts to bear the burden of the guilt, forbidding the other the comfort of sharing even the bond of culpability:

> Julietta: Oh! Can'st thou love! And yet forbid my grief?
>
> Thou deal'st not by me with the Rule of Justice.
>
> Would'st thou not grieve were I to dye like thee?
>
> Yes, yes, thou wou'd'st, my *Claudio*, for my shame,
>
> Tho fortify'd with innocence, just now
>
> Shook thy dear Soul with Agonies of Grief.

> And wilt thou rob me then of the sad Priviledge
>
> Of my misfortunes?
>
> No I will grieve as long as I have life,
>
> For Life has no joys t'appease my sorrows.
>
> What can I see thee leaving me for ever?
>
> For ever! oh dismal! cursed sound!
>
> And part without a pang or tear!
>
> No I'll indulge so just a grief, and melt,
>
> Dissolve into a watry Deluge, that shall
>
> Bear down the damms of Life, and drown my Woe. (*BBA* 37)

Claudio begs her to be "moderate" in her grief since he is only going, as he tells her, "to make ready a retreat for thee," but she responds with "Oh! oh! my heart." then "*Weeps, and shews great sorrow and impatience.*" Claudio, as a result, breaks down with "Good Heaven assist thee, for thy grief unmans me./And I dissolve in tears too, like a woman." In the process, the play "dissolves" into a standard weeping comedy.

Gildon's Claudio gives way to another sentimental outburst in his speech to Isabella. Whereas in Shakespeare's version Claudio asks Isabella to sacrifice her virtue to save his life, in Gildon's he begs her only to protect and guide Julietta and their child who will have to go on living without him. Scenes like this one are indicative not only of Gildon's, but also of the Restoration's penchant for the sentimental.

Gildon's *Roman Bride's Revenge* is a tragedy, not a comedy, and as such provides even more opportunity for scenes of excessive sentimentality and altruistic heroism. Especially evident in the love scenes between Portia and Martian, most notably the scene in which she desires to go into exile with him as well as the heroic, melodramatic death scene, the sentimental element pervades the whole of the play.

William Burnaby once again defies expectations by eliminating tragic and sentimental elements from his version of *Twelfth Night*. Where the initial situation of *Twelfth Night* rests on the shipwreck which landed Viola in Illyria and apparently drowned her brother (*TN* 1.2.3.), in *Love Betray'd*, Viola has willingly left her brother and their home to come to woo Moreno (*LB* 12). Far from being the sister so deeply affected by her brother's death that she has decided to retire from the world for a time, Villaretta is the hard, cynical widow who rejoices that her husband's death has freed her from tyranny (*LB* 21). The love-stricken Moreno (Orsino) shows a sceptical side in Burnaby as he observes to Cæsario that not only are women in general not to be trusted (*LB* 16) but that his own adored Villaretta is herself the most "Merciless, Insolent" (*LB* 7) of all. Gildon similarly transforms the semi-tragic figure Malvolio, duped by his own vanity into courting Olivia in such a ludicrous fashion that he is locked up as a lunatic, into Taquilet, who admits from the beginning, "I'm so overjoy'd with the greatness of my good Fortune, that I have quite forgot the unlikelyhood of its being true" (*LB* 26). He is not tragic, just ridiculous.

Both the tragic and sentimental elements missing from Burnaby's *Love Betray'd* are crucial to Shakespeare's *Twelfth Night* since they provide the situation and a focus for the plot. Rather than gratuitously exploiting sentimentality, Shakespeare exposes the dangers of submitting to excessive emotion in Orsino's overpowering infatuation for Olivia, an infatuation cured easily enough when she marries Sebastian and Orsino recognizes the true love he has been building for Viola. Shakespeare derides excess sentimentality even more explicitly in Feste's dialogue with Olivia when he shows her that since she believes her brother to be in heaven, she is merely indulging her passions by overly grieving.

The virtual omission of sentimental elements from *Twelfth Night* is typical of Burnaby, whose comedy harks to the earlier, more cynical Restoration comedy. His *Reform'd Wife* is devoid of sentimental elements; while *The Ladies' Visiting Day* contains only one instance, the love scene between Fulvia and Polidore:

> Ful. (*In a harsh Voice.*) Then, Sir, know at
> once I do–(*In a softer.*) love you.– [*Aside.*] O dear!
> I hope he did not hear me.
>
> Pol. My Heaven! My All! my *Fulvia*! Food
> of my Eyes! and Transport of my Soul!
>
> Ful. My, *Polidore*! So let me ever call you–I
> long have stifled in my Breast this Fire, which proof
> against the gentler Violence of Love, your moving
> manner and your last resolve, have struck into a
> Flame–Hah!" (*LVD* 226)

Even this scene begins with a harsh voice and an attempt by Fulvia to deny her love for Polidore. Burnaby does introduce one darker note into *The Reform'd Wife* as he has Sir Solomon Empty momentarily consider suicide after learning of his wife's intrigues.

The tragic element of Granville's *Jew of Venice* differs very little from Shakespeare's *Merchant* as both plays hinge on the financial losses of Antonio and the vengeance of Shylock. Granville's Shylock comes across as a less tragic figure than Shakespeare's, primarily because Granville deletes many of Shylock's less crucial passages and edits even the most significant ones to make room for the masque. An excellent example is the condensation of Shylock's discussion of Jessica's elopement (*MV* 3.1.24-30). In Shakespeare this discussion takes the form of a lengthy exchange involving Shylock, Salario, Solanio, and Tubal and spans lines 24-130. Granville cuts the passage to fifty-five lines. The deleted lines flesh out Shylock more fully and lead the audience to understand him better, if not quite to empathize with him. Even more importantly, the relocation of the "Hath not a Jew eyes?"(*MV* 3.1.58) speech to the prison at which Antonio awaits his execution provides further distance for the audience from Shylock as he is no longer addressing the youthful Solario and Solanio who aided in his daughter's escape, but he is vengefully addressing Antonio who stands in shackles before him, a man Shylock himself has condemned to death.

While Shylock's speeches are greatly abridged in *The Jew of Venice*, Antonio's are expanded and, in the process, made slightly more sentimental. He not only risks all for his friend Bassanio as he does in *The Merchant*, but at the same time he endlessly enumerates the duties and extols the glories of true friendship. As with Shylock Granville makes the most profound change by introducing the scene in which Antonio stands shackled before his creditor to listen to Shylock's rantings as he wonders why the "impenetrable Curr" could possibly want a pound of his flesh (*JV* 29). Granville also heightens the melodrama, if not the sentimentality, in Antonio's "parting" speech to Bassanio. In Shakespeare's version, the merchant proclaims his deep and abiding love for Bassanio and his willingness to give his life for his friend. Granville's Antonio wishes to prove his affection for Bassanio graphically:

> . . . Once more farewell:
> Grieve not my Friend, that thus you lose a Friend,
> For I repent not thus to pay your debt
> Even with my Blood and Life: Now, do your Office,
> Cut deep enough be sure, and whet thy Knife
> With keenest Malice; for I would have my Heart
> Seen by my Friend. (*JV* 35)

His friend responds in kind:

> Stand off. I have a word in his behalf,
> Since even more than in his Avarice,
> In cruelty, this Jew's insatiable;
> Here I stand for my Freind [*sic*], Body for Body,
> To endure the Torture. But one pound of Flesh
> Is due from him: Take every peice [*sic*] of mine,
> And tear it with Pincers: whatever way
> Invention can contrive to torture Man,

> Practice it on me. (*J V* 35)

Neither of Shakespeare's characters dwells on the gory, sensational character of Antonio's proposed punishment, a punishment with an almost Websterian quality. Their concern, rather, is with the personal loss which will result if Antonio must pay his debt with his life.

Portia is not an overly sentimental character in either version of the play, though Granville's heroine does tend to employ more excessive language. The difference is slight, but obvious in Portia's attempt to dissuade Bassanio from choosing too soon. Shakespeare's Portia expresses her love for Bassanio in objective, though compelling terms:

> ... Beshrew your eyes,
> They have o'erlooked me and divided me.
> One half of me is yours, the other half yours–
> Mine own, I would say, but if mine, then yours,
> And so all yours. O, these naughty times
> Puts bars between the owners and their rights;
> And so, though yours, not yours. Prove it so,
> Let fortune go to hell for it, not I.
> I speak too long, but 'tis to peize the time,
> To eke it, and to draw it out in length
> To stay you from election. (*MV* 3.2.14-23)

Granville's Portia, on the other hand, uses overt sentimentality and a tragic tone to sway her lover:

> Yet, let me perswade you: If for your self
> You cannot fear, tremble for her–
> For her, to whom you have so often sworn,
> More than your self, you love her: Think! oh Think!
> On *Portia's* Fate: Who may not only lose

The Man, by whom she wishes to be won,

But being lost to him, remain expos'd

To some new Choice; another must possess

What Chance denies to you. O fatal Law!

Lost to each other were a cruel Doom,

But 'tis our least Misfortune; I may live

To be enjoy'd by one I hate. And you

May live to see it. (*JV* 21)

Where Shakespeare's Portia rebukes "these naughty times" which place "bars between the owners and their rights," Granville's exclaims against the "fatal Law" and the "cruel Doom" which not only keeps the two apart but may bestow her hand on another. No weak, simpering maid, Shakespeare's Portia does not wallow in despair over her situation but heartily proclaims, "Let fortune go to hell for it, not I" and admits that she is speaking to "peize the time" and keep Bassanio from making his choice. Granville's Portia can only curse the fate which may give her to one other than Bassanio.

Like Portia, Bassanio becomes a more cloyingly sentimental lover in Granville's *Jew of Venice*. The ring exchange is representative of the change. Shakespeare's Bassanio speaks movingly, emotionally in 3.2.175-85:

Madam, you have bereft me of all words.

Only my blood speaks to you in my veins,

And there is such confusion in my powers

As after some oration fairly spoke

By a belovèd prince there doth appear

Among the buzzing pleasèd multitude,

Where every something being blent together,

Turns to a wild of nothing save of joy

Expressed and not expressed. But when this ring

Parts from this finger, then parts life from hence.

O, then be bold to say Bassanio's dead!

Granville's version excludes the objective metaphor, addresses Portia not as "Madam" but in the overstated "my Mistress and my Queen," and finishes by reiterating his subjection to Portia in even more exaggerated terms:

> Dye first, *Bassanio*, my Mistress, and my Queen
>
> As absolute as ever shall you reign,
>
> Not as the Lord, but Vassal of your Charms,
>
> Not as Conqueror, but Acquisition.
>
> Not one to lessen, but enlarge your Power.
>
> No more but this, the Creature of your Pleasure,
>
> As such receive the passionate *Bassanio*.
>
> Oh there is that Confusion in my Powers,
>
> As Words cannot express: But when the Ring
>
> Parts from this Finger, then part Life from thence;
>
> Then say, and be assur'd, *Bassanio's* dead. (*JV* 25)

By intensifying not only the sentimental element in *The Jew of Venice* but also adding a melodramatic aspect to the play–implicit, but never developed in Shakespeare's play–Granville takes Shakespeare's problem play and turns it into more of a tragicomedy.

Granville's *Reform'd Wife* is devoid of both tragic and sentimental elements. *The She-Gallants* contains some sentimentality, though fewer instances than in his *Jew of Venice* because of the situation. *The Jew*, after all, centers on the deep friendship of Antonio and Bassanio as well as the love of Bassanio and Portia, love which "hazards all." The main plot of *The She-Gallants*, on the other hand, centers on a broken engagement which Bellamour nonchalantly passes off as a matter of fortune. He tells the disguised Angelica, "It was my fortune to see *Angelica*, and to love her. It was my fortune to be absent from her, and to forget her" (*SG* 20). Bellamour, indeed, repudiates the idea of any strong emotion even on Angelica's part. When his disguised mistress suggests that perhaps Angelica now hates him as much as she used to love him, he responds, "Not hate me: I would not have her hate me; only not love so much; and not injure her self by any extravagance of Passion, nor by any over-fondness be burthensome to me" (*SG* 21). Later, after Angelica reveals her identity to Bellamour, the repentant lover begs her forgiveness, ". . . Oh! forgive your Kneeling Penitent. For 'tis resolv'd, and irrevocably fixt in this Perjur'd heart, either you must forgive, or with this Sword that was brought hither to be employ'd against you, I will wash away my Guilt, and Pardon'd be, or Pity'd!" As she turns from him, he continues his plea, vowing ever to "haunt" her for he has recognized what his "folly" has renounced. He waxes poetic, "I have consum'd a vast Estate, and sums immense, in search of Toyes unprofitable and airy Treasures: I have forfeited a promis'd Heaven, to reach at fruit, scarce worth the plucking." Angelica quite appropriately responds by weeping and is encouraged to do so by Bellamour, "You weep–Are they for me, those Tears? Then Weep again, give pity a full entrance: Where there is Pity, sure there will be Mercy" (*SG* 68). Granville is able thereby to elicit the most sentimental speeches in the play from the most hardened cynic.

Tragic elements are lacking in Shakespeare's *The Merry Wives* as well as in John Dennis' *The Comical Gallant* and *A Plot and No Plot*. Since the didactic element of both *The Comical Gallant* and *A Plot and No Plot*, unlike that of *The She-Gallants*, does not focus on the love interest, and the characters in both who bear the brunt of the lesson–Falstaff, Bull, Sr., and Batt Bull all expose the *ridiculum*–neither play offers a real opportunity for exploitation of the sentimental. Dennis' Anne Page and Fenton could hardly be considered more sentimental lovers than Shakespeare's couple even though the original lovers only appear onstage together for a very brief period in act three scene four. In this scene, Fenton tells Anne that he cannot obtain her father's approval. The sole note of sentimentality in the entire speech comes after he admits that her money was what first attracted him to her, then adds "'tis the very riches of Thyself/That now I aim at" (*MW* 3.4.16-17). Anne ignores this admission and responds with further encouragement to gain Page's blessing.

In Dennis' version the couple spends most of their time bickering, and even their endearments sound rather harsh. When Fenton upbraids her for letting him "languish at Windsor three tedious days" without seeing her, rather than inundating him with vigorous protestations of love, Anne calls him "unjust" and reminds him that not only has she been "watch'd perpetually" but she has "been pelter'd both with Spiritual and Temporal Fools." Her response to his "Do you love me?" similarly avoids the overly romantic as she returns, "If you doubt I hate you" (*CG* 2).

The conversation between Belvil and Sylvia in *A Plot* is even less sentimental and affecting. Belvil greets Sylvia at the Playhouse with "But Sylvia comes adorn'd with every Grace, and Love and Death sit sporting in her Eyes," and her reaction is quite peculiar: "And for what weighty reason, Mr. Belvil, have you drawn me hither?" The rest of their tête à tête is spent in discussing Belvil's rival, Batt Bull, as Belvil recounts Batt's lack of wit and Sylvia counters by praising his looks. Sylvia brings an end to the conversation by confronting Belvil for wooing her by degrading her new suitor, "And do you think to make Court to a Woman by saying this?" Belvil, ever the gallant, acquiesces, "Yes, to a Woman who can despise the little follies of her Sex, as much as she detests their Vices." After only four or five more lines of this extremely touching dialogue, Sylvia agrees to marry Belvil if he can obtain his uncle's consent within the next two hours, an acceptance she tempers as she adds, "Upon that condition I may promise any thing and run no risque of performance" (*PNP* 29). Sylvia, at this point, takes her leave of Belvil, refusing even to accept his offer to see her to her chair.

The only emotional speeches in the entire play ironically take place between Frowzy and Batt Bull about his supposed courtship of her daughter, Friskit, and represent a parody of sentimental comedy. When Frowzy assures Batt that her daughter is madly in love with him, he responds with what he assumes to be continental fervor, "Ouy: Le Dieu me dam-me, Je l'adore." Frowzy's aside notes the artificiality of the sentiment: "This fellow is at last come in a proper style for fiction." To prove his love for Friskit, Batt avows that he also made an "English declaration in France" to Friskit and calls for a boy to sing a song proving his affection for her daughter. Since Batt's protestations have still not convinced Frowzy that her daughter is now safely betrothed, she extracts a clearer vow from Batt as she asks him point-blank, "And are you ready to own this in England for her reputation and your honour? For you may assure your self, that no one will believe you that you could frequent any one person of quality, without conversing with us, because we frequented them all" (*PNP* 40-41), of course, swaying him to make an open declaration based entirely on his own self-consequence. Batt's love, counterfeited to gain a titled spouse, backfires on him and wins him only a former prostitute for wife.

These adaptations, as well as the adapters' original plays, exhibit various degrees of tragicomedy and sentimental comedy dependent once again on the main situation of the play. Both *Measure for Measure* and *The Jew of Venice* show some intensification of the sentimental-tragic component. Gildon virtually transforms *Measure for Measure*, the most tragicomic of the plays in its original form, into a heroic play, eliminating all the comedy and playing the tragic aspects to the hilt. Granville's characters become more saccharine in expressing their love and dwell on the melodramatic aspects of Antonio's bond to a much greater extent than Shakespeare's. Only Burnaby and Dennis refrain from indulging the audience's emotions. Burnaby, ever the renegade, takes a play in which the sentimental element is overstated for a reason and eliminates the sentimentality and, in the process, robs the play of its deeper import. In the hands of an entirely witless adapter *The Merry Wives of Windsor* conceivably could have spawned a sentimental adaptation. Though not a great playwright, John Dennis, at least, restrained any lachrymose tendencies in his characters and was content to settle for laughter in *The Comical Gallant*.

Summary

These plays, on the whole, become more like Restoration comedies, and, or so their adapters believed, more closely aligned with critical theory in their diversity, their more conscious manipulation of events by characters, their primary focus on the foibles of the upper classes, their separation of the farcical from the serious, and their increased use of sentimentality. Even when the changes are minor, they affect the whole fabric of the play. Although Granville's version of *The Merchant of Venice* primarily represents an abridgement, the entire tone of the play is different because of the elimination of Lancelot Gobbo, the inclusion of the masque, and the heightened melodrama. More than anything else, these three features, the removal of low characters, the inclusion of the "entertainments," and the more blatant appeal to softer emotions, characterize the difference between Shakespeare and the adaptations as comedies. The removal of the low characters by Gildon, Burnaby, and Granville is probably the most critical mistake caused by the misbegotten zeal of the adapters. The follies of all the Vaunters and Sir Solomon Emptys put together cannot compare with the foibles of an Elbow. Only Sir John Falstaff himself is capable of that.

CONCLUSION

Although the Restoration critics and playwrights seem never to have realized it, their adaptations have proven to all who have come since that Shakespeare has not as yet been improved. Isolated lines may be clarified, or in rarer instances made more sonorous, more poetic, more beautiful. Plots may be tightened and unified to eliminate extraneous action, to tie subplots to the main plot more clearly. Characters may be drawn more consistently. A moral, whether supplied or inadvertently suggested in Shakespeare, may be more pointed and beneficial. The whole design may be more superficially perfect, more of a piece. These requisites for a good play, requisites proclaimed from Aristotle on down, may be more strictly embodied in an adaptation, yet each of these adaptations fails abysmally to surpass or even approach the beauties of the original version. The rich texture, the amazing panoramic view of human character and emotion, the piercing beauty of Shakespeare's words, all are missing from the altered versions. In their place remain second- or third-rate plays, entertaining when judged on their own merits, lacking when pitted against the originals.

The attempts of the Restoration playwrights may nonetheless be excused, partly because the tastes of the public had been altered by exposure to classically correct French plays during the exile and partly because they were desperate to boost the flagging business of the theatre. The number of theatres had dwindled from six thriving playhouses in a much smaller London before the war to a mere two after 1660. According to J. Paul Hunter, the two decades immediately preceding the eighteenth century were even worse for the theatre business as only one of those playhouses had regular seasons for a period of fourteen years.[1] Playwrights, as a result, had to find a way to woo audiences back to the theatre. The most obvious ploy they used was the introduction of comic diversity and entertainments. Altered versions of old plays served in the same capacity as they provided the audience with something familiar, yet still offered the element of surprise. Hunter explains the anxiety behind the extravagance of the tamperers of the Restoration:

> ... Attempts to spice up old plays parallel the search for new
> ways to entertain audiences beyond the limits of verbal possibility,
> and the gimmicks of stage machinery, the importation of operatic
> spectaculars and the addition of songs, dances, pantomimes, and
> variety shows to evenings of drama all share a common fear that
> plays are not sufficient to hold an audience in the eighteenth
> century English theatre. (274)

The Restoration chose to assign another reason for their adaptations. Honestly trying to reestablish the English theatre in the best traditions of both the classical ages and recent past, some playwrights were sincerely bent on perfecting the genre.

If the theatre was declining in popularity, one reason had to be that the plays were simply not good enough. John Dennis expresses just such an opinion

---

[1]J. Paul Hunter, "The World as Stage and Closet," in Shirley Strum Kenney, ed.,

in "A Large Account of Taste in Poetry" when he tells why he altered *The Merry Wives of Windsor*. He chose the play initially because it was "by no means a despicable Comedy," yet he also "believed it not so admirable, but that it might receive improvement" (LATP 279). Like his fellow tamperers, Dennis graciously attributes the imperfections of the play to something other than Shakespeare's inability. In this case he claims that the play was written so quickly that it could not be perfect. The faults in the play, he feels, are responsible for its lack of success in revival. "And that tho something like this may very well happen to a living Author without any just Cause," he explains, "yet that there must be reason for it, when it happens to an Author who has long been dead, or whose Reputation has been long established." He finds the causes for its lack of success in its "strange Defects," which include three actions "independent one of another," irrelevant scenes, and a "stiff and forced and affected" (LATP 280) style. In correcting these "Errours," Dennis hopes he has made the play fit for contemporary audiences, a double triumph since he has not only brought the play nearer to perfection when judged against the standards of drama, but he has also, he hopes, formed a play more likely to command a large audience. John Dennis, like most adapters, failed to attain either objective.

To say that all the adaptations were economic and artistic failures is to overstate the case. Many of them, Dryden's *All for Love* and Granville's *Jew of Venice*, for instance, had some measure of success, artistic and economic, respectively. If they failed in everything else, the four adaptations under consideration here all did succeed in adhering more literally to critical doctrine in some way. Often this close attention to Aristotelian ideals was the prime consideration of the playwright, a consideration evident in an examination of their

British Theatre and the Other Arts, 1660-1800 (Washington: Folger Books, 1984), p. 272.

original plays, which generally show an even closer relationship to accepted critical practice than the alterations.

The unities of time, place, and action were prized highly by the Restoration as is obvious in Dennis' quote on the faults of *The Merry Wives of Windsor*. Charles Gildon and William Burnaby both condense the time span in their altered plays. Gildon's *Measure for Measure* is well within Dryden's recommended thirty hours while Shakespeare's version spans several days; and *Love Betray'd*, though it covers six days, much compresses the original three months which elapse in *Twelfth Night*. In this case, the playwrights most concerned with unity of time in the alterations show a variable concern with it in their own plays. Although Gildon's *Roman Bride's Revenge* exceeds the prescribed time limit by spanning several days' time, Burnaby's *Reform'd Wife* covers two to three days while his *Ladies' Visiting Day* takes place in little more than the actual time of performance. Granville and Dennis did little or nothing to alter the time that elapses during their plays, *The Jew of Venice* and *A Comical Gallant*. The first covers several months in both versions while *The Merry Wives of Windsor* and *A Comical Gallant* represent a time period almost identical to the acting time. In his own play, *The She-Gallants*, Granville interestingly follows unity of time as stringently as Dennis does in *A Plot and No Plot*.

Unity of place, not one of Aristotle's original precepts, appears in the broadest sense in three of Shakespeare's four comedies discussed here: *Measure for Measure, The Merchant of Venice*, and *The Merry Wives of Windsor*. Only *The Merchant of Venice* ventures from one city to another, moving from Venice to Belmont and back again. The adaptations follow the pattern of the originals in the primary setting. All four adaptations nonetheless evidence a move towards unity of place either in the centralization of the action, the reduction of the number of settings–Gildon's four to Shakespeare's eleven; Burnaby's four to Shakespeare's ten; and Dennis' three to Shakespeare's seven–and, even more significantly for the stage crew in an age of more extensive scenery, a vast decrease in the number of scene shifts. Shakespeare has fifteen shifts in *Measure for Measure* in contrast to Gildon's eight; seventeen to Burnaby's ten; eighteen to Granville's eight; and fifteen as opposed to Dennis' five.

The playwrights once again approach unity of place variously in their own plays. *The Roman Bride's Revenge* makes nine scene shifts to five different settings, three of which are located within the same building so that the action is placed almost exclusively in or around the palace. Burnaby, on the other hand, switches about in his *Reform'd Wife*–eight shifts to five different places–and *Ladies' Visiting Day*–fifteen shifts to five different locales–much more than in his *Love Betray'd*. Like Gildon, Granville and Dennis both avoid needless scene shifts and changes of setting in their own plays. *The She-Gallants* is set in three places, shifting scenes only within one act, act four, which moves from the park to Lady Dainty's chambers. *A Plot and No Plot* is the most regular of all, changing scene only as it changes act and remaining in the same place for the final three acts.

Unity of action in the four plays poses a special problem. For though each adapter proclaims an interest in unity of action, two of the four, Gildon and Granville, include a masque in their adaptations. Burnaby also included a masque which, much to his dismay, was cut for the performance as well as the published version of the play. Dennis' play already contained a masque. Only in *The Merry Wives* does the masque serve as an essential device in the plot. None of the four playwrights, interestingly enough, includes such extensive entertainment or spectacle in his own plays.

The adapters do achieve greater unity of action in the plays by omitting scenes that Shakespeare inserts primarily for comic effect or to provide thematic content, such as Lancelot Gobbo's exchange with his blind father and Pompey's day in court. Even more significantly, three of the playwrights, Gildon, Granville, and especially Dennis, rearrange scenes and refocus the action so that each dialogue and each action builds to the climax. Gildon's *Measure for Measure* eliminates the subplot dealing with the Duke's problems with Vienna and ties every action to the unfolding of Angelo's true character through his misuse of power. Granville, though he makes few changes in the story line, does manage to bring greater unity to the plot by eliminating the minor characters, Lancelot Gobbo and the princes of Aragon and Morocco, thereby keeping the focus more clearly on the main characters at all times. One of the major flaws John Dennis saw in *The Merry Wives of Windsor* was the three distinct actions it contained, and he quite effectively unifies the plot by having Fenton instigate the gulling of Falstaff and Ford to provide a distraction so that he can elope with Anne Page. In this way both the happy plot and the gulling plot are neatly bound.

With the possible exception of Granville's *She-Gallants* all the plays by the adapters follow unity of action as closely as, or even more than their adaptations. Every action in *The Roman Bride's Revenge* is necessary to the conflict between the Emperor and Portia and to the idea of vengeance. It contains no subplots or digressions. Burnaby disavowed any interest in the unities and attempted to write plays with subplots that would show the broad compass of his abilities. Even in *The Reform'd Wife* and *The Ladies' Visiting Day*, he had difficulty in escaping unity of action; his subplots are dependent on the main plot–the Cleremont scenes aid in exposing Sir Solomon's character in *The Reform'd Wife*, while the Courtine/Lovetoy subplot serves to further the main plot in *The Ladies' Visiting Day*. Granville's *She-Gallants* is not made up of the type of double plot prescribed by Aristotle, but comprises two interwoven stories concerning the two women who pose as men to win and test the men they love. Although in this instance Dennis includes several scenes primarily for comic effect, *A Plot and No Plot* conforms to Aristotle's double plot in Belvil's cozening of his uncle, Bull, Sr., so that he can marry Bull's ward, Sylvia.

The adapters definitely move the plays toward greater unity of time, place, and action. The gains made in unity not only cause corresponding losses to the grace and fluidity of the action but they also signal a lessening of complexity in action, theme, and tone. Though Shakespeare's plays do not appear to be confined by the unities, they are nonetheless often more truly unified than the adaptations which closely follow the rules of time, place, and action.

Extending far beyond the mechanical rules of the unities, the changes made to the plays encompass the revision of language to make it clearer, more civilized and acceptable to the Restoration ear, and even went so far as to attempt to refine the morals of the age by exposing affectation and folly, impressing the idea of poetic justice on the audience, and drawing characters who act consistently through the play. In order to counter the attacks of Jeremy Collier and his cohorts, playwrights had to show that the theatre offered moral benefits to the audience. The exposure of foolish, pretentious behavior and the concept of poetic justice, an Aristotelian doctrine, were both very important to a theatrical system trying to prove its worth to hostile critics. With the dispensation of poetic justice to sanction the inclusion of amoral characters and tawdry situations, Restoration plays could justify their existence in that they showed the outcome of wickedness. Since poetic justice provides the most effective lesson when applied to characters who are either wholly good or wholly evil, the persons in Restoration plays became predictable, relatively simple, unambiguous characters.

Charles Gildon simplifies both the characters and situations in *Measure for Measure* so that the audience receives a clear-cut moral from the play. Rather than showing the selective justice present in Shakespeare's play, a justice which can condemn the gentleman Claudio for making love to his fiancé while it condones, or at least cannot punish, the pimp Pompey, Gildon's play presents an idealized justice which rewards the good and punishes the evil. In order to endow the play with a definite moral, Gildon makes several important changes. He eliminates the roles of Pompey and Mistress Overdone, makes Claudio and Julietta as well as Angelo and Mariana legally married, and resolves ambiguities in the characters of Angelo, the Duke, and Claudio. In Shakespeare, Angelo first appears to be a judicious, good man and later shows himself to be hypocritical and cold. Gildon, on the other hand, exposes Angelo's duplicity from the outset by suggesting that he has condemned Claudio to help Julietta's guardians keep her dowry for themselves, ennobles Claudio by having him accept the blame for a sin he has not even committed, and idealizes the Duke by giving him good reason to observe Angelo's behavior secretly.

Love Betray'd does not deal with the life-and-death situation present in *Measure for Measure*. Burnaby does not make the play accord with the law of poetic justice to any greater degree than Shakespeare had originally. He does utilize the concept by doling out humiliation in return for pride and true love for patience and persistence. The widow Villaretta, who cruelly disdains the love of Moreno but keeps him enthralled to satisfy her own lust for power, is repaid by the disdain of the "boy" Cæsario. Finally, in an odd way, she receives her just reward by marrying "Cæsario"–actually Sebastian–and coming under the bondage of a man once again. Viola, on the other hand, receives the love of Moreno at the end due to her tenacity and hard work; Moreno's misguided love for Villaretta is redirected to the deserving Viola; and Sebastian, whose love for his sister has led him from his home to search for her, gains the love of Villaretta. Burnaby's characters, unlike those of most adaptations, are not more consistent than Shakespeare's; their inconsistencies indeed do not add complexity to the characters but merely serve to confuse the audience.

Granville's *Jew of Venice* also does not show any appreciable heightening of poetic justice in the events of the play. His play is, in fact, more pedantic than Shakespeare's original in that he includes explicit comments on poetic justice throughout. By rearranging several scenes, particularly having Shylock deliver his "Hath not a Jew eyes" speech to an imprisoned Antonio, Granville makes Shylock a slightly more evil figure, or, at least, one who garners even less sympathy than Shakespeare's character.

If moral instruction was important to Granville and Gildon, it is the driving force behind Dennis' version of *The Merry Wives of Windsor*. Dennis consciously manipulates events to focus on the basic moral issues which are included but not stressed, in Shakespeare's play–the vanity of Falstaff, the foolishness of unreasonable jealousy, the horrors of forced marriages, and the problems that arise when children marry without parental consent. Making Ford, and not Falstaff, the recipient of the fairies' pinches and taunts perhaps changes the complexion of poetic justice more than anything else in *A Comical Gallant* as Shakespeare's Ford receives no repayment for his insane jealousy. Another major difference is the ending of Dennis' play. In his version, Anne Page and Fenton do not actually marry, but wait for the blessing of her parents.

Gildon, Granville and Dennis also express an interest in the moral function of the play in their original works. *A Roman Bride's Revenge* is based on the dictum that the duty to one's country supersedes all other responsibilities. The

Emperor, Perennius, and Lætus receive their due for the evil they have committed, but Martian's death is also necessary to the moral of the play since he had abandoned Rome in its time of need and now must die to preserve the state. Portia's fate, on the other hand, seems appropriate since she has no ties remaining on earth and can only find joy in heaven.

Granville's *She-Gallants* rewards Angelica's constancy when Bellamour turns his affections back to her, punishes the folly of Vaunter and Sir John Aery, and deals most appropriately of all with Lady Dorimen who is left alone with the recollection that she has been wooing a woman disguised as a man, yet poetic justice is not consistent in this play. Though Vaunter and Sir John are humiliated countless times throughout the play, at the end, they are allowed to choose among Frederick's sisters for wives. Bellamour's case is different: true, he does not deserve Angelica's love, because he has been unfaithful to her, but he does reform when he learns her true identity.

Like his *Comical Gallant*, Dennis' *A Plot and No Plot* is as a vehicle for moral instruction. That old plotter, Bull, Sr., is adequately repaid for his contentiousness and avarice in the sham conspiracy. By the end of the play, he has lost control over the fortune of Sylvia, his ward, whom he had designed for his son Batt, a fop; in place of a wealthy young lady for daughter-in-law, he now has a prostitute; and, he has willingly given away five thousand pounds to regain his freedom. Bull's lesson has been delivered for a purpose. Belvil has deluded his uncle into believing his life is ruined to keep him from being so easily drawn into conspiracies and thereby protect him in the future. As the play closes, Belvil, who is ill-treated by his relatives yet stops short of vengeance, receives the only real poetic justice when he wins the hand of Sylvia.

Burnaby disavowed any interest in the moral function of the drama, yet even his plays instruct the audience to behave more prudently. Poetic justice threatens to reign in Burnaby's plays, but, as in *A Plot and No Plot*, mercy eventually prevails. In exhibiting the tribulations of the jealous husbands, their straying wives, and the young men who are courted by them, Burnaby attempts to show the audience the disastrous possibilities of such situations, hoping at the same time to entertain the audience with the ridicule of vice and the exposure of folly.

The refinement of style was perhaps even more important to the Restoration than the refinement of morals. Clarity, once again, was the prime consideration of these adapters of Shakespeare. Since they were so consumed by the idea of simplicity of style, the adapters eliminated much of the poetry from the plays and wound up with dialogue that is easier to understand, open to fewer interpretations, and eminently less beautiful. The few changes Gildon makes to Shakespeare's language are designed primarily to reduce ambiguity. Burnaby, in contrast, rewrites most of the dialogue, sometimes clarifying Shakespeare's words, at other times obscuring them. Like Gildon, Granville uses much of Shakespeare's original dialogue. In achieving his goal of clarity, Granville modernizes some words, edits certain speeches and expands others to make their meaning unmistakable. Dennis' aim in *A Comical Gallant* was to make the conversation more natural. He retains most of Shakespeare's original language throughout the play and reserves most of his changes for the dialogue between Anne and Fenton which he turns into prose. As is true of the other adapters, Dennis succeeds sometimes but fails even more frequently at making the language clearer.

If the adapters were concerned with refining the plays so that they would conform to the unities as well as present a clear moral statement in lucid, simple language, they were equally concerned with revising the plays to bring them into harmony with critical ideas about the genre of comedy. One of the most readily apparent changes each of the adapters, except Dennis,[2] made to the plays was the inclusion of a masque. As Hunter's statement quoted earlier shows, the Restoration playwrights were desperate to revive the floundering business of the theatre. The recent rise of the Italian opera, the popularity of the "entertainments" given during the Interregnum, along with Aristotle's approval, inspired them to draw on such spectacle, song and dance in order to build an audience.

Although *Measure for Measure* deals with weighty subjects, Charles Gildon adds "the Mask of Dido and Aeneas in four parts" to a play whose only original "entertainment" was one brief song. Ostensibly included to melt Angelo's heart so that he will pardon Claudio, the masque makes use of spectacular stage effects. Furies fly about; ships appear; Phœbus and Venus ride their chariots as sprightly Tritons cavort; and a grand dance ends the play. The masque Burnaby wrote for *Love Betray'd* never reached publication; because of that failure, his play actually has less diversity–it contains only two songs–than Shakespeare's *Twelfth Night*, which contains four. Although Burnaby's *Reform'd Wife* does not have any songs and dances, his *Ladies' Visiting Day* evidences his concern with variety as it includes three songs and a dance by some Moors. Granville, like Gildon, adds a masque in *The Jew of Venice*. This masque, which is included as part of Bassanio's farewell feast, is tied thematically to the plot but does not further the action in any way. *The She-Gallants*, on the other hand, contains a couple of catchy songs but no spectacle. Dennis was provided with the most successful masque of all in *The Merry Wives*, but his play, *A Plot and No Plot*,

---

[2] *The Merry Wives of Windsor* already contained a masque.

also makes room for several songs and dances, including a drinking song by Wycherley and a dance to the fiddles.

Spectacle and music are optional in comedy. Deception and trickery, on the other hand, are essential to the genre. Even in *Measure for Measure* which becomes more of a heroic play and less of a comedy in Gildon's hands, the deception remains as the Duke disguises himself as a friar to observe Angelo's rule. Most of the other adapters carry the idea of trickery even farther than Shakespeare had in the original version. Burnaby's Viola does not have her masquerade thrust upon her as Shakespeare's had, but she chooses it willingly so that she can be near Moreno. His *Reform'd Wife* and *Ladies' Visiting Day* also depend on deception. Astrea pretends to hate men so that she can carry on intrigues without Sir Solomon's opposition. Polidore, Lady Dolt, and Courtine all use trickery in order to achieve their goals. Granville makes few changes in the nature of trickery in his *Jew of Venice*, but his *She-Gallants* concerns two women who dress as men to win their lovers. The whole plot of *A Comical Gallant* also centers on the deception of Falstaff and Ford by Mrs. Page and Mrs. Ford with the main difference between this play and Shakespeare's *Merry Wives of Windsor* resting in the intentional use of deception in Dennis' version. The same is true of Dennis' *A Plot and No Plot* in which Belvil sets out to con his uncle Bull into a sham conspiracy and prove to him the dangers of gullibility. In this play a couple of prostitutes pretend to be a Countess and her daughter while Bull's own house becomes first Newgate and then Bedlam. The main contrast between all these Restoration plays and Shakespeare's plays is that deception is more by design in the later plays and seemingly accidental or spontaneous in Shakespeare's.

Shakespeare frequently made use of nobility in his comedies, but this digression from the rules on his part evidently did not bother the adapters excessively as they make only minor changes to lessen the social stature of their characters. Granville's characters appear to be of a lower rank than Shakespeare's, and Dennis omits any reference to the Court at Windsor. In their own plays, these men do not include rulers but dwell on the foibles of ordinary, though wealthy people.

Two of the adapters, on the other hand, made extensive changes with regards to wit and humour in these comedies. Gildon eliminates both equally from *Measure for Measure* and winds up with a sentimental rather than comic play. Burnaby replaces the true humour and real wit of Shakespeare with his pale imitations, but he is more successful with both witty dialogue and humour in his own characters, particularly Sir Testy Dolt and Sir Solomon Thrifty. Granville and Dennis, in contrast, retain much of Shakespeare's wit as well as the humours characters. In their own plays, Granville depends on wit and humour, while Dennis adheres more closely to classical teaching and primarily relies on humours characters to provide comedy.

One of the more striking changes the adapters made to Shakespeare's comedies was to remove farcical elements from the plays. Gildon rids his play of Pompey, Justice Shallow, and Elbow, thereby eliminating all horseplay, puns, and physical humor. Although Burnaby includes some weakly farcical scenes centering on the servant Pedro in *Love Betray'd*, he totally demolishes the subplots containing the farcical scenes with Malvolio and Sir Andrew Aguecheek by combining the two characters into Taquilet. Burnaby's own plays include a couple of instances of horseplay, the beating of Captain Strut and Mrs. Friendlove's horror at Freeman's marriage. Granville removes all farce from his *Jew of Venice* by omitting Lancelot Gobbo, while he has Sir John Aery and Vaunter brought on stage tied to chairs in *The She-Gallants*. Dennis keeps some of the broader comedy present in *The Merry Wives*, Falstaff's escape in the buckbasket, for example, while he eliminates other instances like Mistress Quickly's malapropisms. His own play, *A Plot and No Plot*, paradoxically, is comprised primarily of low comedy due, he says, to the insignificance of the subject. All the adapters seem to include or exclude farcical elements depending on the weight of the topics introduced in the play so that in a play like *The Jew of Venice* which deals with the socially significant ideas of justice and mercy, all farcical elements are missing while in a play like *Love Betray'd*, in which love is the major topic, farce is acceptable.

If the Restoration disliked farce, it looked with great favor upon tragicomedy and sentimental comedy. As with farce sentimental elements are added or removed from the comedies depending on the situation depicted in the play. *Measure for Measure* and *The Merchant of Venice*, both of which deal with important issues, undergo the transformation to sentimental plays under Gildon and Granville. In the first, Gildon places more emphasis on Julietta and Claudio, giving them long, bathetic speeches to deliver in which each tries to wrest the blame for their situation from the other. In *The Jew of Venice*, Granville heightens the sentimentality of Antonio's and Bassanio's avowal of friendship for each other and has Portia and Bassanio gush with their love for each other. In their own works, the two rely on sentimentality in various degrees. Gildon's *Roman Bride's Revenge*, a heroic tragedy, is extremely dependent on melodrama and is permeated with sentimentality in the story of a perfect woman and an ideal hero who die to save their country. Granville's *She-Gallants* is only sentimental in the reunion of Angelica and Bellamour. Neither Burnaby nor Dennis adds sentimental or tragic elements to his plays. Burnaby's plays reflect the sophisticated, jaded comedy of Congreve, while Dennis' deal only with the softer emotions to a limited extent and serve primarily to expose ridiculous pretensions. When Dennis does employ sentimental speeches they serve, as in Batt Bull's courtship of Friskit, as a parody.

Each of the adapters tried in some way to bring to Shakespeare's plays a closer attention to critical doctrine. Gildon and Burnaby both reduce the amount of time covered in their adaptations. All four greatly cut the number of scene shifts, and all but Granville decrease the number of settings. Each adapter unifies action either by eliminating subplots or tying them more closely to the main plot even though three of the four add a masque to their version. Moral issues, similarly, are refined by all the adapters except Burnaby as they heighten the workings of poetic justice, obliterate ambiguities of characterization, or merely offer choric comment on the vices and affectations of the age. Also in the interest of clarity, each of the adapters tried to refine the language of Shakespeare's plays. As far as the genre of comedy is concerned, only Dennis actually makes an effort to produce a classical comedy by stressing humour over wit while Granville and Gildon eliminate both, opting for sentimental comedies or heroic plays.

These adaptations, then, did accord more closely with critical doctrine than Shakespeare's original plays. In almost every instance bringing the plays more closely in line with classical criticism only serves to rob them of their natural exuberance and beauty. The Restoration begrudgingly acknowledged at least this aspect of genius which pervaded Shakespeare's plays. The subtleties of Shakespeare's art eluded them. The action depicted in Shakespeare's plays might occur over three months' time, as it does in *Twelfth Night*, rather than thirty hours. The play might consist of three separate actions as *The Merry Wives of Windsor* does. The characters, like Angelo, might be so complex as to be neither wholly good nor evil, but merely human. The language, finally, might be archaic and open to multiple interpretations. Shakespeare's plays, nonetheless, far exceed the adaptations made from them in artistic excellence often through a unity of atmosphere. All the various motions and emotions, the multiplicity of character in separate individuals and existing within one person, the beauty and density of the language, the intricate weaving of plot and theme, all prove that Shakespeare, and not the adapters, actually attained mimesis, the highest goal for literature set by Aristotle.

BIBLIOGRAPHY

Aristotle. *Poetics*. Edited and Translated by Stephen Halliwell. The Loeb Classical Library. G. P. Goold, Ed. Cambridge, Mass.: Harvard University Press, 1995.

Bahlman, Dudley. *The Moral Revolution of 1688*. New Haven: Yale University Press, 1957.

Bateson, F. W. "Second Thoughts: II. L. C. Knights and Restoration Comedy" *Essays in Criticism* 7 (1957):56-67.

Berkeley, David S. "The Penitent Rake in Restoration Comedy" *Modern Philology* 99 (1952):223-233.

_____. "The Art of Whining Love" *Studies in Philology* 52 (1955):478-496.

_____. "*Preciositè* and the Restoration Comedy of Manners" *Huntington Library Quarterly* 18 (1955):109-128.

Bordinat, Philip, and Sophia Blaydes. *Sir William Davenant*. Boston: Twayne Publishers, 1981.

Bradbrook, Muriel. *Elizabethan Stage Conditions: A Study of Their Place in the Interpretation of Shakespeare's Plays*. London: Cambridge University Press, 1968.

_____. *English Dramatic Form*. New York: Barnes and Noble, 1965.

_____. *The Growth and Structure of Elizabethan Comedy*. London: Chatto and Windus, 1962.

_____. *The Living Monument: Shakespeare and the Theatre of His Time.* Cambridge: Cambridge University Press, 1976.

Brown, John Russell. *Shakespeare and His Comedies.* London: Methuen, 1962.

_____. *Shakespeare's Dramatic Style.* New York: Barnes and Noble, 1971.

Budd, F. E. Introduction to *The Complete Dramatic Works of William Burnaby*, by William Burnaby. Edited by F. E. Budd. London: E. Partridge, The Scholartis Press, 1931.

Burnaby, William. *Letters.* In *The Complete Dramatic Works of William Burnaby*, by William Burnaby. Edited by F. E. Budd. London: E. Partridge, The Scholartis Press, 1931.

_____. "Critical Essay." In *The Complete Works of William Burnaby*, pp. 327-39.

_____. *Love Betray'd, or the Agreable Disappointment.* London: D. Brown, 1703; reprint ed., London: Cornmarket Press, 1969.

Burnaby, William. *The Ladies' Visiting Day.* In *The Complete Dramatic Works of William Burnaby*, pp. 197--271.

_____. Prologue to Mrs. Centlivre's *The Perjur'd Husband.* London: Bennet Banbury, 1700; Three Centuries of English Drama (1701-1750), TCD-E-1469.

_____. *The Reform'd Wife.* London: Thomas Bennet, 1700; Ann Arbor, Mich.: University Microfilms, B5745, 1973.

Cairns, Edward A. *Charles Gildon's MEASURE FOR MEASURE: A Critical Edition.* New York: Garland Press, 1987.

Castelvetro, Lodovico. "A Commentary on *The Poetics* of Aristotle." *In Literary Criticism: Plato to Dryden*, pp. 305-57. Edited by Allan H. Gilbert. New York: American Book Company, 1940.

Cecil, C. D. "Libertine and *Preciéux* Elements in Restoration Comedy." *Essays in Criticism* 9 (July 1959):239-53.

Charlton, H. B. *Castelvetro's Theory of Poetry.* Manchester: University Press,

1913.

_____. *The Dark Comedies*. New York: Haskell House Publishers, 1972.

_____. *Shakespeare's Comedies: The Consummation*. New York: Haskell House Publishers, 1972.

Cinthio, Giraldi. "On the Composition of Comedies and Tragedies." In *Literary Criticism: Plato to Dryden*, pp. 252-61. Edited by Allan H. Gilbert. New York: American Book Company, 1940.

Clark, W. S. "The Definition of the Heroic Play in the Restoration Period" *Review of English Studies* 8 (1932):437-444.

_____. "The Sources of the Restoration Heroic Play" *Review of English Studies* 4 (1928):49-63.

Collier, Jeremy. "A Short View of the Immorality of the English Stage." In *Critical Essays of the Seventeenth Century*, vol. 3, pp. 253-91. Edited by J. E. Spingarn. Bloomington: Indiana University Press, 1957.

Congreve, William. "Concerning Humour in Comedy." In *Critical Essays of the Seventeenth Century*, pp. 242-52. Edited by J. E. Spingarn. Bloomington: Indiana University Press, 1957.

_____. Prologue to *The Way of the World*. In *British Dramatists from Dryden to Sheridan*, pp.307-48. Edited by George H. Nettleton and Arthur E. Case. Revised by George Winchester Jones, Jr. Carbondale: Southern Illinois University Press, 1969.

Cooper, Lane. *Aristotelian Theory of Comedy*. New York: Harcourt Brace, and Company, 1922.

Cook, Albert. *Shakespeare's Enactment: The Dynamics of Renaissance Theatre*. Chicago: Swallow Press, 1976.

Corneille, Pierre. Dedicatory Epistle to *La Suivante*. In *Literary Criticism: Plato to Dryden*, pp. 574-75. Edited by Allan H. Gilbert. New York: American Book Company, 1940.

_____. "Discours des Trois Unities." In *Literary Criticism: Plato to Dryden*, pp. 577-79.

248 Bibliography

Cox, James E. *The Rise of Sentimental Comedy.* Philadelphia: R. West, 1977.

Deane, Cecil V. *Dramatic Theory and the Rhymed Heroic Play.* London: Oxford University Press, 1931; reprint, Philadelphia: R. West, 1972.

Dennis, John. "The Advancement and Reformation of Poetry." In *The Critical Works of John Dennis,* vol. 1, pp. 197-278. Edited by Edward Niles Hooker. Baltimore: The Johns Hopkins University Press, 1939.

_____. "The Characters and Conduct of Sir John Edgar." In *The Critical Works of John Dennis,* vol. 2, pp. 181-99.

_____. *The Comical Gallant.* London: A. Baldwin, 1702; Three Centuries of English Drama (1701-50), TCD-E-1546.

_____. Dedication to *The Invader of His Country.* In *The Critical Works of John Dennis,* vol. 1, pp. 176-80.

_____. "A Defence of *Sir Fopling Flutter.*" In *The Critical Works of John Dennis,* vol. 2, pp. 241-50.

_____. "Essay on the Genius and Writings of Shakespear." In *The Critical Works of John Dennis,* vol. 2, pp. 1-17.

_____. "A Large Account of Taste in Poetry." In *The Critical Works of John Dennis,* vol. 1, pp. 279-95. Edited by Edward Niles Hooker. Baltimore: The Johns Hopkins University Press, 1943

Dennis, John. Letter to Walter Moyle. In *The Critical Works of John Dennis,* vol. 2 p. 386.

_____. Letter to William Congreve. In *The Critical Works of John Dennis,* vol. 2, pp. 385-86.

_____. *A Plot and No Plot.* London: F. Parker, 1687. Three Centuries of English Drama (1642-1700), TCD-852.

_____. "The Stage Defended, from Scripture, Reason, Experience, and the Common Sense." In *The Critical Works of John Dennis,* vol. 2, pp. 300-21.

_____. "To Henry Cromwell, on the *Vis Comica.*" In *The Critical Works of John*

Dennis, vol. 2, pp. 169-61.

Dobrée, Bonamy. *Restoration Comedy, 1660-1720*. Oxford: Clarendon Press, 1924; reprint ed. London: Oxford University Press, 1962.

Dobson, Michael. *The Making of the National Poet: Shakespeare, Adaptation, and Authorship, 1660-1769*. Oxford: Clarendon Press, 1992.

Draper, John W. "The Theory of the Comic in Eighteenth-Century England" *Journal of English and Germanic Philology* 37 (1938):207-223.

Dryden, John. "A Defence of 'The Epilogue'." In *"Of Dramatic Poesy" and Other Critical Essays*, vol. 1, pp. 169-83. Edited by George Watson. New York: E. P. Dutton and Company, Inc., 1962.

_____. "Essay: Of Dramatic Poesy." In *"Of Dramatic Poesy" and Other Critical Essays*, vol. 1, pp. 10-92.

_____. "The Grounds of Criticism in Tragedy." In *"Of Dramatic Poesy" and Other Critical Essays*, vol. 1, pp. 243-61..

_____. "Heads of an Answer to Rymer." In *"Of Dramatic Poesy" and Other Critical Essays*, vol. 1, pp. 210-20..

Dryden, John. Letter to John, Lord Haughton. In *"Of Dramatic Poesy" and Other Critical Essays*, vol. 2, pp. 274-79.

_____. "Parallel of Poetry and Painting." In *"Of Dramatic Poesy" and Other Critical Essays*, vol. 2, pp. 181-208.

_____. Preface to *Albion and Albanus*. In *"Of Dramatic Poesy" and Other Critical Essays*, vol. 2, pp. 34-43.

_____. Preface to *Don Sebastian*. In *"Of Dramatic Poesy" and Other Critical Essays*, vol. 1, pp. 44-51.

_____. Preface to *An Evening's Love*. In *"Of Dramatic Poesy" and Other Critical Essays*, vol. 1, pp. 144-55.

_____. Preface to *Troilus and Cressida*. In *"Of Dramatic Poesy" and Other Critical Essays*, vol. 1, pp. 238-43.

_____. To Mr. Congreve, on His *The Double Dealer*, prefixed to Congreve, *The*

Double Dealer (1694). In *"Of Dramatic Poesy" and Other Critical Essays*, vol. 2, pp. 169-72.

_____. Prologue to *Secret Love*. In *The Prologues and Epilogues of John Dryden: A Critical Edition*, pp. 10-11. Edited by William Bradford Gardner. New York: Columbia University Press, 1940.

Ellis, Frank H. *Sentimental Comedy: Theory and Practice*. New York: Cambridge University Press, 1991.

Flecknoe, Richard. "A Short Discourse of the English Stage." In *Critical Essays of the Seventeenth Century*, vol. 2, pp. 91-96. Edited by J. E. Spingarn. Bloomington: Indiana University Press, 1957.

Freehafer, John. "The Formation of the London Patent Companies in 1660." *Theatre Notebook* 20 (October 1965-July 1966): 6-30.

Fujimura, Thomas H. "The Appeal of Dryden's Heroic Plays" *PMLA* 75 (1960):37-45.

_____. *The Restoration Comedy of Wit*. Princeton: Princeton University Press, 1952.

Gallaway, Francis. *Reason, Rule, and Revolt in English Classicism*. New York: Octagon Books, 1965.

Genest, John. *Some Account of the English Stage from 1660 to 1830*. Bath: H. E. Carrington, 1832.

Gewirtz, Arthur. *Restoration Adaptations of Early Seventeenth Century Comedies*. Washington, D. C.: University Press of America, 1982.

Gildon, Charles. *A Comparison Between the Two Stages*. New York: Garland Publishing, Inc., 1973.

_____. *The Complete Art of Poetry*. 2 vols. New York: Garland Publishing, Inc., 1970.

_____. *The Laws of Poetry*. New York: Garland Publishing, Inc., 1970.

_____. *Measure for Measure, or, Beauty, the Best Advocate*. London: D. Brown, 1700; reprint ed., London: Cornmarket Press, 1969.

_____. Preface to *The Marriage Hater Match'd*, by Thomas D'Urfey. London: for Richard Parker and Sam Briscoe, 1692; Three Centuries of English Drama, (1642-1700), TCD-E-911-rev.

_____. "Some Reflections on Mr. Rymer's *Short View of Tragedy*." In *The Important Critick and Miscellaneous Letters and Essays by Charles Gildon*. Edited and with an introduction by Thomas Arthur Freeman. New York: Garland Publishing, Inc., 1973.

_____. *The Roman Bride's Revenge*. London: John Sturton, 1697; Ann Arbor, Mich.: University Microfilms, G 736.

Granville, George. *The Jew of Venice*. London: Ber Lintott, 1701; reprint ed., London: Cornmarket Press, 1969.

_____. *The She-Gallants*. London: Henry Playford, 1696; Three Centuries of English Drama (1642-1700), TC-II-569.

Grebanier, Bernard. *Then Came Each Actor*. New York: David McKay Company, Inc., 1975.

Green, C. C. *The Neo-classic Theory of Tragedy in England during the Eighteenth Century*. Cambridge, Mass.: Harvard University Press, 1934.

Guarini, Giambattista. "The Compendium of Tragicomic Poetry." In *Literary Criticism: Plato to Dryden*, pp. 505-33. Edited by Allan H. Gilbert. New York: American Book Company, 1940.

Hammond, Anthony. "'Rather a Heap of Rubbish Then a Structure': The Principles of Restoration Adaptation Revisited." In *The Stage and the Eighteenth Century*, pp. 133-48. Edited by J. D. Browning. New York: Garland Publishing, Inc., 1981.

Harwood, John T. *Critics, Values, and Restoration Comedy*. Carbondale: Southern Illinois University Press, 1982.

Higgons, Bevill. Prologue to *The Jew of Venice*, by George Granville. London: Ber Lintott, 1701; reprint ed., London: Cornmarket Press, 1965.

Holland, Norman. *The Dynamics of Literary Response*. New York: Oxford University Press, 1968.

Hooker, E. N. Introduction to *The Criticial Works of John Dennis*, vol. 2. Edited by E. N. Hooker. Baltimore: The Johns Hopkins University Press, 1943.

Horace. "The Art of Poetry." In *Literary Criticism: Plato to Dryden*, pp. 128-43. Edited by Allan H. Gilbert. New York: American Book Company, 1940.

Hotson, Leslie. *The Commonwealth and Restoration Stage*. New York: Russell and Russell, Inc., 1962.

Howard, Sir Robert. Preface to *Four New Plays*. In *Critical Essays of the Seventeenth Century*, vol. 1, pp. 97-104. Edited by J. E. Spingarn. Bloomington: Indiana University Press, 1957.

_____. Preface to *The Great Favourite*. In *Critical Essays of the Seventeenth Century*, vol. 1, pp. 105-111.

Hume, Robert. *The Development of English Drama in the Late Seventeenth Century*. Oxford: Clarendon Press, 1976.

_____. *The Rakish Stage: Studies in English Drama, 1660-1800*. Carbondale: Southern Illinois University Press, 1983.

Hughes, Derek. "Providential Justice and English Comedy 1660-1700: A Review of the External Evidence." *The Modern Language Review* 81:2 (April 1986): 273-292.

Hunter, J. Paul. "The World as Stage and Closet." In *British Theatre and the Other Arts, 1660-1800*, pp. 271-87. Edited by Shirley Strum Kenny. Washington, D. C.: Folger Books, 1984.

Kaul, A. N. *The Action of English Comedy: Studies in the Encounter of Abstraction and Experiences from Shakespeare to Shaw*. New Haven: Yale University Press, 1970.

Ker, W. P. Introduction to *Essays of John Dryden*, vol. 1. Edited by W. P. Ker. Oxford: Clarendon Press, 1976.

Kewes, Paulina. "Gerard Langbaine's 'View of *Plagiaries*': The Rhetoric of Dramatic Appropriation in the Restoration." *The Review of English Studies* ns 48:189 (February 1997): 2-18.

Kirsch, Arthur C. "Dryden, Corneille, and the Heroic Play." *Modern Philology* 59

(1962):248-264.

_____. *Dryden's Heroic Drama*. Princeton: Princeton University Press, 1965.

Knight, G. Wilson. *The Golden Labyrinth: A Study of British Drama*. New York: Norton, Inc., 1967.

Knights, L. C. "Restoration Comedy: The Reality and the Myth" *Scrutiny* 6 (1937):122-143.

Langbaine, Gerard. *An Account of the English Dramatick Poets*. London: by L. L. for George West and Henry Clements, 1691; Ann Arbor, Mich.: University Microfilms, TC-II-358.

Leech, Clifford. "Restoration Comedy: The Earlier Phase" *Essays in Criticism* 1 (1951):165-184.

Levison, William S. Restoration Adaptations of Shakespeare as Baroque Art. Ph.D. dissertation, University of Illinois at Urbana-Champaign, 1972.

Loftis, John. "The Social Milieu of Early Eighteenth-Century Comedy" *Modern Philology* 53 (1955):100-112.

Longinus. "On Literary Excellence." In *Literary Criticism: Plato to Dryden*, pp. 146-98. Edited by Allan H. Gilbert. New York: American Book Company, 1940.

Love, Harold. "The Myth of the Restoration Audience." *Komos* 1 (1967):49-56.

_____. "Who Were the Restoration Audience?" *Yearbook of English Studies* 10 (October 1980):21-44.

Marsden, Jean. *The Re-Imagined Text: Shakespeare, Adaptation, and Eighteenth-Century Literary Theory*. Lexington: University Press of Kentucky, 1995.

_____. Introduction to *The Appropriation of Shakespeare: Post-Renaissance Reconstructions of the Works and the Myth*. New York: St. Martin's Press, 1991.

Martz, William J. *Shakespeare's Universe of Comedy*. New York: David Lewis, 1971.

McClellan, Kenneth. *Whatever Happened to Shakespeare?* New York: Barnes and Noble, 1978.

McCollum, William G. *The Divine Average: A View of Comedy*. Cleveland: The Press of Case Western Reserve University, 1971.

McMillan, Dougald. "The Rise of Social Comedy in the Eighteenth Century" *Philological Quarterly* 41 (1962):330-338.

Merchant, W. Moelwyn. "Shakespeare 'Made Fit.'" In *Restoration Theatre*, pp. 195-220. Edited by John Russell Brown and Bernard Harris. New York: St. Martin's Press, 1965.

Moore, Robert E. *Henry Purcell and the Restoration Theatre*. Westport, Conn.: Greenwood Press, 1974.

Mudrick, Marvin. "Restoration Comedy and Later." In *English Stage Comedy*, pp. 98-125. Edited by W. K. Wimsatt, Jr. English Institute Essays. New York: Columbia University Press, 1954.

Nethercot, Arthur H. *Sir William Davenant: Poet Laureate and Playwright Manager*. New York: Russell and Russell, 1966.

Nettleton, George H. *English Drama of the Restoration and Eighteenth Century*. New York: The Macmillan Company, 1914; reprint, New York: Cooper Square Publisher, 1968.

Nicoll, Allardyce. *A History of English Drama, 1660-1900*. 6 vols. Cambridge, Mass.: Harvard University Press, 1952-1959.

Noyes, Robert G. "Conventions of Song in Restoration Tragedy" *PMLA* 53 (1938):162-188.

Odell, George. *Shakespeare from Betterton to Irving*. 2 vols. New York: Benjamin Blom, Inc., 1963.

Parsons, "The English Heroic Play" *Modern Language Review* 33 (1938):1-14.

Perry, H. V. E. *The Comic Spirit in Restoration Drama*. New Haven: Yale University Press, 1925.

Powell, Jocelyn. *Restoration Theatre Production*. Boston: Routledge and Kegan Paul, 1984.

Price, Herewood T. "Shakespeare as Critic." *Philological Quarterly* 20 (July 1941):390-99.

Raddadi, Mongi. *Davenant's Adaptations of Shakespeare*. Stockholm: Almqvist and Wiksell International, 1979.

Rabkin, Norman. *Shakespeare and the Problem of Meaning*. Chicago: Chicago University Press, 1981.

Rothstein, Eric. "English Tragic Theory in the Late Seventeenth Century" *English Literary History* 29 (1962):306-323.

_____. *Restoration Tragedy*. Madison: University of Wisconsin Press, 1967.

Rymer, Thomas. "The Tragedies of the Last Age Consider'd and Examin'd by the Practice of the Ancients and by the Common Sense of Each Age." In *Critical Essays of the Seventeenth Century*, vol. 1, pp. 181-208. Edited by J. E. Spingarn. Bloomington: Indiana University Press, 1957.

Salingar, Leo. *Shakespeare and the Traditions of Comedy*. Cambridge: Cambridge University Press, 1974.

Scheil, Katherine West. "Sir William Davenant's Use of Shakespeare in 'The Law Against Lovers' (1662)." *Philological Quarterly* 76.4 (Fall 1997): 369-87.

Sengupta, Shivagi. "Shakespeare Adaptations and Political Consciousness." *Mid-Hudson Language Studies* 4 (1981): 58-67.

Shakespeare, William. *Measure for Measure*. In *The Norton Shakespeare*, pp. 2021-2090. Edited by Stephen Greenblatt, et. al. New York: W. W. Norton Company, 1997.

_____. *The Merchant of Venice*. In *The Norton Shakespeare*, pp. 1081-1145.

_____. *The Merry Wives of Windsor*. In *The Norton Shakespeare*, pp. 1225-1291.

_____. Prologue to *Pericles*. In *The Norton Shakespeare*, p. 2720.

_____. *Twelfth Night*. In *The Norton Shakespeare*, pp. 3047-3107.

Sherbo, Arthur. *English Sentimental Comedy*. East Lansing, Mich.: Michigan State University Press, 1957.

Sidney, Sir Philip. *An Apology for Poetry.* Edited by Forrest G. Robinson. Indianapolis: Bobbs-Merrill Company, Inc., 1970.

Singh, Sarup. *The Theory of Drama in the Restoration.* Bombay: Orient Longmans, 1963.

Sorelius, Gunnar. "The Early History of the Restoration Theatre: Some Problems Reconsidered." *Theatre Notebook* 33.2 (1979).

_____. *"The Giant Race Before the Flood": Pre-Restoration Drama on the Stage and in the Criticism of the Restoration.* Uppsala and Stockholm: Almqvist and Wiksells, 1966.

Southern, Richard. *Changeable Scenery: Its Origin and Development in the British Theatre.* London: Faber and Faber, 1952.

Spencer, Christopher, ed. *Five Restoration Adaptations of Shakespeare.* Urbana, Ill.: University of Illinois Press, 1965.

Spencer, Hazleton. *Shakespeare Improv'd: The Restoration Versions in Quarto and on the Stage.* New York: Frederick Ungar Publishing Co., 1963.

Stevenson, David L. "Design and Structure in *Measure for Measure.*" *English Literary History* 23 (December 1956):256-70.

Summers, Montague. *Shakespeare Adaptations.* New York: Benjamin Blom, Inc., 1922; reprint ed., New York: Benjamin Blom, Inc., 1966.

Sutherland, James. *English Literature of the Late Seventeenth Century.* New York: Oxford University Press, 1969.

_____. "Prologues, Epilogues and Audience in the Restoration Theatre." In *Of Books and Humankind*, pp. 37-54. Edited by John Butt. London: Routledge and Kegan Paul, 1964.

Symons, Julian. "Restoration Comedy (Reconsiderations II)" *Kenyon Review* 7 (1945):185-197.

Taylor, Gary. *Reinventing Shakespeare: A Cultural History, From the Restoration to the Present.* New York: Weidenfeld and Nicholson, 1989.

Trissino. "Poetica." In *Literary Criticism: Plato to Dryden*, pp. 213-32. Edited by Allan H. Gilbert. New York: American Book Company, 1940.

Van Lennep, W. B., et. al., eds. *The London Stage, 1660-1800.* 11 vols. Carbondale, Ill.: University of Southern Illinois Press, 1960-1969.

Verbruggen, John. Epilogue to *Measure for Measure, or, Beauty, the Best Advocate.* Attributed to Charles Gildon. London: D. Brown and R. Walker, 1700; reprint ed., London: Cornmarket Press, 1969.

Vernon, P. F. "Marriage of Convenience and the Moral Code of Restoration Comedy." *Essays in Criticism* 12 (1962):370-381.

Vickers, Brian. "Shakespearean Adaptations and the Tyranny of the Audience." In *Das Shakespeare-Bild in Europa zwischen Aufklarung und Romantik,* 37-59. Bern: Peter Lang, 1988.

Weimann, Robert. *Shakespeare and the Popular Tradition in the Theatre: Studies in the Social Dimension of Dramatic Form and Function.* Baltimore: The Johns Hopkins University Press, 1978.

Wells, Stanley. "Elusive Master Shakespeare." *Forum* 11 (1973-74): 2-3; 6-10.

Wheeler, David. "Eighteenth Century Adaptations of Shakespeare and the Example of John Dennis." *Shakespeare Quarterly* 36.4 (Winter 1985): 438-449.

Wickham, Glynne. "The Restoration Theatre." In *New History of Literature, III: English Drama to 1710,* pp. 375-79. Edited by Christopher Ricks. New York: Bedrick, 1987.

Wikander, Matthew H. "The Spitted Infant: Scenic Emblem and Exclusionist Politics in Restoration Adaptations of Shakespeare." *Shakespeare Quarterly* 37 (Autumn 1986): 340-58.

Williams, Edwin E. "Dr. James Drake and the Restoration Theory of Comedy." *Review of English Studies* 15 (1939):180-191.

Wilson, John Harold. *Preface to Restoration Drama.* Boston: Houghton Mifflin, 1965.

Wood, F. T. "The Attack upon the Stage in the XVIII Century." *Notes and Queries* 163 (1937): 218-222.

_____. "The Beginnings and Significance of Sentimental Comedy" *Anglia* 55 (1931):368-392.

_____. "Sentimental Comedy in the Eighteenth Century" *Neophilologus* 18 (1953):281-289.

Wright, Louis B. "The Reading of Plays during the Puritan Revolution" *Henry Huntington Library and Art Gallery Bulletin* 6 (1934):73-108.

INDEX

preciosité, 161
principles of classical drama, 24, 49, 91
private theatricals, 8
probability, 19, 20, 20 n. 7, 21, 30, 33, 43,
    65, 70
problem play, 129, 215, 223
prose, 33, 34, 47, 54, 48, 55, 185, 189, 237
Providence, 20, 132, 148, 159, 162
Puritans, 7, 10, 12, 18, 128
Quintilian, 19, 53
Rabkin, Norman, 7, 21 n. 10, 44
Racine, 9
Raddadi, Mongi, 7, 7 n. 15
rank, 52, 199, 200, 201, 242
Reason, reason, 17, 18, 19, 30, 33, 36, 45,
    50, 58, 163 n. 29
reasons for adaptation, 5, 228, 229;
    innovation, 6; mandated by charter, 7;
    theatrical realities, 5 n. 9; political
    realities, 5 n. 9, 18
reduce, reduction, reductive, 19, 21 n. 10,
    28, 44, 56, 62, 189, 209, 214, 230, 237,
    242
refinement of wit, language, and manners, 8,
    45, 56, 127, 128, 148, 158, 164, 175,
    177, 180, 182, 188, 189, 233, 237, 242
revels, revelry, 192
rhymes, 1, 33, 34, 47
Ridiculum, ridiculous, 37, 40 n. 48, 42, 49,
    50 n. 74, 54, 58, 148, 149, 154, 168,
    172, 173, 217, 223, 243
Rochester, 11
role of nobility, 191, 199, 200, 201, 242
Roscians of the Red Bull, 10
Rowe, Nicholas, 19, 19 n. 4
ruler, 136, 144, 199, 200, 240
"Rules" of art, the, 2, 3, 12, 13, 15, 17, 18,
    19, 20, 21, 25-33 passim, 36, 39, 61, 64,
    96, 118, 136, 188, 199, 233, 239
Rymer, Thomas, 14 n. 40, 20, 30, 59, 191
    n. 1
Salingar, Leo, 22, 23, 24 n. 15, 24, 29, 44
    n. 60, 48 n. 72, 58, 192, 196, 199
Salisbury Court, 9
satire, satirize, (satyr, satyrize), 39, 40 n.
    48, 41, 164, 170
Scaliger, 3, 23, 28, 58
scene shifts, 68, 69, 71-76 passim, 83, 87,
    93, 95, 97, 104, 109, 113, 114, 231, 242
scenery, use of, 7, 23 n. 14, 68, 231
Scheil, Katherine West, 7 n. 15
science, 2, 13
Second Shepherd's Play, The, 196 n. 3
Secretary Thurloe, 10
Sengupta, 5 n. 9

sentence construction, 181
sentimental, 41, 58, 141, 144, 153, 191,
    202, 210 , 214-226 passim, 240, 241,
    242
Shakespeare, William, 1-8 passim, 12, 14,
    15, 17, 18, 19, 22, 24, 25, 30, 31, 34,
    40, 44-48 passim, 50, 56, 58, 59, 61-73
    passim, 78-82 passim, 85, 88, 90, 101-
    107 passim, 112-118 passim, 123, 124,
    125, 129, 130, 131, 132, 133, 135-142
    passim, 149, 149 n. 22, 150, 151, 151 n.
    23, 153, 158, 159, 160, 164-171 passim,
    175, 176, 177, 179, 180-185 passim,
    188, 189, 191-200 passim, 203-226
    passim, 227-243 passim; *Comedy of
    Errors,* 24; *Henry V,* 12; *King Lear,* 1;
    Measure for Measure, 1, 3, 58, 70, 71,
    75, 76, 78, 83, 124, 129, 130, 131, 133,
    136, 140, 192, 193, 196, 199, 201, 202,
    210, 211, 214, 215, 216, 225, 230, 231,
    234, 238, 239, 240, 241; *Merchant of
    Venice, The,* 40, 68, 72, 73, 101, 103,
    104, 106, 177, 178, 182, 183, 188, 188
    n. 37, 192, 194, 206, 213, 214, 219, 221,
    230, 241; *Merry Wives of Windsor, The,*
    24, 66, 74, 75, 76, 112, 114, 117, 118,
    119, 123, 164-170, 174, 184, 185 n. 38,
    186, 188, 192, 195, 198, 199, 200, 207,
    209, 223, 225, 229, 230, 231, 235, 238,
    239, 241, 242; *Pericles,*1; *Tempest, The,*
    24, 49; *Twelfth Night,* 64, 65, 70, 71,
    72, 76, 85-91 passim, 148, 151, 151 n.
    23, 152, 153, 176, 181, 192, 193, 194,
    196, 202, 204, 211, 212, 217, 230, 238,
    242
Sidney, Sir Philip, 2, 57
simile, 46, 177, 177 n. 35
simplification (of language, tone, and/or
    meaning); simplify, 5 n. 9, 15, 48, 129,
    134, 138, 177, 182, 188, 189
Singh, Sarup, 12 n. 32, 14, 29 n. 23 and n.
    24, 57
singleness of artistic purpose, 33
Sophocles, 22
Spencer, Hazleton, 5, 5 n. 9, 7, 61, 177,
    185, 191 n. 1
song(s), 48, 49, 50, 56, 92, 109, 121, 162
    n. 29, 192, 193, 194, 195, 225, 228, 238,
    239
Sorelius, Gunnar, 7 n. 15
spectacle(s), 49, 51, 192, 194, 195, 231,
    238, 239
St. Paul, 36
Summers, Montague, 6
stage machinery, 194, 228

Stevenson, David L., 129
struggle for perfection, 2, 229
Suckling, Sir John, 33 n. 29
Tate, Nahum, 1
Taylor, Gary, 6, 23 n. 14
Terence, 23; *Self-Punisher*, 23
tennis courts, 9
theory of comedy, 19, 50, 51, 53, 190-226
  passim
tragicomedy, 56, 57, 58, 210, 214, 222,
  225 241
tragedy, 3, 19, 22, 27, 29 n. 23, 31, 32 n.
  35, 39, 45, 46 n. 65, 50, 51, 52, 54, 57,
  58, 142, 199, 202, 210, 216, 241
trickery, 191, 195-201 passim, 239
Unities, The, 3 n. 6, 21-30 passim, 61, 62,
  65, 67, 76, 91, 124, 125, 175, 191, 230,
  232, 233, 237
unity of action, 14, 23, 24, 25, 28, 32, 33,
  62, 76, 77, 82, 87, 92, 93, 96, 101, 106,
  118, 123, 124, 231, 232
unity of atmosphere, 215, 243
unity of emotion (emotional unity), 14
unity of place, 12, 23, 25, 28, 30 n. 25, 31,
  67-76 passim, 230, 231
unity of taste, 14
unity of time, 23, 25, 28, 62-67 passim, 74,
  230, 233
variety (and as hallmark of English genius),
  13, 26, 27, 29, 37, 47, 48, 49, 55, 192,
  193, 194, 195, 228, 238
Vega, Lope de, 13; "The New Art of
  Making Comedies," 13
Verbruggen, John, 2
vice, 21, 34 n. 35, 35, 40, 41, 43, 50 n. 74,
  79, 127, 141, 156, 158, 161, 208, 237
verisimilitude, verisimility, 25, 26, 115
weeping comedy, 217
Weimann, Robert, 8, 14
Wells, Stanley, 4 n. 9
Wheeler, David, 42 n. 55
Whigs, 58
wickedness of the age, 161
Wikander, Matthew H., 5 n. 9
Williams, Aubrey L., 33 n. 33
wit, 8, 26, 42, 53, 54, 55, 56, 162, 169,
  176, 189, 191, 195, 201-209 passim,
  224, 240, 242
Wit Without Money, 10
wordplay, puns, 177, 178 n. 36, 185 n. 38,
  205, 208
world view, *Weltanschauung*, (changing
  Restoration) 8, 17, 20, 61, 62
  (Shakespeare's) 8

Wycherley, William, 11, 38, 39 n. 48, 52
  n. 80, 122, 195, 241; *Plain Dealer*, 39

STUDIES IN COMPARATIVE LITERATURE